SERIES IN PSYCHOLOGY

Other books by Gordon H. Bower:

*AN INTRODUCTION TO
MATHEMATICAL LEARNING THEORY,*
by R. C. Atkinson, G. H. Bower, and E. J. Crothers,
John Wiley and Sons, 1965.

THEORIES OF LEARNING (third edition),
by E. R. Hilgard and G. H. Bower,
Appleton-Century-Crofts, 1966.

ATTENTION IN LEARNING:
Theory and Research

TOM TRABASSO
University of California, Los Angeles

GORDON H. BOWER
Stanford University

with the collaboration of
ROCHEL GELMAN
University of California, Los Angeles

 John Wiley and Sons, Inc.   New York   London   Sydney

This book is
respectfully
dedicated to our
teachers who inspired
and influenced our
studies of behavior:

Neal E. Miller   (for G. B.)

Frank A. Logan   (for G. B.)

Frank Restle   (for T. T.)

PREFACE

This book reports our research on stimulus selection by human subjects during their learning of elementary discrimination or classification problems. Research that views the experimental subject as a selective processor of stimulus information is almost forced to discuss these matters in terms of *attention,* and so it is in this book. In crisp terms, this book is concerned with developing hypotheses about the operation of attentional processes in the human subject when he is involved in learning classifications. Part of the theoretical task here is developing an appropriate system of constructs for representing attentional processes, how these change with the experience of the learner, and how these processes function in organizing or encoding the perceptual environment of the learner. After reviewing a range of earlier thought and experimentation in Chapter 1, we propose such a set of constructs in Chapter 2. Chapters 3 through 7 may be viewed as experimental tests of the validity of the theory stated in Chapter 2. Chapter 8 gives a final overview and suggestions for extensions and modifications of the theory to make it handle the more salient failings of the earlier theory.

It is a truism that scientific research is a stepchild of the prevailing *Zeitgeist,* and that it is most often only a modest extension of what has gone before. These generalizations surely describe the work presented herein. Attention, as a respectable topic worthy of scientific interest, certainly has been "in the wind" for the past fifteen to twenty years. Contributors to this interest include the neurophysiologists with their emphasis on habituation, arousal, and the reticular activating system of the brain stem, the human-performance psychologists with their view of man as a limited-capacity information processor, and the learning theorists with their views of stimulus encoding, selectivity, and the learned distinctiveness of cues.

Our work falls within the province of the learning psychologist, and the kind of ideas and results to which we address ourselves have been recurrent for many years in the literature of discrimination learning. The writings of Lashley, Krechevsky, Lawrence, Sutherland, Mackintosh, Wyckoff, and Zeaman may be viewed as the proper progenitors of the present work. A large portion of the experimental literature on this topic has been concerned with discrimination learning by animals, particularly mammals. Despite our concentration on the adult human subject, we review this literature on animal discrimination learning because it has been and remains a fertile base and source for theoretical ideas and experimental paradigms. Also, in this way, we are led to compare the similarities in results when rats and college sophomores learn discrimination tasks that, from a theoretical point of view, are formally equivalent.

As with many scientific inquiries, the investigations to be reported began by happenstance, and, not unusually for psychologists, with some disturbing pieces of data. In 1963 at Stanford University we were collaborating on a series of experiments in which human subjects solved concept-identification problems. We were testing an elementary, all-or-none learning model that implicitly assumed rather drastic stimulus selection by the subject. In that theory, the learning subject was viewed as formulating and testing hypotheses (about the correct solution) based on stimulus attributes selected from the experimental displays, and for mathematical simplicity we had assumed that subjects attended to only one attribute at a time. At that time we were concerned primarily with testing the statistical features of the all-or-none model and were momentarily blind to the model's implications concerning exactly what subjects should learn. The single-attribute selection idea implied that subjects could learn about only one cue for correct classification even though two or three other cues might be redundant and equally good for doing the classification. A small pilot study run at that time gave results that provided a distinct jar to these firm implications. When a theorist's preconceptions are shaken up by an experimental finding, his automatic reaction is to question the finding, and proceed to try to replicate or extend the experiment. This we proceeded to do, and with the same disturbing outcome: the results simply showed again that our notions about single-attribute sampling by the subject were all wrong, and that a richer system of constructs was needed to explain the orderly, but nonetheless puzzling, results regarding the subjects' mode of solution.

These disturbing results led to some constructive thinking. Under the influence of some earlier theoretical ideas of Frank Restle, we evolved an unpublished "working paper" that was later developed into the sampling theory described in Chapter 2. This theory led to a variety of predictions about the way in which subjects would solve multiply determined classification problems. From that moment onward, an increasing portion of our research efforts was directed toward the testing of these implications. The first full-scale testing of the theory was the experiment reported in Chapter 3. This yielded orderly results for which the model gave excellent numerical predictions, so we were encouraged to continue our investigations. We extended the theory and experimentation to transfer of training of classifications (Chapter 4) and to stimulus selection in paired-associate learning (Chapter 5). The work on cue selection in paired associates was strongly influenced by the then-current review of this problem by Benton Underwood, whereas the transfer study was motivated by general considerations regarding the assessment of attention in learning. The research reported in Chapter 6 on cue salience and mode of solution in classification learning was testing some direct implications of the sampling theory. The research on overtraining reported in Chapter 7 was testing for the significance of factors that were not then incorporated in the specific model we had developed.

At several stages throughout this work, we faced the decision of whether to report our findings piecemeal in the technical journals or to accumulate further experiments to report in a longer monograph. By degrees it eventually became apparent that given the experiments, the literature related to them, and the number of things we wished to say about them, the only feasible alternative was a research monograph integrated around our particular version of attention theory.

The historical and personal factors that lead scientists into a particular line of research are diverse and multiply determined. However, we would like to single out a few individuals who, in some way, have contributed to making this book possible. First, we owe a special debt of gratitude to our teachers, most notably the three men to whom this book is dedicated. These men introduced us to the scientific issues discussed in this book, inspired us to search for answers, shaped by example and deeds our attitudes and methods of approach to scientific problems, and generally had a profound influence upon our intellectual development. Dedication of this book to them is meager pay for the valuable guidance they gave us in our formative years. Second, a number of our students contributed directly to this research and to these we owe our special thanks. Dr. Gelman's contribution, acknowledged by her collaborative authorship, was primarily in terms of designing the experiments on transfer and overtraining reported in Chapters 4 and 7; she also contributed through discussions and questions to the general ideas in the book. Those students who aided in the collection and analysis of data and to whom we are indebted are Sharon Deans, Steve Harp, Douglas Hintzman, Mark Le Vine, Kathryn Nash, Jack Rawlings, Robert Rosenbaum, Benson Schaeffer, Herman Staudenmayer, and Feng Chu Wong. Financial support for this research was generously provided by the United States Public Health Service, National Institutes of Health, grants MH 08741 to T. Trabasso and HD 00954 and MH 13950 to G. Bower. We thank the American Psychological Association and the Academic Press for permission to reproduce tables or figures that appeared in papers published in their journals. Specific acknowledgment of the authors is made at the appropriate places in the text.

Tom Trabasso

Gordon H. Bower

January 1968

CONTENTS

ATTENTION IN LEARNING:
Theory and Research

1

ATTENTION IN LEARNING

This book concerns discrimination learning. Discrimination is a basic and important psychological concept and discrimination learning has long been a central issue for psychologists. Discrimination implies a capacity for variability in behavior and a correlation between changes in behavior and changes in environmental stimulation. The process by which these correlations arise, where they otherwise were absent, is called discrimination learning.

The fact that an organism responds differently to two situations implies the existence of differential stimuli, and further that these differential elements, in part, are controlling its behavior. It does not mean, however, that all differential elements are equally controlling; some elements may exert a powerful controlling influence, and others none at all. Psychologists, recognizing the possibility of differential control, now distinguish between the "nominal" stimulus variables or the full set of differential elements, and the effective or "functional" stimulus variables which, in fact, control the behavior. The theoretical conundrum is then to explain *why* some differential elements become converted into effective stimuli, whereas others remain only nominal during the course of learning. Some theoretical notions of selectivity or "abstraction" are clearly needed here. To indicate that the issue involved in this discussion is not a modern discovery, the following passage from Wundt (1894), written over seventy years ago, may be used to characterize the process of abstraction:

> By *abstraction* we generally mean the process by which certain constituent parts are eliminated from a compound idea or from several such ideas and what remains is retained as the elements of a concept. Moreover, abstraction is the principal means of forming general concepts (p. 11).

The quotation from Wundt can be dressed, but not without some esthetic loss, into the modern clothes of learning theory by translating

1

"compound ideas" as stimulus patterns with many variable features ("constituent parts"), and saying that, in learning, the person selects or samples ("abstracts") criterial features ("concepts") to guide his behavior. The content is about the same either way. In each case, however, the statement describes the outcome of a selection process without really telling us *how* it comes about. One seeks more detail, more "mechanism" theory to describe the process and to guess at the variables that will influence its selective outcome. In short, one wants a theory for calculating or specifying the effective stimulus.

The principal theoretical candidates for attempting to solve this puzzle involve *attention* constructs. The effective stimuli are those to which the subject attends. Attention concepts have had a long and checkered career in psychology, and part of that history is reviewed in the next section. There has been a clear resurgence of interest in attention, and this interest has been reflected in modern theories of discrimination learning. To place our research in proper perspective, then, these theories, the evidence supporting them, and the particular kinds of attention problems to which they have been or should be addressed are reviewed in this chapter.

SOME HISTORY OF THE ATTENTION CONSTRUCT

Attention, as a systematic concept for reconstructing mind, has undergone many shifts in popularity, swinging from belief that it was an absolutely indispensable construct to the opposite belief that it was a vague, useless, irrelevant construct. The early English empiricist school of psychologists—Locke, Hume, the Mills, Spencer—gave no recognition to the notion, perhaps because its implication of capricious spontaneity went counter to their aim of mechanizing the operation of the mind by the laws of association applied to initially raw sense impressions. Later, both functionalists and structuralists, given more to introspective descriptions of mental faculties, accorded a high status to attention. William James (1890) in his *Principles of Psychology* devoted a full chapter to a descriptive account of the operation of attention, an account to which modern work can add surprisingly little. The following quotations illustrate the importance he ascribed to attention:

> Millions of items of the outward order are present to my senses which never properly enter into my experience. Why? Because they have no *interest* for me. *My experience is what I agree to attend to.* Only those items which I *notice* shape my mind—without selective interest experience is an utter chaos. . . . It varies in every creature,

2

but without it the consciousness of every creature would be a gray chaotic indiscriminateness, impossible for us even to conceive. (James, 1890, pp. 402–403, italics his.)

Or again:

> Everyone knows what attention is. It is the taking possession by the mind, in clear and vivid form, of one out of what seem several simultaneously possible objects or trains of thought. Focalization, concentration, of consciousness are of its essence. It implies withdrawal from some things in order to deal effectively with others, and is a condition which has a real opposite in the confused, dazed, scatterbrained state which in French is called *distraction*. . . . (James, 1890, pp. 403–404.)

Despite such eloquent accounts of attention and its operation, there was early difficulty in staking out a specific experimental domain in psychology to which the notions firmly applied and from which they could be developed. For this and other reasons, the early status of the construct of attention rested upon introspective reports or intuitive assumptions, usually prefaced by the remark "It is well known that. . . ." Thus, not having a firm experimental toehold, attention was one of the first mentalistic concepts to be cast aside in the behaviorist revolution. It was said to be a vague construct which explained too much or too little, which added complications of indeterminism to the S-R framework, which rested on little systematic evidence except introspections, and whose sole factual content (insofar as it was unambiguous) referred to a motoric readiness to react to particular stimuli upon which the receptors (eyes) were focused. Attention was decried as part and parcel of the homunculus, or inner-demon, view of behavior; and explaining a person's response to complex stimulation by appeal to the operations of this inner homunculus was scientifically vacuous and detrimental—the problem to be explained was merely translated "inward," to an uncertain domain that could only hinder the conduct of a functional analysis of behavior. As late as 1954, in summarizing a scattered literature on investigations of attention, Woodworth and Schlosberg (1954) justifiably complained of its disjointedness and lack of organization, and they commented:

> In spite of the practical reality of attending, the status of attention in systematic psychology has been uncertain and dubious for a long time. Early psychologists thought of it as a faculty or power, akin to the Will. . . . Any such view was strongly opposed by the associationists who wished to recognize as forces only sensory stimulation and association. The Gestalt psychologists also have regarded any

3

force of attention as extraneous to the field forces which in their view are the dynamic factors in human activity. The behaviorists have rejected attention as a mere traditional mentalistic concept. (Woodworth & Schlosberg, 1954, pp. 72–73.)

In more recent times, mostly from 1950 onward, there has been a strong swing back to an interest in attention and a gradual staking out of several experimental domains relevant to the topic. The three major domains are discrimination learning, neurophysiological research, and studies of rapid information processing in humans. The applications of attention constructs to discrimination learning began in recent times with Lashley and Krechevsky, and have been materially advanced by recent research and theorizing by Lawrence, Sutherland, Mackintosh, Wyckoff, Zeaman and House, and the Kendlers. Their work and views will be reviewed later. The neurophysiological laboratories have discovered impressive evidence for peripheral attenuators that gate out information at lower levels of the sensory pathways, this work being carried out by Hernandez-Péon, Galambos, Livingston (cf. Lindsley, 1957), and many others in recent times. The most detailed elaboration of attention theories has developed from investigations of human information processing in dichotic listening experiments, with major impetus being given by early work done by Cherry, Broadbent, Moray, and Treisman among others. Broadbent (1958), Egeth (1966), and Treisman (1964) provide reviews of this work.

DISCRIMINATION LEARNING AND RECEPTOR-ORIENTING THEORY

Modern accounts of discrimination learning have their intellectual beginnings with a paper in 1936 by Spence entitled "The Nature of Discrimination Learning in Animals." In this paper, which has the status of a true "classic" in the field, Spence brought to the analysis of discrimination learning the basic concepts of habit strength, reinforcement, inhibition, nonreinforcement, and habit summation which Hull (1930) had used earlier in accounting for simple trial-and-error learning. The basic view was that discrimination phenomena would yield to understanding by systematic application of these concepts which were familiar from other experimental contexts. The main assumptions, stated with reference to a simultaneous or a single stimulus ("go-no go") discrimination, were as follows:

1. If a subject approaches a stimulus complex and is rewarded, then all stimulus components affecting his sensorium at the initiation of this

4

approach response receive an increment in their association to this approach response.

2. Similarly, if the approach response is not rewarded, all stimulus components affecting the subject's sensorium at the time receive a decrement in their association to the approach response.
3. The net tendency to approach a stimulus complex is determined by summation of the associative strengths of the individual components constituting that complex.
4. Given a choice between approaching two or more stimulus complexes, the subject chooses that alternative having the higher net reaction tendency.

These general assumptions, supplemented by specific quantitative formulas for the increments and decrements mentioned in items 1 and 2, were then used by Spence to account for a variety of phenomena of animal discrimination learning. Examples are his accounts (Spence, 1936, 1938, 1940) of systematic responses prior to learning (typically, position habits in rats), the sudden breakup of position habits, the retarding effect of presolution reversals, the effect of the previous history of reinforcements and nonreinforcements of the two discriminative stimuli upon the difficulty of learning a new problem involving them, the prior basis for sudden versus gradual solutions to discrimination problems, and other phenomena. Further, by adding the assumption of stimulus generalization of the habit and inhibition tendencies, Spence was able to account for transposition (relational choices) of behavior along a stimulus continuum (Spence, 1937a and b, 1942).

The status of Spence's theory with respect to an attention construct was brought out clearly in his discussions of a series of presolution reversal experiments which were central to what has come to be called the "continuity-noncontinuity controversy." There were several logically separable issues involved in those experiments—incremental versus all-or-none (insight) views of learning, hypothesis versus habit summation, and so on—but clearly one of the points at issue was whether all, or only selected, stimulus components present became associated with the response. In interpreting one of Krechevsky's experiments which had failed to find retarded learning following presolution reversal, Spence (1940) pointed out that associations should develop only with respect to those stimulus components affecting the animal's sense organs, that in certain experimental arrangements the critical cues may be so located that they are not received by the animal unless certain receptor orientations or adjustments are made, and so these receptor-orienting acts may

5

have to be learned in certain circumstances. In an earlier publication, he had anticipated this issue with the following footnote:

> Moreover, the animal learns many other responses in addition to the final selective approaching reaction. Prominent and important among these are what have been termed, for want of a better name, "preparatory" responses. These latter consist of the responses which lead to the reception of the appropriate aspects of the total environmental complex on the animal's sensorium, e.g., the orientation and fixation of head and eyes towards the critical stimuli. That is, the animal learns to "look at" one aspect of the situation rather than another because of the fact that this response has always been followed within a short temporal interval by the final goal response. Responses providing other sensory receptions are not similarly reinforced in a systematic fashion and hence tend to disappear. (Spence, 1937b, p. 432.)

This notion of peripheral orienting responses was a sensible extension of S-R principles to account for some of the gross effects ascribed to attention. It is true enough that a potential visual stimulus will not become an *effective* stimulus for reaction unless it impinges upon a sensitive retina. Furthermore, the basic approach of reinforcement theory provides a plausible account of how and why particular orienting responses are learned. That is, the orienting response is an early member of a behavior chain that ends in reinforcement, and the orienting response is strengthened because it produces or clarifies a discriminative stimulus (secondary reinforcer) that controls a later, goal-directed response. With this functional analysis in hand, experiments on "chained schedules" are relevant (Kelleher & Gollub, 1962); it is further possible to set up explicit analog situations in which an overt response plays the role of the observing reaction. This is illustrated in the work of Atkinson (1961), Prokasy (1956), Wyckoff (1952), and several others.

It is possible to interpret such orienting reactions as operating at one of two levels, which we will label as molar and molecular. These are exemplified most easily in vision. The molar level corresponds to gross orientation of the receptor—for example, looking in that corner of the room where the experimental displays are presented. The molecular level corresponds to fine scanning of details of a visual display; in particular, it allows for different scanning movements to be correlated with different features of the visual pattern—for example, the scan may differ whether one is processing information about the shape of a figure, the number, orientation, and locations of the figures, and so forth.

It is our view that if orienting-response theory refers only to molar adjustments, then considerable evidence can be quickly amassed to show

6

the inadequacy of this formulation to deal with discrimination learning. On the other hand, if the orienting-response theory is interpreted in terms of molecular scanning, it is more difficult to show its inadequacy, and one instead must invoke implausibility arguments against its various accounts. To demonstrate the inadequacy of the molar level interpretation of orienting responses, it suffices to demonstrate selective learning of components in a compound stimulus discrimination under conditions that ensure the subject's gross orientation of the relevant receptor toward the stimulus display. Such demonstrations now abound. For example, training a visual discrimination between a red triangle (the reinforced complex) and a green circle (the nonreinforced complex) may be followed by the demonstration that a subject primarily cued its response to the shape of the stimulus and not to its color component, or vice versa (e.g., Reynolds, 1961). But since the components were configurated, it is impossible to have the animal's retina stimulated by the shape but not the color of the figure. In this gross sense of "receive," both components were equally received before the response and reinforcement, so both should have been equally associated to the response if Spence's theory were correct.

There are essentially two ways to deal with such demonstrations without invoking something like selective attention operating as a central mechanism. One is by appeal to a construct like Hull's (1943) "afferent neural interaction"; the other is by shifting to a molecular-scanning interpretation of orienting reactions. Let us discuss them in that order.

THE AFFERENT INTERACTION POSTULATE

Hull (1943) introduced the notion of "afferent neural interaction" between simultaneous stimulus traces to afford recognition to the facts about stimulus patterning. Pavlov (1927), Woodbury (1943), and others had demonstrated experimentally the commonsense fact that animals can be trained to respond positively to a compound of two stimulus elements (e.g., a light and a tone) but not to respond to either element presented singly. Organisms are equally capable of learning the reverse patterning, to respond to single elements but not to the compound. This competence at patterning is inconsistent with the simple habit summation postulate of Spence's theory mentioned earlier. Hull's solution to this puzzle was the proposal that the afferent input from a given stimulus component differed depending upon whether the component occurred alone or in combination with other components presented simultaneously. If components S_1 and S_2 separately produce afferent traces s_1 and s_2 when acting singly, then the combination $S_1 + S_2$ produces the

7

interactive afferent trace $s'_1 + s'_2$, each part of which becomes separately associated to the response reinforced to the compound.) Depending then upon the habit strength conditioned to s'_1 and the similarity of s_1 to s'_1 on a generalization gradient, the response conditioned to $S_1 + S_2$ will generalize in some degree to S_1 presented singly. And because of the dissimilarity between s_1 and s'_1, the subject can be trained to give differential responses to the single elements versus the compound. Hull proposed no laws concerning the extent of change in s'_1 versus s_1 except to offer the conjecture that elements within the same sense modality might interact more than elements from different modalities.

In the absence of rules specifying the ordinal amount of change from s_1 to s'_1 under particular interactive circumstances, Hull's formulation has little predictive power beyond the obvious assertion that pattern discriminations are possible. Typically the degrees of freedom or number of unknowns in the theory would equal the degrees of freedom in transfer data that were to be explained. Thus, if the subject transfers responding to S_1 but not S_2 following compound training on $S_1 + S_2$, the theory need only assume post hoc that the neural interaction was such that s'_1 was similar to s_1 but that s'_2 was very different from s_2. A determinate prediction of this scheme however, is that if transfer is perfect from $S_1 + S_2$ to S_1 alone, indicating essential identity of s'_1 and s_1, then it should prove impossible to train a perfect discrimination between $S_1 + S_2$ versus S_1. But there is sufficient evidence available, some of ours to be reported plus other results, to reject this strong implication. The fact that following simple compound conditioning the subject transfers perfectly to one of the components does not imply in general that he cannot be specifically trained to differentiate between the compound and that component. Thus this one determinate prediction of the afferent interaction postulate cannot be supported in general.

A further weakness of the afferent interaction postulate is its implication that the kind or amount of interaction between two components is determined by their physical properties, and is independent of the past experience of the subject in dealing with these dimensions of stimulus variation. But we know this is false, the relevant evidence having been supplied first in an admirable series of experiments by Lawrence (1949, 1950) and since replicated by others (cf. Mackintosh, 1965b). Roughly speaking, Lawrence's experiments showed that prior training of rats on problems in which stimulus dimension A was relevant and dimension B irrelevant established a systematic "bias" in the rat to use dimension A in preference to dimension B in later discrimination learning problems. This trained bias toward using a particular dimension (A) can be made to show itself by comparison with "unbiased" control subjects during the

8

learning of a new problem that is so arranged as to obviate *direct* transfer of S-R habits from the earlier learning tasks. The bias can be demonstrated by one of three methods: (1) facilitation of learning when the relevant cue is still in dimension *A;* (2) retardation of learning when dimension *B* becomes relevant whereas dimension *A,* though present, is now irrelevant to the correct solution; and (3) a preference for learning mainly about cue *A* (rather than *B*) when cues *A* and *B* are made redundant and equally relevant in the new problem.

The latter result, differential learning of cue *A* or *B* in the compound *A + B,* is critical to the independence prediction of the afferent interaction postulate. If the transfer from *A + B* training to *A* or *B* alone is manipulable by prior training which logically could not directly produce the transfer differential, then the "similarity" of s_a to s'_a and s_b to s'_b must be determined by psychological, not purely physical stimulus, variables. And this, in conjunction with the other deficiencies of the hypothesis, discredits the afferent interaction postulate as an adequate account of stimulus selectivity during discrimination learning.

OBSERVING RESPONSES AS MOLECULAR SCANNING PATTERNS

The afferent interaction postulate having failed to account for the pattern of results in the compound-to-component transfer experiments, we turn to the alternate explanation of peripheral S-R theory, namely, molecular scanning. That is, the orienting response of the theory is identified with different sequences of finely graded receptor movements which are controlled by (or which track) selected features of the stimulus field. Such differential orientation is plausible for stimulus dimensions differing in their modality of reception since the receptor adjustments are relatively gross in these cases: for example, a rat could turn its head and ears to localize the source of a sound, or it could scratch its paws over the maze floors to detect differences in the roughness of a sandpaper flooring used as a cue, or sniff rapidly to detect odor cues and move along an odor-intensity gradient, or move its head and eyes to fixate the upper or lower part of a visual stimulus card to which it jumps, and so forth. The proposal would be to try to carry through this style of analysis at a molecular level to account for differential attention to particular attributes of a stimulus complex, all of whose attributes are in the same modality, such as visual or auditory. For example, if the compound patterns presented on a response key to a monkey are a green spot inside a white outlined triangle on a dark background or a red spot inside a white outlined square, one could imagine different sequences of eye movements that generally would be favorable to, or increase sensitivity

9

to, form or color. The fixation sequence appropriate to form would be to locate a black-white contour and then move the fixation point along this contour; for color, locate a black-white contour, then move the fixation point "inward" to put the color spot onto the fovea. When one of these orienting sequences unwinds, the attribute controlling it would provide maximal foveal stimulation, whereas the alternate component would fall on peripheral retinal cells and be degraded. And one might consider such scanning sequences as "proto-demons" (Selfridge, 1959) for doing selective information processing of particular stimulus dimensions, and suppose further that their learning and maintenance accounts for the selective biasing encountered, for example, in the Lawrence experiments.

There are several problems with this molecular view of orienting-response theory, with the more serious objection regarding the implausibility of its account of various cases of configured components. For example, it should be possible to construct patterns of two or more closely tied attributes wherein any orientation sequence that sets out to extract information about one of the attributes must perforce be fully exposed to the information in the other attribute (e.g., colored outline drawings; see Chapter 7). Further, tachistoscopically presented stimuli would not be of sufficient duration for any peripheral scanning to occur, yet selective attention operates in such conditions (cf. Egeth, 1966, for a review). The work on stabilized retinal images (Hebb, 1963), wherein eye movements do not shift the retinal image, shows that identification of most visual properties occurs effortlessly without scanning. Moreover, the scanning sequence is halfway plausible only in those cases in which the receptor can move relative to the proximal stimulus. But it is an implausible account of selectivity in other cases, such as a person's ability to follow a selected one of two messages read into one earphone simultaneously by two different speakers, or his ability to make separate judgments of the pitch and loudness of the same series of tones. The selective analyzers in such cases are unlikely to be found in the peripheral activity of the receptor. Lawrence (1963) has pointed out the further problem that if such orienting responses are considered to be responses conditioned by reinforcement to the general experimental context, then one cannot on this basis account for the sudden shifts in stimulus-response correlations that a person exhibits when he is instructed to judge (or rank order) a stimulus series first on one and then another attribute.

Our opinion is that this orienting-response interpretation of attention can be sustained only at the expense of inelegant and implausible

10

confabulations. The initial bias in favor of this view—which would overlook such inelegances—developed from a history in which peripheral reference was a main desideratum for psychological constructs. But that bias clearly has faded and hypotheses regarding central processes are no longer anathema. Whatever its worth, the peripheral-versus-central distinction has become increasingly harder to sustain, certainly in terms of neurophysiological results relevant to attention. The distinction is doubtless the wrong kind for psychologists to be worried about, let alone to use as a criterion for evaluating scientific constructs.

The purport of our remarks here is to lay to rest the view that peripheral orienting acts will get us very far in analyzing attention phenomena. If attention is to be identified as a response process ("attending response"), let it be clear that "response" is being used here in only a metaphorical or analogical sense; it is just another hypothetical construct, on equal footing with other interpretations of attention. We think "peripheralism-versus-centralism" is a dead issue, at least in this branch of psychology; we beat the horse dead again here, so we need not stomp on the nag periodically throughout this book.

ATTENTION THEORIES IN DISCRIMINATION LEARNING

The germinal ideas underlying attention theories of discrimination learning were expressed by Lashley and Krechevsky during the 1930's. The following quotation from one of Lashley's papers illustrates his view of what the animal is doing during discrimination learning:

> A definite attribute of the stimulus is "abstracted" and forms the basis of the reaction; other attributes are either not sensed at all or are disregarded. So long as the effective attribute is present, the reaction is elicited as an all-or-none function of the attributes. Other characteristics may be radically changed without affecting the reaction. (Lashley, 1938, p. 81.)

In more recent times these ideas have been developed by Bower and Trabasso (1964a), Lawrence (1963), Levine (1966), Lovejoy (1965, 1966), Restle (1955, 1962), Sutherland (1959), Trabasso (1963), Wyckoff (1952), and Zeaman and House (1963). In this section, we will relate what we perceive to be the common core assumptions of these theories without trying to highlight the small differences among them.

11

The first assumption is that stimulus patterns are first analyzed into their constituent parts by analyzers sensitive to variations in particular features of stimulation. The analyzers typically are identified with properties or possible *dimensions* of variation of the stimulus. These stimulus analyzers may be learned (e.g., counting the number of figures), unlearned (e.g., detecting brightness or color), or a combination of learned and unlearned mechanisms (e.g., shape discrimination).

Figure 1.1 illustrates the general diagram of a set of these analyzers arranged in parallel to analyze patterns of geometric figures that vary in

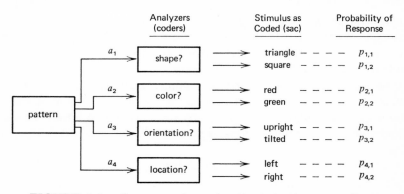

FIGURE 1.1. *Pattern analyzers for discrimination responding.*

shape, color, orientation, and location. For example, the first analyzer listed encodes the shape of the figure. In this case, its output or the stimulus-as-coded (sac) is one of two values correlated with whether the presented figure is a triangle or a square. If a triangle were presented, then the "triangle-output" line of the shape analyzer would be active. In human subjects, these analyzer outputs would often be coordinate with or would elicit an implicit verbal label for the attribute. This point, however, or related ones about conscious awareness of the attributes analyzed need not be appended to the basic theory. It is clear, for example, that humans discriminate many more stimulus variables than they have labels for (Gibson, 1963, 1967). In lower animals, of course, the verbalizations are absent.

There is rarely any commitment in these theories as to how many analyzers there are, how many are brought to bear upon a particular discrimination problem, whether new analyzers or compounds of previous analyzers are developed during the course of discrimination learning, or whether all possible analyzers are available in the system at the outset of training and only their strengths or probabilities of usage are modified during learning. These questions represent the vague fringes of

12

the theories, and few theorists have attempted to discuss these points.* Typically, in representing a given experimental situation, the theorist first enumerates the dimensions of stimulus variations employed, and then assumes that the subject has an analyzer for each such dimension. The evidence that an organism has a particular analyzer is inferred from prior experiments showing that members of this species can be taught a discrimination utilizing variations in this stimulus dimension.

To return to the model diagram in Figure 1.1., the response probabilities p_{ij} listed in the right-hand column give the probability of some particular reference response (e.g., approaching this value, or saying "classification A," etc.) when output j is given by analyzer i. A response probability is brought into play when and only when its corresponding antecedent output occurs. The p_{ij} typically are learned variables established by the reinforcement history on those occasions when output j of analyzer i occurred. The common assumption is that reward or nonreward of the reference response to output ij increases or decreases p_{ij}, respectively. For example, if in Figure 1.1 shape is the relevant dimension with triangles belonging to class A and squares to class B, then the probability of saying A to the "triangle output" ($p_{1.1}$) should converge to unity whereas the probability of saying A to the "square output" ($p_{1.2}$) should converge to zero.

The analyzers in Figure 1.1 are presumed to vary in their strengths, which we have denoted by a_1, a_2, and so on. The main assumption in all attention theories is that not every analyzer is used or is active on a single trial, but rather that only a subset of the total number of analyzers is active. The strengths, a_i, in conjunction with a *sampling* assumption determine the subset of analyzers that will be switched in and possibly also how strongly they are switched in (i.e., how much weight is given to each analyzer in determining the response).

The simplest assumption is that only a single analyzer is active on any given trial. Following Zeaman and House (1963), we will call this the "one-look" model. For the one-look model, major interest centers on the analyzer that is selected on each trial, and the theory is to specify the

---

* Uhr and Vossler (1963) have addressed these problems of perceptual learning in their computer program for pattern recognition. For recognition of visual shapes, for example, their analyzers roughly correspond to asking whether small patches of retinal cells have been activated in a particular constellation by the input pattern. Their program randomly generates its own analyzers for extracting information from local retinal patterns, and then evaluates these during a training series. Analyzers that contribute relevant information for making successful discriminations are increased in their weight or importance; analyzers contributing useless information are decreased in weight, eventually being discarded and replaced by new, self-generated analyzers.

probability that a particular analyzer is selected. In this instance, the a_i can be interpreted directly as selection probabilities, or they can be treated as strengths which are convertible to selection probabilities by some rule such as Luce's (1959) choice axiom (see pages 51–52, Chapter 2, in this book).

Typically, the a_i are considered to be learned variables, influenced by the occurrence of reward and nonreward for responses following selection of analyzer $i;$ but the a_i are also considered to be functions of such variables as the perceptual salience of a dimension, instructional set, and prior experience. In the learning context, the usual assumption is that the selection probabilities are altered according to a "win-stay, lose-shift" principle. That is, the probability of selecting analyzer i is increased if its selection is followed by reward for the subsequent instrumental response or if selection of an alternate analyzer is followed by nonreinforcement; the probability of selecting analyzer i is decreased if its selection is followed by nonreinforcement or if selection of an alternate analyzer is followed by reward.

To review the operation of the system, at the beginning of a trial the subject selects an analyzer, using analyzer i with probability $a_i;$ if value j of dimension i is presented, then the analyzer output is $ij,$ and to this the subject then makes the reference ("correct") response with probability $p_{ij}.$ If reward is provided at the end of this sequence, then there is an increment added to a_i and to the probability of the reinforced response to output $ij;$ if the sequence is nonreinforced, then a decrement is subtracted from a_i and from the probability of the error response to output $ij.$

The obvious implication of this system is that stimulus dimensions that are not analyzed on a given trial (1) do not influence the response made on that trial, and (2) do not have their output-response associations modified by the reinforcing outcomes of that trial. In other words, features that are not noticed neither influence performance nor are learned on such trials. Another implication is that if the subject has an analyzer for the relevant cue of a solvable discrimination problem, then this system expects him to learn the problem eventually. By a trial-and-check process, the subject will try first one and then another analyzer, gradually developing a strong bias toward using the analyzer appropriate to the relevant dimension, and also learning the correct (reinforced) instrumental responses to the outputs from this relevant analyzer.

This formulation of the process in terms of the learning of mediated stimulus-response associations can easily be recast in the cognitive language of hypothesis testing. Indeed, Levine (1966) and Restle (1962) have preferred this formulation. In their terms, the subject's selection of an hypothesis to test corresponds in Figure 1.1 to setting some one $a_i = 1$ (and other $a_i = 0$) and simultaneously setting $p_{i,2} = 1$ and $p_{i,1} = 0$ (or vice versa), all of this being done in one trial. That is, selection of an hypothesis ("choose triangles") corresponds to a dual selection of an analyzer and a response probability. Thus the hypothesis-testing theories are special cases of the general framework depicted in Figure 1.1.

The one-look model supposes that many features of the stimulus have no influence on the response. In other words, such information that enters the receptor is blocked at some point in the nervous system. There are logically two places where this extraneous information could be blocked from issuing into response, namely, before the analyzer or after it. In the first case, information on nonselected channels is not analyzed at all; in the second case, it is analyzed but is not passed on into further memorial or motor-output processes. Although Treisman (1964) has reported evidence that the former view appears the more appropriate, this issue is not of consequence to the results reported here. That is, either view of blocking of unselected channels could be adopted without materially affecting the interpretation of the theories under discussion.

A further issue is whether the blocking is a complete stoppage or only a significant attenuation of the discriminability of the "signals" on the unanalyzed channels. With sufficient attenuation, the signals would carry little, if any, differential information, and so differential responses would not be learned to differentially reinforced signals that were so attenuated. However, interpreting inattention as attenuation rather than complete blockage of an analyzer does allow for the organism noticing particularly important or novel stimuli coming in over the unattended channel (Deutsch & Deutsch, 1963).

A final comment regarding the one-look model. This concerns the "win-stay, lose-shift" reinforcement rule for altering the analyzer-selection probabilities, the a_i. An alternative rule, proposed by Sutherland (1959) and Wyckoff (1952), is that the strength of an analyzer should depend on the *differential* in reinforcement correlated with the two or more outputs from the analyzer. That is, a_i should depend on $p_{i,1} - p_{i,2}$. The intuitive notion is that if the outputs from an analyzer have no correlation with presence versus absence of reinforcement for responding, then it provides no useful information and could be ignored. The two alternative rules deliver the same predictions in most circumstances (i.e., relevant analyzers become strong, irrelevant analyzers become weak), but they differ in certain cases. In particular, they differ concerning their prediction of what will happen to the strength of the relevant analyzer if, following initial learning, one were to begin rein-forcing each value equally often. An experimental realization would be as follows: a rat is first rewarded for approaching a white door and nonreinforced for approaching a black door, with training continuing until the brightness analyzer is selected on every trial; the rat then receives a series of forced trials to black and white doors with equal, 100 percent reward. The "win-stay, lose-shift" rule predicts that the strength of the rat's brightness analyzer will be undiminished by the equal-reward series because the selection of that analyzer begins at 100 percent and is always rewarded. The differentiation rule implies that the animal will detect the equality of reinforcement for approach to black and white values during the second phase (that $p_{i,1} - p_{i,2}$ converges to zero) and so will switch out his brightness analyzer.

Although there is some evidence for the latter view in one of Wyckoff's (1951) dissertation experiments, the circumstances for a crucial test were absent; Wyckoff used intermittent reinforcement and an observing response that competed in some degree with the instrumental response, so the issue is still open. A major conceptual problem with the differentiation view is how to formulate this notion in terms of changes in a_i resulting from single-trial events—that is, how to write difference equations stipulating the trial-to-trial changes in a_i as a function of the analyzer output and trial outcomes that occur. It is not presently known how to do this.

MULTIPLE-LOOK MODELS

The one-look model is an extreme example of a theory involving stimulus selection. It assumes total concentration of attention upon a single dimension or attribute of the stimulus complex. Without wishing to prejudge the range of data explicable in these terms, we can admit the possibility that in some situations the subjects notice more than one attribute per trial. Indeed, the evidence to be presented requires it. Additionally, the fact that subjects *can* learn configural or patterned discriminations also requires that compounds of two or more dimensions can act as single cues. For example, in a two-key Skinner box, pigeons can be trained to peck the left key when both keys are red and to peck the right key when both keys are green. Here the effective stimuli are compounds of a color plus a position: red-on-left and green-on-right become positive compounds, whereas red-on-right and green-on-left become negative.

There are several ways to interpret such configural learning (cf. Estes, Hopkins, & Crothers, 1960; Trabasso & Bower, 1964a; Zeaman &

House, 1963). The simplest conceptual device is simply to postulate a *separate* anaylzer appropriate to detection of compounds of two primary attributes, and that the "one-look" is at the output (one of four, in our example) from this compound analyzer. The conceptual status of the compound analyzer is then the same as the one-dimensional analyzers, and one could hopefully use the theory to estimate the probability that such analyzers are selected over a block of trials. This solves the conceptual problem of patterned learning, but leaves for later filling in many of the very knotty problems regarding generalization of conditioned responses from components to patterns and vice versa (cf. Estes, Hopkins, & Crothers, 1960; Friedman, Trabasso, & Mosberg, 1967).

But ignoring configural learning—which involves special training conditions that were obviated in our experiments—we may still ask whether we can formulate a multiple-look model of attention. That is, each selection would be of a single analyzer but there would be several such selections made per trial, perhaps either successively (in series) or all simultaneously (in parallel). The important rule is that the response would not be specifically conditioned to the unique pattern of active analyzers, but rather would be determined by *averaging* over the conditional connections (the $p_{i,j}$) of the independent analyzers active on a given trial.

When the goal is stated in this manner it becomes perhaps obvious that the stimulus sampling model of Estes and Burke (1953) is an appropriate representation of the desired multiple-look theory. Thus we have independent, stimulus-component sampling probabilities, the θ_i of the Estes and Burke model. Although in the one-look model the a_i probabilities were interpreted as summing to unity, there is no similar constraint on the θ_i of the multiple-look model (except $\Sigma_{i=1}^{N} \theta_i \leq N$). Thus, for this scheme, the effective stimulus on a trial becomes a randomly sampled subset of the outputs from the N stimulus analyzers, and performance is determined by averaging over the conditional connections of this sample. Spence's earlier theory represents the special case when $\theta_i = 1$ for all attributes i that impinge on the receptors, and the $p_{i,j}$ are replaced by habit strengths that are summated. Restle's (1955) earlier discrimination model can be formulated in this manner, with the restriction that the sampling probabilities for irrelevant dimensions are gradually reduced to zero as training continues.

We have found this model involving N *independent* looks to be mathematically intractable for our special purposes. In Chapter 2 we develop a model similar in spirit, but more tractable in detail, based on the idea that the subject takes a fixed sample of size s (with replacement) at the beginning of each trial. However, because he may select the

17

same analyzer several times during the sampling, effectively *weighting* that analyzer more heavily, the number of different analyzers selected can vary from 1 to s on any given trial. A scheme is also given whereby irrelevant dimensions may be temporarily eliminated from sampling. But we are getting ahead of our story, and further elaborations can best wait until Chapter 2. The main point here is that our model will be a multiple-look model that differentially weights the outputs of the N analyzers, where the weights for all analyzers are restricted to sum to a constant. The advantages of this scheme will become apparent as we relate the research conducted around it.

With this digression into attention theories of discrimination learning behind us, we return to the main course of our discussion.

AIMS OF THIS RESEARCH

Our primary goal is to offer new theory and new results regarding selective attention in discrimination learning. We are particularly concerned with characterizing what the subject learns in particular discrimination problems, and are hopeful of developing a theory to predict these results. We believe (as does Berlyne, 1960) that an ideal experimental paradigm for studying selectivity during learning is afforded by "redundant relevant cues" (RRC) problems. An example of an RRC problem involving, say, geometric figures would be one in which a human subject were to learn to put red circles into class A and blue squares into class B, while ignoring irrelevant dimensions such as the size, location, and numbers of the figures. Here both color and shape are relevant dimensions since they correlate perfectly with the correct classification. They are also perfectly redundant: all circles are red and all squares are blue, and other combinations simply do not occur in the training series. Thus, by forcing the subject to learn this classification, we are forcing him to key his responses to something about these two relevant dimensions. Within this constraint, however, there are still a variety of alternative ways the subject could key his responses to the relevant elements, and the discrimination history has not forced a particular outcome here.

The stimulus control exerted by the particular cues can be evaluated by a series of transfer tests, by seeing how well the subject can maintain the learned classification during test series without information feedback, using each cue singly while removing or neutralizing the other redundant relevant cue. The procedure is similar in many respects to that employed by Pavlov (1927) in carrying out salivary conditioning to

18

a compound conditioned stimulus consisting of two elements (e.g., a light and a bell), and then testing for transfer of the conditioned response to the elements singly. The light and bell are redundant, relevant cues in our sense, since presence versus absence of each correlated perfectly with presence versus absence of the reinforcing stimulus. Results from such procedures will be discussed later.

In light of the foregoing discussion, the aims of this research are to investigate the following questions:

1. *What* has the subject learned in a problem involving redundant relevant cues (RRC's)?
2. What conceptions of *how* the subject goes about learning RRC problems will lead us to predict what he learns?
3. What are the variables that influence *how fast* and *what* the subject learns in RRC problems?

The experimental results to be reviewed are largely ambiguous regarding the answer to question 1, mainly because of methodological flaws. Our experiments provide a more definitive answer, at least for adult human subjects. In reply to question 2, we propose a simple attention learning theory, describing an abstract machine (or mathematical model) that samples cues according to their attention values. This theory relates learning rate to attention values of the relevant cues (like the a_i in Figure 1.1) and, as a by-product, predicts what subjects learn in RCC problems. The theory also suggests some partial answers to question 3, the variables influencing how fast an RRC problem is learned and what is learned.

ALTERNATIVE VIEWS OF WHAT IS LEARNED

It is apposite to begin our discussion of what is learned in RRC problems by giving four alternative views on the matter. All of them are somewhat plausible, and indeed at any one time at least a few psychologists can be found to argue for any of the views. This discussion is merely to show that the answer to the question is not obvious. Later we will further explode the reader's prior biases by showing that a single formulation can produce average results in line with either of the four alternatives depending on parameters of the situation that are not represented in the alternative views of what is learned.

The alternative hypotheses regarding what is learned in RRC problems will be labeled the configural, cue-dominance, pattern-component transfer, and habit-distribution hypotheses.

19

The Configural Hypothesis

This supposes that the subject associates responses to the configurated pattern of the two relevant cues as they appear together, and that presentation of a single cue (with the other absent) constitutes a new pattern to which little, if any, transfer will occur from the configurated pattern. This is similar to the Gestalt dictum that a configurated "whole" is not psychologically analyzable into its separate parts. The notion has been proposed for discrimination learning by Estes (1959) and Razran (1965), among others. In Estes' pattern model, responses are associated with entire patterns, with no transfer to other patterns containing common elements. In a concept identification task, one could identify the patterns of interest either as the entire set of configurations of relevant and irrelevant cues or as the configurations of only the relevant cues (blue triangle versus red circle), ignoring the irrelevant cues. By the former view, deletion or alteration of an irrelevant cue would cause severe degradation in performance. But in an earlier experiment (Bower & Trabasso, 1964a, p. 49), we showed this to be false; for example, subjects trained to give response 1 to the patterns ax and $ay,$ and response 2 to bx and $by,$ will transfer perfectly to a or b alone when the irrelevant cues x and y are deleted. Therefore the most plausible interpretation of the configural hypothesis for RRC problems is the second view, which identifies the effective stimuli as patterns of the two *relevant* cues.

The Cue-Dominance Hypothesis

This is the outcome expected by the one-look theories of attention. The subject's attention allegedly is restricted to one dimension at a time, and when he eventually finds a relevant dimension that solves the problem for him, he searches no further. The view was put forth by Lashley (1938, 1942), Lashley and Wade (1946), and many others, including ourselves in an earlier paper (Bower & Trabasso, 1964a, p. 49). The expectation is that the subject will learn one relevant dimension (the "dominant" cue) but not the other. To the former cue, he will respond nearly perfectly in various transfer tests; to the latter cue, he will respond at the chance level in transfer tests. The hypothesis supposes that different subjects and experimental conditions may differ in what is selected to be the dominant cue, but that each subject learns only one cue. The basic dependent variable, according to this hypothesis, is the probability that dimension A dominates B when both are redundant relevant cues. The hypothesis can be elaborated further by specifying

20

some of the variables that will affect this dominance probability (cf. Bower & Trabasso, 1964a; Trabasso, 1963).

The Pattern-Component Transfer Hypothesis

Atkinson and Estes (1963), Friedman (1966), and others have proposed the "mixed" model which assumes conditioning both of stimulus patterns and of components within patterns. Specifically, when the pattern xy is conditioned to response 1, at the same time the elements x and y separately become conditioned to response 1, and these associations will be evidenced by performance to any novel pattern containing x or y as elements. If the associations to be learned are xy-1 and xz-2, and if the xy pattern is learned first, then response 1 will generalize to xz, thus causing errors. Eventual conditioning of xz-2 would stop the generalization errors since, by assumption, the subject responds first to the conditioning of the entire pattern; if the pattern is not conditioned, then performance is determined by averaging over the conditional connections of the elements making up the pattern. As with the configural hypothesis, the model's performance on transfer tests when one relevant cue is removed depends on whether or not the theorist assumes that strictly irrelevant cues are ignored. If irrelevant cues are ignored, and conditioning is to the pattern of relevant cues, then transfer will be essentially perfect to each cue tested singly; if irrelevant cues are not ignored in testing transfer, then the transfer percentage of correct responses will be $(2 + i)/(2 + 2i)$, where i is the number of irrelevant attributes in the test stimulus. As mentioned before, for symmetric concept identification tasks, it appears one can ignore the presence of irrelevant cues on transfer tests, so only the first interpretation—perfect transfer to components—will be considered in this context.

The Habit-Distribution Hypothesis

According to this view, following learning of a RRC discrimination, the subject is expected to show an intermediate degree of transfer to each relevant cue tested singly, but the two cues need not show equal transfer. This follows from Spence's or Hull's theory of RRC learning, whether or not one appends the afferent neural interaction postulate to the theory. Because the two relevant cues always appear together in training, the habit differential (favoring the correct response) produced by each cue is summated as a unit. The problem is learned whenever this summated habit differential is sufficient to offset any fortuitous habit differential allied on any trial against the relevant cues by the irrelevant cues (see Spence, 1936, for details). Thus removal of one of the

21

relevant cues following learning can only reduce the habit differential favoring the correct response, and thus probably leads to errors on transfer. The exact outcome depends on many unknown parameters of the theory (e.g., the initial habit strengths to the various components), but the general expectation is of a decrement in performance on transfer. The decrement need not be the same for both relevant cues, since one cue may have built up a larger habit differential than the other owing to more favorable initial values at the outset of discrimination training. Adding the afferent interaction postulate to the system does not affect matters, since it simply adds more unknown parameters (generalization decrements from s'_i to s_i) to a system that already suffers from too many unknowns. Insofar as it is considered, afferent interaction will simply reduce the amount of transfer some indeterminate amount below what it would be ignoring the interaction effect (which is already indeterminate).

It is apposite to note that the one-look models can imply results demonstrating either dominance (one cue learned) or pattern-component transfer (both cues learned). The transfer outcome depends on the attention probabilities to the relevant dimensions by the end of discrimination training. Although the model is constrained to look at only one relevant cue per trial, it could be looking alternately at both relevant cues over a series of asymptotic learning trials. Let a_1 and a_2 denote the probabilities of attending to the first and second relevant cues. Then the fact of errorless performance at the end of training requires that $a_1 + a_2 = 1$. Any further information about the values of a_1 and a_2 must be given by the attention-learning axioms. For example, the all-or-none learning assumptions of our earlier one-look model (Bower & Trabasso, 1964a) imply that $a_1 = 1 - a_2 = 1$ or 0 is the only admissible set of values. Similarly, the incremental learning axioms of Zeaman and House (1963) and Lovejoy (1966) impose a positive feedback or "trapping" effect on a_1 or a_2 whereby one of them eventually converges to unity and the other to zero. If the attention-learning operators keep a_1 and a_2 bounded away from unity, however, or if the transfer tests occur before complete convergence, then perfect transfer to both relevant cues could be predicted. This line of thinking incidentally raises the question for the Zeaman and House and Lovejoy models regarding how one calculates the attention probabilities when the learning situation is altered by removing some cues or adding new cues during transfer tests. Something like Luce's (1959) choice axiom is needed to renormalize the old probabilities to get the new analyzer-selection probabilities for the reduced situation (e.g., what happens if $a_1 = 1$ and cue 1 is removed?).

22

A COMPOSITE MODEL FOR TRANSFER

To demonstrate the uncertainty involved in inferring what is learned from transfer results, we will present a simple miniature model for transfer. We do not intend to defend the model, but it nevertheless illustrates the equivocation between theory and results on this question. The model follows the same line of thinking presented by Restle (1959), although we develop it somewhat differently.

Assume the RRC's are color and shape, and suppose that the analyzer strengths at the outset of training are given by the weights w_c for color, w_s for shape, and w_i for the combined set of irrelevant cues. The sampling probability θ for an analyzer is given by its relative strength, namely,

$$\theta_c = w_c(w_c + w_s + w_i)^{-1}$$
$$\theta_s = w_s(w_c + w_s + w_i)^{-1}$$
$$\theta_i = w_i(w_c + w_s + w_i)^{-1} = 1 - \theta_c - \theta_s$$

The parameters θ_c and θ_s control the learning rate of the initial problem. Assume that during initial learning both relevant cues are learned perfectly, and that the strength of irrelevant analyzers, w_i, is habituated to zero, whereas w_c and w_s remain constant. Assume further that, on transfer tests where one relevant cue is removed (or neutralized), the novelty of the stimulus context releases habituation of the irrelevant cues, and they recover a fraction d of their former strength w_i. Assume finally that on the transfer test, the subject samples one analyzer, responding correctly with probability 1 if it is a relevant analyzer, responding correctly with probability .50 if it is an irrelevant analyzer.

With these assumptions about learning and transfer, the following equation gives the probability of a correct response on a transfer test with color present and shape removed:

$$p_c = \frac{w_c + .50dw_i}{w_c + dw_i} = \frac{\theta_c + .50d\theta_i}{\theta_c + d\theta_i} \tag{1.1}$$

The identity on the right follows upon dividing each w on the left by the sum of the w's. A similar equation holds for p_s, transfer to shape with color removed; to obtain p_s, replace θ_c in Equation 1.1 by θ_s.

We will suppose that $d = .50$ but any other nonzero value would do almost as well for our illustration. Table 1.1 then gives some patterns of transfer outcomes expected by Equation 1.1 for different choices of θ_c and θ_s. Here .50 is the chance level, indicating no transfer whatsoever.

A glance at Table 1.1 shows that the composite model can produce predictions consonant with either of the four hypotheses depending upon

TABLE 1.1. PROPORTION OF CORRECT RESPONSES TO COMPONENTS ON TRANSFER
TESTS RELATED TO THE LEARNING RATE (θ) OF EACH COMPONENT

Learning Rate		Proportion of Correct R's		
Color	Shape	Color Tests	Shape Tests	Hypothesis Supported
.05	.05	.55	.55	Configural
.75	.02	.95	.59	Cue dominance
.45	.45	.95	.95	Pattern-component transfer
.25	.25	.75	.75	Habit distribution

the learning-rate parameters for the two relevant cues. The larger the
learning rate of a cue, the greater the amount of transfer to it following
RRC learning. If the learning rate of one cue is very high relative to
the other, "cue dominance" in transfer results. It is important to realize,
however, that the outcomes in Table 1.1 were predicated on the assumption that both relevant cues were equally conditioned to a high degree.
The differential transfer results from then dishabituating the irrelevant
cues, which then makes performance depend on the relative weight of the
conditioned stimulus in the test pattern. Presumably if the irrelevant cues
were removed or neutralized for the transfer tests, the conditioning of both
relevant cues would be more in evidence.

Our introduction of this composite model should serve mainly to
start the reader thinking about the relation between learning rate on
particular cues in the RRC problem and the pattern of transfer results
that can be obtained following RRC training. There are firm intuitive
reasons for expecting a positive relationship here. The rate of learning a
problem in which dimension A is relevant should depend on the salience
or "attention value" of that dimension. And by the same token, the
extent of learning of cue A during RRC training with $A + B$ should
increase with its attention value. In the following, therefore, we often
will be concerned with this question of relating learning rate on a cue to
its possible dominance in a RRC problem. In the course of subsequent
discussions, the composite model briefly developed here will be discarded since it can be shown to be inadequate in particulars despite its
generality.

LEARNING RATE AND CUE ADDITIVITY

The first point we wish to make about learning rate in discrimination problems is that it is very sensitive to the stimulus structure of the

problem. In particular, learning rate increases with the salience and number of the relevant dimensions and decreases with the salience and number of irrelevant dimensions. This relationship has been demonstrated many different times in discrimination learning, with both animals and human subjects.

An illustration of the relationship is provided by an experiment on monkeys by Warren (1953). The monkeys learned problems involving simultaneous choice between two stimulus objects presented in a Wisconsin General Test Apparatus. The left-right position of the two objects was varied randomly over trials and was irrelevant. The two objects could differ in their color (C), form (F), or size (S), or in any two of these features, or in all three features. A problem was set up by choosing one object to be positive (rewarded by a peanut) and a second object differing from it in one, two, or three attributes to be negative (nonrewarded). For example, for a color-form problem, the two objects would differ in color and in form, but not in size. A subject would be trained on a particular problem like this for ten trials, and would then be shifted to a new problem involving new stimulus objects. Within a learning-set design, each monkey had seven different ten-trial problems per day for thirty days, with the order of the seven types of problems (see Table 1.2) randomized within the day. Warren assessed the speed of learning the various problems by calculating the percentage of errors for trials 2 through 10 (trial 1 was a guess) averaged over all problems of a given type. The results appear in Table 1.2.

The results in Table 1.2 show that learning was slightly faster with more relevant cues, but that the color cue alone was a very dominant cue

TABLE 1.2. PROPORTION OF ERRORS ON TRIALS 2–10 FOR DISCRIMINATION PROBLEMS THAT DIFFER IN COLOR, FORM, SIZE, OR COMBINATIONS OF THESE

Differential Features	Proportion of Errors
$C + F + S$	.07
$C + F$	.08
$C + S$	.08
C	.09
$F + S$	.21
F	.23
S	.26

(Data from Warren, 1953.)

25

for these subjects. The proportions of errors for all compounds containing color are only slightly less than the errors when only color was relevant. Because of the dominant control over learning rate by the color cue in this instance, it would be expected that single-cue transfer tests following $C + F + S$ training would show performance to be keyed primarily to color and not to the form or size differential.

The Warren experiment shows the influence of a dominant cue without providing very convincing evidence for the additive effects of redundant relevant cues. We move on now to two experiments in which the additive effects of cues on learning rate or performance are quite large. The first experiment to be reviewed, that by Bourne and Haygood (1958), involved human subjects learning concept identification problems having differing numbers of relevant and irrelevant dimensions, each of which appears, from the results, to have had about equal weight or salience. The second experiment, by Hara and Warren (1961), using cats as subjects, provided behavioral assessment of the salience of particular cue differences, and then demonstrated improved performance to additive stimulus combinations upon testing.

TABLE 1.3. ADDITIVITY OF CUES: RESULTS OF ADDING NUMBERS OF RELEVANT AND IRRELEVANT DIMENSIONS ON THE RATE OF LEARNING [a] AND PREDICTIONS FROM ALL-OR-NONE MODEL [b]

Experimental Condition	Number of Dimensions		Observed Mean Errors	Predicted
	Relevant	Irrelevant		
1	1	1	4.3	4.5
2	2	1	3.2	3.4
3	3	1	3.1	3.0
4	4	1	3.1	2.8
5	5	1	2.7	2.7
6	6	1	2.1	2.6
7	1	3	8.2	9.0
8	2	3	6.5	5.6
9	3	3	5.7	4.5
10	4	3	3.9	3.9
11	1	5	13.6	13.5
12	2	5	7.4	7.8

[a] From Bourne & Haygood, 1959.
[b] From Bower & Trabasso, 1964a.

In the Bourne and Haygood study, ten college students were run in twelve different conditions, learning concept identification problems involving binary dimensions (color, form, size, etc.) and two responses. The twelve conditions are listed in Table 1.3 where the number of redundant relevant and independent irrelevant dimensions corresponds to a given condition. The entries in the fourth column of Table 1.3 are the average errors to a strict learning criterion for the ten subjects learning that problem.

A very elementary one-look model of the all-or-none type will suffice to describe these data fairly well. It will be sketched only briefly here (see Bower & Trabasso, 1964a, for details). Assume the subject can be described at any trial as being in one of two states: attending to and responding correctly to a relevant attribute, or attending to an irrelevant attribute and responding so as to be correct 50 percent of the time. Assume further that a correct response preserves his state for another trial, whereas upon making an error (to an irrelevant cue) he chooses another cue at random to attend. The probability of his choosing a particular cue upon such error occasions is presumed to be proportional to the weight of that cue relative to the weights of all the alternative cues. If the weights of the R redundant relevant cues are $w_1, w_2, \ldots, w_R$, and the weights of the I independent irrelevant cues are $w_{R+1}, \ldots, w_{R+I}$, then the net probability that the subject selects one of the relevant cues following an error is:

$$c = \frac{k \sum_{i=1}^{R} w_i}{\sum_{j=1}^{R+I} w_j} \tag{1.2}$$

Here, k is the proportionality constant. If all the stimulus dimensions have equal weights, then the weight per dimension cancels from Equation 1.2 and we have

$$c = k \frac{R}{R + I}$$

If the probability of learning per error is c, then the average number of errors before learning will be $1/c$. Therefore the function

$$\text{Total errors} = \frac{R + I}{kR} = \frac{K(R + I)}{R}$$

was fit to the error score in Table 1.3 by the least-squares method. The least-squares estimate of K was 2.24, and the predictions are shown in the right-hand column of Table 1.3.

The data in Table 1.3 show an increase in errors as the number of irrelevant cues is increased or as the number of redundant relevant cues is decreased. The results are described quite well by the Restle-type formulation (see Restle, 1955) that (1) learning rate depends on the proportion of relevant cues, and (2) total errors during learning bear a reciprocal relation to the learning rate. For further illustrations of such additivity predictions, see Restle (1955, 1957, 1962) or Bower and Trabasso (1964a).

The cue-sampling model just described is a one-look or single-cue model. According to such an idea, adding redundant relevant cues simply increases the probability that the cue the subject selects for testing will be a relevant cue, one that he then can use to solve the problem. On this view, the habit differentials of the relevant cues are not adding to help each individual; rather we are only altering the probability that the subject solves after each error. By this scheme, of course, the subject is expected to learn only one of the R relevant cues, and will show no transfer to the $R-1$ unlearned cues. In Chapter 2 we develop a multiple-look model that implies the same additivity effects in learning rate but allows for more varied outcomes on single-cue transfer tests.

The next experiment to be discussed, by Hara and Warren (1961), illustrates the effects of adding together cues that systematically differ in their salience or discriminability. The subjects were nine cats and the task was a simultaneous choice between two rectangles that differed in size, brightness, and form (ratio of height to width). Each cat first received a prolonged series of tests wherein each stimulus dimension was scaled for discriminability by the method of constant stimuli. For example, in the brightness-scaling series, the two rectangles for choice were the same size and form, but differed somewhat in brightness. One of the two stimuli (the "constant" stimulus) remained the same brightness throughout whereas the brightness of the other (the "variable" stimulus) was varied over trials. The cat was always reinforced for choosing the brighter of the two stimuli; that is, a press on the panel showing that rectangle caused food to be delivered to the cat. By this method, one pair of brightness values was found which the cat could correctly discriminate about 70 percent of the trials, and another pair was found which it discriminated 80 percent correctly. We will call these two brightness pairs the "weak" and "strong" brightness cues, to be denoted as b and B, respectively. In a similar fashion, the dimensions of size and form were scaled for discriminability, and strong (80 percent) and weak (70 percent) pairs of size cues (S and s) and form cues (F and f) were selected.

Following these series of scaling trials, the cats then received many

28

trials with a variety of cue combinations which should have had an additive effect on performance. For example, when size and brightness were added, the positive stimulus was both larger and brighter than the negative stimulus; since the cat had learned to choose larger and brighter stimuli in the prior series of scaling trials, transfer of that learning to the combination test stimuli should be additive. Hara and Warren tested a variety of combinations, obtained by sampling one, two, or three cues from the set $(B$ or $b)$, $(S$ or $s)$, or $(F$ or $f)$. One major simplification of the results is that the three strong cues, B, S, and F, were equally potent as were the three weak cues, b, s, and f. This was to be expected, of course, since these cues were chosen to be equally discriminable (80 percent for strong, 70 percent for weak cues). Thus, in our treatment of the results, we need only distinguish the test combinations according to how many strong and weak cues were allied with the correct alternative. The test stimuli and results are shown in Table 1.4 where the notation C denotes a strong cue and c a weak cue. The "preoperative" data were obtained from all nine cats. The "postoperative" data were obtained four months later from four of the cats that suffered surgical damage to the visual cortex of the brain during the intervening period.

The qualitative ordering of the results in Table 1.4 are quite regular for both pre- and postoperative series. The strong cue produces more

TABLE 1.4. PRE- AND POSTOPERATIVE PROPORTIONS OF CORRECT RESPONSES TO COMPOUND AND COMPONENT TESTS VARYING IN DISCRIMINABILITY

Test Condition	Preoperative		Postoperative	
	Observed	Predicted	Observed	Predicted
c	.718	.747	.683	.676
C	.822	.853	.852	.862
cc	.817	.831	.794	.761
Cc	.883	.886	.864	.880
CC	.900	.914	.902	.920
ccc	.875	.873	.817	.810
Ccc	.948	.906	.917	.894
CCc	.940	.926	.948	.926
CCC	.990	.939	.989	.944
Estimate of:	$a = .978$		$a = .545$	
	$b = 2.394$		$b = 2.629$	

(Data from Hara & Warren, 1961.)

correct responses than does the weak cue. The more weak or strong cues added together, the higher the proportion of correct responses.

The predictions entered into columns 3 and 5 of Table 1.4 come from the elementary sampling model outlined in the previous section. It is assumed that both strong and weak cues are associated with correct responses, but that strong cues have larger weight relative to the set of irrelevant cues in the situation (e.g., position, stray odors, etc.). Let w_1, w_2, and w_i represent the weights for the strong, weak, and irrelevant cues, respectively. The proportion of correct responses to a test combination is given by one times the probability that one of the relevant cues is sampled plus one-half times the probability that the irrelevant cues are sampled. The following formula will illustrate a few of the cases:

$$p(C) = \frac{w_1 + .5w_i}{w_1 + w_i}$$

$$p(Ccc) = \frac{w_1 + 2w_2 + .5w_i}{w_1 + 2w_2 + w_i} \tag{1.3}$$

As we add more relevant cues, we add their weights in the numerator and denominator. This says that the cat is twice as likely to sample a relevant cue if you give it two as opposed to one weak (or strong) relevant cues. Equations similar to 1.3 can be written for each of the nine test combinations. If we divide each term in such equations by w_i, it is apparent that there are only two parameters to the system, namely $a = w_2/w_i$ and $b = w_1/w_i$. Therefore we have obtained least-squares estimates of a and b to best fit the nine data points, treating the preoperative and postoperative data separately. These estimates are shown in the bottom rows of Table 1.4. As can be seen, the predictions are fairly accurate in most cases, except the triple compound proportions are consistently underpredicted by the model. Even so, the average discrepancy between predicted and observed proportions is only .022 for the preoperative data and .020 for the postoperative data. This is well within the range set by the standard deviations of the observed mean proportions.

The relative accuracy of these predictions lends at least some plausibility to the weighted-average model. The prediction equations were derived from the assumptions of the one-look model: on test trials, the subject is assumed to attend to only one cue and respond according to its conditioning, and the probability that he attends to a particular cue depends on its weight relative to the weights of the alternative cues. The effect of adding relevant cues in the test patterns is simply to increase the probability that the one cue sampled is a relevant cue, thus producing a correct response. But for a subject who responded to relevant cue A, his

30

performance in a sense is independent of whether or not relevant cue *B* was also present. This, at least, is the way the one-look model views the situation. Of course, multiple-look models are easily developed that imply basically the same predictions of results.

Although these Hara and Warren results illustrate nicely the behavioral effect of testing with additive combinations of relevant cues, it appears that by the nature of the task the results cannot be used to differentiate between one-look and multiple-look models of the learning or performance processes. To differentiate between these theories, the appropriate experiments are those investigating transfer to single components following RRC learning. This paradigm also gives us a better opportunity to investigate the relationship between the learning rate on a cue and the extent to which it is learned in a redundant relevant cue compound.

GROUP TRANSFER DATA FOLLOWING RRC TRAINING

In this experimental design, subjects are first trained to criterion on a RRC problem, and are then given a transfer problem in which one relevant cue is retained and the other cue is removed in some way. Transfer performance is supposed to reflect the amount learned about the retained relevant cue. Typically, the transfer problem is run until the subject meets some learning criterion, and the performance measure is the number of errors on the transfer task before meeting this criterion.

There are several ways to remove a cue in making up transfer stimuli following RRC training. If training involves choice between two simultaneously presented stimuli (e.g., red triangle-positive versus green square-negative), then a stimulus differential can be removed by presenting both choice stimuli with the same value of that dimension, and this value can be either one of those seen in training or a novel value of that dimension. Thus, to test the potency of the form cue with color removed, the choice set might be red triangle versus red square, or yellow triangle versus yellow square. On the other hand, if training was by the single-stimulus, successive method (e.g., say "A" to a red triangle, say "B" to a green square), then a training dimension is best removed by giving it a new, "neutral" value that is equally distant on a generalization gradient from the two training values. Thus, to remove the red-green differential one presents black figures, to remove the triangle-square differential one presents circles, and so on.

A variety of these types of transfer studies has been done, but we shall review only a few of them here. Some more are reviewed in Chapter 4 where we develop our theory for transfer learning in more

31

detail; others involving paired-associates learning are reviewed and treated theoretically in Chapter 5.

Another experiment by Warren (1954) serves as a useful entry point to this class of experiments. He trained four rhesus monkeys on a series of ninety-six problems, each for fifteen trials. These problems were simultaneous discriminations, and during trials 1 through 6 the positive stimulus differed from the negative stimulus in color, form, and size. Thus there were three redundant relevant attributes and one irrelevant attribute (left-right position of the positive stimulus). On trials 7 through 15 of each problem, the number of relevant cues was reduced by eliminating the differences in one or two dimensions. For example, the initial problem for trials 1 through 6 might be large, red triangle (positive) versus small, green square (negative), and the transfer problem for trials 7 through 15 might be large, red triangle (positive) versus large, red square (negative). In this example, the test is for transfer from color-form-size (*CFS*) to form (*F*). Labeling the six types of transfer problems in terms of the relevant cues retained for trials 7 through 15, the conditions were *CS, CF, FS, C, F,* and *S.* Each problem type was presented sixteen times over the course of the experiment with a different random order for each subject.

In acquisition, the average probability of a correct response on trial 6 was .90, indicating fast learning of the *CFS* problem. In transfer, the results of interest are the averaged proportions of errors over trials 7 through 15; these are listed in Table 1.5 in the second column. Also listed there are the average error proportions from Warren's (1953) earlier study relating acquisition rate to the nature of the relevant cues; these are repeated from our Table 1.2.

In transfer testing as in acquisition, color was the strongest cue. Error proportions for all transfer cases involving color are less than for those involving either form, size, or both. Transfer to both form and size was greater than that to either form or size alone, indicating some additive effect. Comparing the two columns of figures in Table 1.5, a direct relation obtains between the rate of learning of a stimulus combination and the amount of transfer from *CFS* to that same combination. The rank order of the error proportions is essentially the same in the two columns except for the *CF* versus *CS* difference in transfer, which was not reliable. Thus the rate of learning a stimulus component correlates well with the degree of transfer to that component after training on that component in a RRC problem.

Similar findings have been reported by Miles and Jenkins (1965) for pigeons trained on a "go-no go" discrimination to a light-tone compound stimulus. The positive stimulus was a tone plus the lighting of the response key at a bright value, denoted as L_1. The negative stimulus

TABLE 1.5. PROPORTIONS OF ERRORS FOR COLOR, FORM, AND SIZE DISCRIMINATIONS BY MONKEYS

Problem	Transfer [a]	Training
CFS	—	.07
CF	.13	.08
CS	.08	.08
C	.11	.09
FS	.19	.21
F	.25	.23
S	.31	.26

(Data from Warren, 1953, 1954.)
[a] Transfer data were obtained following CFS training.

was no tone plus the lighting of the response key at a dimmer brightness, denoted L_2. Different groups of birds were run with one of four different light differentials, L_1-L_2, and for each condition a control group was run learning the L_1 versus L_2 difference without the tone as an added stimulus. Acquisition proceeded faster with larger L_1-L_2 differences, and was facilitated in all cases by addition of the redundant relevant tone. In fact, our calculations on their data show that average error scores of their additive groups are well predicted by our simple formulation (cf. Equation 1.2) using, for estimation purposes, the error scores of the L_1-L_2 and the TL_1 versus L_1 control subjects. Of greater interest are a series of transfer tests carried out (during extinction) with subjects trained in the TL_1-L_2 conditions. The light intensity on the key was varied, presenting each intensity with or without the tone, and the amount of responding to each stimulus combination was recorded. A measure of tone control over responding was assessed by the difference between the intensity generalization gradients taken with or without the tone present. The neat outcome of this study was that degree of tone control over responding in the TL_1-L_2 discrimination was higher the smaller the L_1-L_2 difference. The more difficult was the brightness discrimination, the more the subject tended to "solve" the TL_1-L_2 compound problem on the basis of the easier tone cue. However, for large brightness differences (bright versus completely dark key), key brightness became the dominant, controlling stimulus and the tone-no tone cue was relegated to a secondary role. To summarize this experiment then, learning of a compound $T + L$ discrimination proceeded at a rate pre-

33

dicted by adding the separate T and L rates; and degree of control of T over responding was very large or very small depending on the salience (learning rate) of T relative to the salience of L.

We shall not review here further studies reporting group average transfer data following RRC training, although such studies are fairly plentiful. Practically all of them are defective for one or another reason for inferring answers to questions regarding what individual subjects learn in RRC problems. Investigators typically have assumed that the group average outcome is representative of the transfer of each individual subject. This sort of inference from group average to individual behavior is known to be fallacious for learning curves (e.g., Estes, 1956), and it probably is fallacious as well for inferring the transfer for an individual subject. A group transferred to a component problem following RRC training probably contains an assorted mixture of "learnings" by various individuals; some may have learned only cue A, some only cue B, some may have learned a little about both cues, and group transfer reflects a crude average over these heterogeneous possibilities. Further, if the transfer problem involves new learning (as opposed to "neutral" test trials that do not alter performance probabilities), then the salience of the new cue to be learned in transfer enters to confound the inference from transfer performance back to what was learned preliminary to the transfer task. A specific and explicit model for transfer and transfer learning following RRC learning is required for making more precise inferences. We attempt to provide this later, in Chapter 4.

Another procedure, used frequently in studying stimulus selection in paired-associates learning (e.g., Underwood, 1963), is to transfer independent groups of subjects to each component of the compound stimulus. The problem with this procedure for inferring what is learned is that each subject is assessed on only one component and not on the other. And the fact that a subject did or did not learn (transfer positively to) one cue gives us no information about whether he learned the other cue in the RRC problem.

For such reasons, the best arrangement for inferring what is learned in RRC problems is provided by extensive single cue tests given on both relevant components with results from individual subjects being reported separately. All of our studies are of this kind; the next section reviews some of the prior studies which have used this assessment procedure.

INDIVIDUAL DATA ON TRANSFER

The evidence from individual subjects, provided by occasional reports scattered throughout the learning literature, tends uniformly to support the "dominance" hypothesis; that is, in a RRC problem the individual subject tends mainly to learn only one of the relevant cues—and he differentially responds quite well to this cue but poorly to the other relevant cues which he did not learn. The configural or habit-distribution hypotheses find no support at all in these data.

The first examples are from studies done in Pavlov's laboratory (reported in Pavlov, 1927, pp. 141–143) wherein dogs were conditioned to salivate to a compound CS consisting of stimuli from different modalities—a touch and a cold stimulus in Palladin's experiment, a tone and three lights in Zeliony's experiment. Following conditioning to the compound, tests with the individual components showed one (the touch or tone) to be dominant and the other (the cold or the lights) to be completely ineffective. The CR to the dominant element alone was as large as to the compound CS. From prior experiments with dogs the ineffective stimuli of the compound were known to be perfectly good cues when conditioned singly. Their ineffectiveness in the compound resulted from their being "overshadowed" (Pavlov's term) by the dominant element.

Later experiments in Pavlov's laboratory showed that when the two stimuli belonged to the same modality (both were sounds), the more intense one, being more discriminable from the background or between-trials stimulation, was usually the dominant element. If the two sounds were of equal intensity, then they tended to be learned equally well in the compound.

Much further work on compound conditioning in the Pavlovian situation has been done, especially in the Soviet Union (see Razran, 1965, for some review), but we will not attempt to review that literature here. In general, the work is not directly relevant to the transfer obtained following *explicit* differential training of compounds involving dimensionalized stimuli.

A study demonstrating selective learning in discrimination of compounds was reported by Jones (1954). Six pigeons were trained in a simultaneous procedure to peck the positive stimulus that differed from the negative stimulus in color, form, and position. Following RRC training, the pigeons received four types of tests to determine component control over choices. However, instead of using test stimuli with one component differential and the others constant, Jones "opposed" the various cues. For example, the positive color and negative form would be pitted against the negative color and positive form. Suppose for illustration that the positive stimulus in training was a green circle on the right, and the negative stimulus was a red triangle on the left. Then the four test patterns, listing first the stimulus presented on the left, would be: (1) red triangle versus green circle, (2) green triangle versus red circle, (3) green circle versus red triangle, and (4) red circle versus green triangle.

From the subject's choices on an interrelated series of such tests, one can infer his cue preferences. For example, the pigeon might peck always on the right, or always the green stimulus, or always the circle. Levine (1966) has used similar opposed-cue tests (without feedback information) during training to infer which of several elementary hypotheses human subjects were using in simple concept-identification tasks. It is clear enough how a subject should respond on such opposed-cue tests if he has learned only one cue in the prior RRC problem—namely, he should always choose the learned cue. The sticky feature of these tests occurs for subjects who may have learned two or all three of the redundant cues; the opposition tests then produce conflict for them. There are two strategies for them to pursue: choose objects randomly when learned cues conflict, or rank order the conflicting cues by chance or preference and choose consistently according to this ordering. The latter strategy that a three- or two-cue learner could follow brings out the main weakness of opposed-cue tests—namely, the sequence of choices by a subject who randomly selected color (after learning color and form) is the same as another subject who only learned color. That is, these tests impose a kind of single-cue preference, or else random responding, upon the multiple-cue learner.

To return to Jones' pigeons, individual animals were quite consistent in their choices to one cue over the series of opposed-cue tests. Four pigeons responded only to color, two to position, and none to form. Jones extended this study by training these same pigeons on later single-component problems, with the two stimuli differing only in color, shape, or position. Measures of learning rates in these problems showed the same general ordering as in the opposed-cue tests: color was learned the fastest, position next, then form the slowest. These data then support the relation between learning rate on a component and the probability that it is learned or becomes dominant in a RRC problem.

Further demonstrations of selective learning of components in RRC discriminations have been reported by Reynolds (1961). Two pigeons were reinforced for pecking a white outline triangle on a red background but were extinguished to a white outline circle on a green background. They were tested later for their response to the four components during an extinction series: red, green, triangle, or circle (the latter cues on a black background). One bird responded solely to the red key and not to the triangle; the other bird responded only to the triangle and not to red (green or circle elicited no responding from either bird).

36

Thus there was complete dominance of the compound discrimination by one component.

A second experiment reported in the same paper involved a conditional (patterned) discrimination. The four stimulus compounds projected successively on the response key were a red triangle, a blue triangle, a red circle, and a blue circle. The conditional cue was a yellow or green lamp going on about 2.5 inches to the side of the response key. The reinforcement rule was this: if the yellow sidelamp were on, responses to red were reinforced but to blue were extinguished (form irrelevant); if the green sidelamp were on, responses to triangle were reinforced but to circle were extinguished (color irrelevant). The pigeons learned these conditional discriminations after prolonged training. Reynolds then altered the sidekey stimuli in several ways to see what features of them were controlling the patterned behavior. By turning on both, or neither, sidekeys when the response key went on, it was determined that the pigeons were primarily coding the yellow-green sidekey cue simply in terms of presence versus absence of yellow. By further tests, substituting white for yellow, red for green, or dimming the yellow sidekey, Reynolds determined that the controlling feature of the yellow-green nominal stimulus was the brightness of the sidekey: sidekeys equally bright as the yellow one elicited the same conditional pattern of responding (to the four response-key stimuli) as did yellow, whereas dim sidekeys produced the "green" pattern of responding. Thus the nominal stimuli of yellow versus green wavelengths, which pigeons can differentiate, were in this instance being coded only in terms of their brightness.

Reynolds' experiment demonstrated selective excitatory control over responding by one component of a compound S^+, with virtual absence of responding to the other component of S^+ or the components of S^-. An experiment by Eckerman (1967) has demonstrated a complementary effect, namely, selective *inhibitory* control of nonresponding by one component of S^-. To demonstrate this, Eckerman first trained his pigeons to respond to four stimulus components (horizontal or vertical line, red or green color) projected singly on the response key; this was followed by prolonged compound training, with green plus vertical line as the reinforced compound and red plus horizontal line as the nonreinforced compound. Subsequent to discrimination learning, tests with the four single components showed that for one of three pigeons inhibition of responding to the compound S^- was controlled primarily by the red color and not by the horizontal line. In fact, for this pigeon the horizontal line (part of S^-) evoked more responses in the test series than did the vertical line (part of S^+). Thus the inhibition that normally would have occurred from extinction to a horizontal line alone was completely overshadowed by the inhibition developed to the more conspicuous color component of the S^- complex.

A further demonstration of selective attention in individual subjects was reported by D'Amato and Fazzaro (1966) using an ingenious technique that can be highly recommended. They trained two monkeys on a compound discrimination between a white vertical line on a red background versus a horizontal line on a green background. On some trials, however, the monkey had the option of seeing only one as opposed to both components of the compound. To initiate a trial, the monkey pushed a switch that set up one of four trial types as follows:

1. The full compound stimuli occurred, one on a left panel, one on the right (randomized locations), with reward for pressing the panel illuminated with the positive compound.
2. A white center key came on which the monkey then had to press to turn on the two compound stimuli on the sidekeys.
3. The white center key came on as did the red and green colors of the two sidekeys; the monkey could respond either to the color alone, or could press the white center key to add the vertical and horizontal lines to the sidekeys before responding.
4. Same as 3 above except the vertical-horizontal lines came on the sidekeys with the white center key, and the monkey could choose on the basis of the horizontal-vertical cue or press the center key to add the colors to the lines before making his choice.

Each of the four types of trials occurred equally often in random order throughout training. The critical data are afforded by trials of types 3 and 4, in which the subject has the option of responding immediately on the basis of the component shown or choosing to see the other component as well before he "risks" a goal-directed response. If the animal chose a sidekey immediately on trials of type 3 but opted for more information on trials of type 4, one would infer that the color component dominates his discrimination. If the opposite pattern obtained, then the vertical-horizontal line component would be the dominant element. The attractive feature of this procedure is that it provides a temporal picture of the development of discriminative control by the components and the compound. Its disadvantage is the extensive pretraining required to get the animals to work on the chained schedule.

Both monkeys in the D'Amato and Fazzaro study showed a strong color dominance, as one would expect from Warren's data reviewed earlier. Throughout the course of learning, the percentage of correct choices to the color alone was almost identical to the percentage correct

38

with the compound stimuli. One animal never responded to the lines alone, always choosing to add the color component before making its goal-directed response. The other animal produced the compound about 80 percent of the time when the trial began with the line stimuli; this animal also showed some learning of the line-orientation cue later in training. The subject that never responded to lines alone was later trained in a special trial series to discriminate the line-orientation cue. When retested in the initial "option" situation, however, this special line training had no effect in overcoming the prior color dominance in that situation.

Demonstrations of selective learning in a RRC problem with rats have been reported by Sutherland and Mackintosh (1964) and Sutherland and Holgate (1966). Using a notion similar to a "conservation of attention" law, they reasoned that in a RRC problem the more the subject attends to and learns about cue A the less it will learn about cue B. Hence, transfer scores for each individual on single-cue tests with A and B should be negatively correlated.

In the Sutherland and Mackintosh experiment, rats were trained on a black-horizontal rectangle (BH) versus white-vertical rectangle (WV) simultaneous discrimination. Following learning, test trials on single components were interspersed among regular RRC trials by holding constant the value of the untested dimension and rewarding the rat for either choice. Specifically, the test patterns for orientation were BV versus BH, and WV versus WH; the test patterns for brightness were BV versus WV, and BH versus WH. Measuring the percentage correct transfer responses for each rat on the two test series, Sutherland and Mackintosh found a negative correlation of $-.42$.

Sutherland and Holgate (1966) replicated this experiment with similar results (their correlation was $-.56$) and found additional effects. One effect was that with prolonged overtraining on the RRC problem, more rats eventually learned both cues, so that the correlation between percentage correct on orientation and brightness tests dropped to zero. Furthermore, if these overtrained rats were nonrewarded (extinguished) throughout a protracted series of single-cue test trials, the negative correlation between component scores reappeared strongly ($r = -.86$). The idea was that overtraining increased the amount learned about the less preferred cue, but it nonetheless was extinguished faster than the preferred cue, thus inducing the negative correlation again during extinction.

We turn now to review some of the evidence for selective learning in RRC problems by human subjects. First are some studies by Luria (1960) on figure-ground relationships. Introspectively, when we attend

39

to some object, we make it "stand out" as a figure on a background. Examining the situation from the other side, it seems reasonable that "figures" capture more attention than backgrounds. Luria was interested in this issue. In one experiment, a child was presented with one of two cards, either a red circle on a gray background or a green circle on a yellow background. In the presence of the first card, he was rewarded for squeezing a ball with his right hand; to the second card, he was rewarded for responding with his left hand. Opposed-cue tests then were given: red circle on yellow ground, and green circle on gray ground. Results were that test responses were those appropriate to the figure color, not the ground.

Luria described two further experiments in which this figure dominance was reversed by language and emphasizer cues. In Martsinovskaya's experiment, before training, the experimenter began by pointing to the background and telling the child to respond with his right hand if it was gray and with his left hand if it was yellow. The extent to which this verbal instruction was understood, remembered, and guided performance on the opposed-cue test (thus reversing figure dominance) increased with the age of the child. Percentages of age groups responding to the background were 44 percent for three to four years, 80 for four to five years, 70 for five to six years, and 90 for six to seven years.

Another study, by Abramyn (see Luria, 1960), involved similar training but replaced the colored circles by drawings of red and green airplanes on gray and yellow backgrounds. During instructions and rewarded training, the experimenter emphasized the background colors of the pictures by meaningful comments such as "The plane can fly when the sun is shining and the sky is yellow" or "When the weather is bad and it rains, the plane cannot fly—it must be stopped." In this condition, all children at the age levels tested responded to the background on the opposed-cue tests. Thus a physical stimulus can be given associative value and emphasis by such language cues, and these facilitate its selection or control over responding to compounds in which it appears.

The studies just reviewed used opposed-cue tests, so they were biased toward results showing single-cue dominance. However, a recent experiment by Suchman and Trabasso (1966b) with young children used "neutralized cue" tests for responding to single components following RRC training; this procedure, of course, does not force the "dominance" outcome. To obtain a possible correlate of which of the RRC cues would dominate in a child's discrimination, Suchman and Trabasso (1966a) employed a simple cue-preference assessment before the dis-

40

crimination problem was given. They measured each subject's preference for the dimensions of form, color, and size of geometric figures by use of a modified "method of triads" (see Torgerson, 1958). The child would be presented with a card containing three figures differing in these dimensions; any two of the three figures were the same on one dimension but differed on the other two dimensions. For example, the three figures might be (a) large red square, (b) small red circle, and (c) large blue circle. The child was asked to select those two figures that were "most alike." If he chose a and b, he was said to have a color preference; if a and c, a size preference; if b and c, a form preference. Over a series of forty such test cards, the children made very consistent choices, with most children preferring color, next most preferring form. There was a reversal in the frequencies of these preferences with age (from three and a half to six years).

In a later experimental session, Suchman and Trabasso (1966b) had these same children learn to sort stimulus cards into left or right bins according to whether the card contained a red triangle or a blue circle. After attaining a learning criterion, the child received single-cue tests without reinforcement. For the color tests, red and blue stars were used, neutralizing form; for the form tests, black outline triangles or circles were used, neutralizing color.

When the group was divided into those assessed previously as preferring color and those preferring form, few errors occurred on the single-cue tests involving the preferred cue whereas many errors occurred on tests with the nonpreferred cue. Across subjects, the correlation between errors on the color and form tests was $-.38$, much as Sutherland and Mackintosh (1964) had found with rats. However, 32 percent of the subjects made no errors on either component test, indicating they had learned both cues.

In another experiment, Suchman and Trabasso (1966b) had children learn discriminations either with color relevant and form irrelevant, or vice versa. As expected, an interaction occurred between cue preference and problem difficulty: children previously assessed as preferring color learned the color problem quickly but the form problem slowly; children preferring form gave the opposite ordering of learning rates.

We may conclude from these two experiments that the triad assessment procedure gives reliable estimates of dimensional preference, at least for children; that this measure correlates well with the child's likelihood of attending to the preferred cue during a discrimination problem, thereby affecting his learning rate (positively if the cue is relevant, negatively if it is irrelevant) and affecting which cue will dominate following RRC training. This is a simple "response-response"

41

correlation, and it can be used in an explanatory sense without any concern at the moment for the reasons why some children prefer color and others prefer form.

SUMMARY COMMENTS

By way of summarizing the evidence reviewed on individual subjects, we have seen that the predominant outcome is that of cue dominance, although to be sure there are occasional subjects who show good learning of both cues. But, in general, negative correlations are obtained between transfer scores on the two cues in the RRC problem. Since most, if not all, experiments involved bringing the subjects to a learning criterion, it is difficult to invoke the argument of insufficient training to explain the absence of learning on the nondominant cue. The individual subject data provide no consolation for the configural or habit-distribution views of RRC learning. On the other hand, they are not particularly consoling for a *strong* form of Lashley's hypothesis, which might suppose that it is always the same dimension that is dominant for each subject and that no subject could learn both cues. Instead, with large enough groups, it appears that a certain proportion of subjects will learn only cue A, another proportion will learn cue B, and still others will learn both cues A and B. Which of these groups a given subject is likely to be in depends on a multiplicity of factors, included among which would be the relative saliences (attention values, learning rates) of dimensions A and B, and preexperimental preferences of the subject for particular dimensions. The relative saliences of dimensions A and B doubtless depend on the discriminability of the two or more values used to exemplify each dimension. Only in the Hara and Warren (1961) study were the stimulus values specifically chosen to make the three dimensions equally discriminable. And only in the Miles and Jenkins (1965) study was the discriminability of one dimension varied across groups to see how this would affect which cues subjects learned in RRC problems. Therefore most of the evidence simply provides demonstrations of stimulus selection in RRC without providing further experimental variables that influence the likelihood of particular dimensions being selected in the RRC problem.

A final word here regarding methodology. Comparing the individual subject results with those reported in terms of group averages in transfer, it is clear that the group averages can give a distorted and grossly misleading picture of what is learned in RRC problems. The group averages doubtless contain mixtures of subjects with heterogeneous learnings, who show a pattern of transfer performances more or less unique to what they have learned. But in averaging over transfer performance of such heterogeneous subjects, the overall results look rather supportive of the habit-distribution idea, or of the idea that relevant cues "add together" in affecting the performance of each individual during learning or during testing. But we have seen that the individual data reject the habit-distribution notion of what is learned, and that the additivity data for learning and multiple-cue testing *could* be explained by a one-look model. In the next chapter we present one version of a multiple-look discrimination learning model that appears to us to be consistent with most of the data we have reviewed. After developing the model and empirically testing its adequacy, extensions, and implications, we will return in the final chapter to noting a few of its failings and how these might be rectified.

2

A MODEL FOR STIMULUS
SELECTION IN LEARNING

Having reviewed some of the evidence for stimulus selection, cue dominance, and cue additivity, we now begin investigation of a theoretical system that will help us to understand the empirical relations. Before commencing this enterprise, however, it is useful to have some statement of the goals or aims of the theoretical search. Any listing of desiderata and facts to be explained is necessarily incomplete and open-ended, since it is continually altered by new experimental evidence. Nevertheless, we think it wiser to list explicitly what we wish the theory to accomplish rather than to have no maps at all to guide us.

GOALS OF A THEORY
FOR STIMULUS SELECTION

The first desideratum of a theory of stimulus selection is that it should provide a useful representation of the salience, or importance, or noticeability, of a cue. This is done later in our discussion of cue weight. Second, the theory should specify some rules or mechanisms whereby certain cues are selected from the overall stimulus display; and further it should provide an explicit connection between the salience of particular cues and their likelihood of being selected. Third, this theory of cue salience and cue selection should be related in an explicit way to rate of learning discrimination problems wherein particular cues are relevant to solution. In particular, the theory should imply that the rate of learning should vary directly with the number and salience of the relevant cues and inversely with the number and salience of irrelevant cues. As a corollary of the foregoing, the theory should accommodate results from experiments on cue additivity and various manipulations of relevant and irrelevant cues. A fourth desideratum is that the theory should provide a sensible way to characterize what the subject has learned at the completion of a discrimination problem involving redundant relevant cues (RRC's). What does he know, and how has he come by this particular knowledge? Given this knowledge, the theory should tell us what kind of transfer performance is to be expected of this subject on one or another subsequent task. For example, in our RRC experiments with cues A and B, it is found that some subjects learn only cue A but know nothing about cue B, other subjects learn only cue B, whereas still other subjects learn both cues. A fifth desideratum is that the theory should predict the likelihood of particular modes of solution or patterns of acquired knowledge (e.g., learn A but not B). Furthermore, these likelihoods should be related in a reasonable way to the structure of the discrimination problem—the saliences of the particular relevant cues, the number of irrelevant cues, and so forth.

To this list of theoretical desiderata, one must, of course, add the most difficult, namely, that most of the testable implications of the theory should be empirically confirmed. Moreover, reasonable interpretations (or specifications as to where the theory is incomplete) should be available for at least the more obvious counterevidence.

SPECIAL RESTRICTIONS

To this general recounting of theoretical goals, we list a few special restrictions under which we have operated. These are listed separately because they constitute strategies subject to controversy, and many readers will differ from us on these points. Our first restriction is that the theory of stimulus selection should be developed with sufficient precision so that it may be cast as a mathematical model, so that important parameters of the theory may be estimated from data and its predictions evaluated according to their numerical accuracy. That is, we wish the theory to operate effectively in the "specific-quantitative" mode in a number of instances. However, it is frequently used for qualitative predictions as well when conditions for numerical predictions are not fully realized. Second, we confine ourselves to theoretical decisions that lead to *tractable* mathematical models; in practice, this requires a preference for simple hypotheses that lead to explicit estimation and prediction equations. For example, we have not pursued theoretical alternatives that lead to unwieldy mathematical expressions that cannot be worked through explicitly (several are briefly mentioned later). This preference for simple mathematical structures in a preliminary investigation results from the ease of deriving implications, estimating parameters, predicting results, and evaluating the model. Partly because of this restriction we do

45

not have high confidence in the empirical accuracy of the exact details of the theory proposed here. But we propose it as a good and useful starting place.

Perhaps the most serious restriction we have placed on our search for a theory of stimulus selection is that it should be consistent with the Markov learning model which Restle and we have used previously to describe acquisition in simple concept-identification problems (Bower & Trabasso, 1964a; Restle, 1962). This reflects a desire for continuity and consistency in our theoretical work. That model was written for a specific situation, namely, the trial-by-trial learning of simple, two-category concept-identification problems by adult human subjects and it was in that context that evidence for the model was originally collected. Since all our studies reported herein involve the same general situation, the desire for consistency is understandable.

There are three essential assumptions to that Markov learning model. The first assumption is that performance can be adequately represented as a two-state process: presolution and solution. The subject in the presolution state is viewed as testing hypotheses based on irrelevant cues, and hence his probability of a correct response to a pattern selected at random would be .50 in a two-category problem. The solution state corresponds to the subject holding the correct hypothesis and responding according to it for the remaining trials. The subject begins the series of acquisition trials in the presolution state, with learning consisting of a discrete change on some one trial into the solution state where the subject remains. On this view, the probability of a correct response over trials prior to the subject's last error should be stationary at .50, and such evidence has been found repeatedly (Bower & Trabasso, 1964a; Erickson, Zajkowski, & Ehmann, 1966; Guy, VanFleet, & Bourne, 1966; Holstein & Premack, 1965; Trabasso, 1963).

The second assumption is that opportunities for learning (entering the solution state from the presolution state) occur only in trials in which the subject makes an error, whereas correct response trials provide no opportunity for the subject to exit from the presolution state. This assumption follows in the spirit of the hypothesis-testing rationale: if an (irrelevant) hypothesis leads to a correct response, it is retained for test on the next trial; if it leads to an error, then another hypothesis (possibly the correct one) is tried. On this view, the correct hypothesis, once adopted, is held indefinitely, simply because it always leads to a correct response. Various indirect tests (Bower & Trabasso, 1964a) and some direct assessments by Levine (1966) have indicated that this assumption is approximately correct in the situations investigated. For example, Levine found that the probability that a person would change

46

his hypothesis following an error was about .98 and following a success was about .05.

The third assumption is that an error is an (uncertain) recurrent event in a subject's sequence of responses. Unpacking this assumption, it assumes that following each error the subject has a constant probability (call it c) of solving the problem. This leads to a geometric distribution of errors before solution. This is the simplest assumption to use in calculations from any hypothesis-sampling theory and several indirect tests of the assumption (Bower & Trabasso, 1964a, b; Trabasso & Bower, 1964b, c) gave no evidence against it. However, recent and more direct evidence (Erickson, Zajkowski, & Ehmann, 1966; Erickson, 1967; Holstein & Premack, 1965; Levine, 1963, 1966, 1967; Suppes & Schlag-Rey, 1965; Trabasso & Bower, 1966) has shown some improvement in c over trials above that to be expected from the subject's rational use of information provided on the error trial; that is, one has to recognize that the subject may carry some past information in memory in making his current hypothesis selection. The subject may recall previous hypotheses tried and rejected, or he may recall previous stimuli and correct responses, and use that remembered information together with the information from the current trial to reject particular hypotheses. By either means, the rejection of irrelevant hypotheses increases the probability of the subject sampling the correct hypotheses.

To illustrate just one of these cases of changing c values, we describe an experiment by Levine (1966) which enabled him to infer on each trial the size of the operative set of hypotheses from which the subject was sampling. The task was a simultaneous discrimination involving the stimulus cards depicted in Figure 2.1. Two complementary figures were shown per trial and the subject's task was to pick the "correct" figure. The dimensions of variation were form (X or T), color (black or white), size (large or small), and position (left or right). There are eight elementary or single-valued hypotheses in this task, corresponding to the rules "Pick X," "Pick the left figure," and so on. Subjects were trained on many problems involving these dimensions, with each elementary hypothesis being correct equally often; this was to teach the subjects the types of solution and to equalize sampling probabilities of the various hypothesis. Then over a long series of similar problems, the data in Figure 2.2 were collected. Figure 2.2 plots the estimated number of operative hypotheses for subjects who made their last error on trial 2, 3, . . . , 9 of a training series. The estimate is simply the reciprocal of a conditional probability, namely, the conditional probability of a criterion run of correct responses immediately following an error on trial n. If subjects had, say, three operative

47

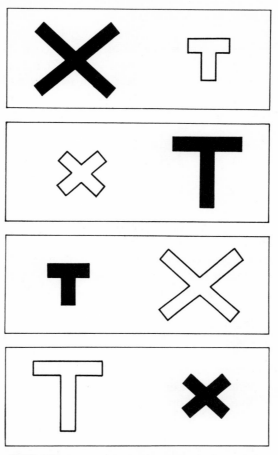

FIGURE 2.1. *Examples of stimuli used by Levine (1966) in a simultaneous discrimination to infer hypotheses used by subjects.*

hypotheses after some error trial and if they selected one of these at random, then with probability 1/3 it would be the correct hypothesis, issuing into the criterion run. Conversely, given a learning probability of 1/3 for those subjects making an error on trial *n,* then we infer three operative hypotheses for subjects at this point in the experiment.

Comparing trial 2 with trial 3 in Figure 2.2, there is a reduction in the number of hypotheses, but there appears to be little consistent change over the following trials. The question is, how much memory for past information need be assumed to account for such results? The general answer seems to be "Not much," and we will try to show the plausibility of this answer. Our hypothesis-sampling model assumes that

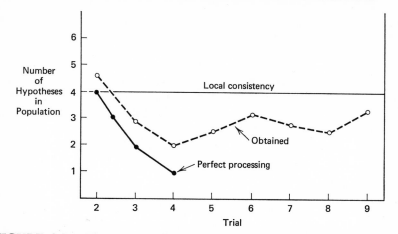

FIGURE 2.2.   *The size of the operative set of hypotheses from which subjects sample on successive trials. Estimates are the reciprocals of proportions of subjects who begin criterion runs on trial* n (*data from Levine, 1967*).

the subject samples only those hypotheses that are consistent with the information provided on the error trial—an assumption Gregg and Simon (1967) have dubbed "local consistency." For example, if the subject made an error on the second card of Figure 2.1 and was told that the figure on the left was correct, then only four (not eight) hypotheses are consistent with this information, namely, X, small, white, and left. A further sampling restriction that could apply on trials after the first would be for the subject not to consider the alternate value within the dimension referred to by the hypothesis he has just disconfirmed on this error trial. Thus, if he came into this trial holding the hypothesis "black is correct" and this was disconfirmed, then he would tend not to try white, but would choose randomly among the remaining three locally consistent hypotheses, namely, X, small, or left. The point is that a locally consistent subject, knowing his hypothesis, knows that "black" was correct on a previous card; after his current "black" error, he now knows that black is inconsistently reinforced (irrelevant), and so by the nature of the problem white also will be irrelevant and should not be sampled on this trial. Following Gregg and Simon (1967), we would label these processing assumptions as "local consistency with local nonreplacement of the disconfirmed dimension."

These assumptions impute very little "memory for past information" to the subject; local consistency requires only that the stimulus and reinforcement of the current trial are available to him, perhaps in short-term memory if not otherwise; local nonreplacement requires in addition that he know the hypothesis used for responding on the current trial. And yet these give values of four or three which are well within the range observed in Levine's experiment. What is not accommodated is the shift from trial 2 to trial 3 in Levine's data.

Such data indicate that the deviations from the local-consistency assumption are relatively small and nearly constant over trials; but even these could be obtained only in a relatively precise experiment in which the number of hypotheses is small, there is simultaneous display of all attribute-value pairs, and the subjects are well practiced in solving such problems involving just these attributes. The discrepancy probably would be even smaller in our experiments where the procedure involves successive presentation of single stimuli, naive subjects, and many dimensions. In the interests of parsimony and simplicity, then, we shall continue to use the assumptions of constant c and local consistency in what follows, even though we are painfully aware that situations can be devised which produce some deviations from this assumption. The theoretical complications needed to handle the small discrepancies (e.g., Erickson, 1967; Trabasso & Bower, 1966) cost more than they are worth in effecting better theoretical fits especially in the following experiments in which this assumption is not central to the issue under investigation.

A process theory of learning, such as we shall propose later, may have a large number of implications about experimental outcomes, but yet only some of these are routinely examined. Owing to tunnel vision, contemporary conventions, or whatever, the theorist simply does not stumble upon the relevance of certain aspects of his data to his theory. In retrospect, we believe that this has occurred in our own case, specifically regarding stimulus-sequence effects in learning. All of our experiments involve random stimulus sequences, different for every subject, and the theory is applied to error measures summed over trials. And in this application the randomness of the stimulus sequence is specifically evoked for making derivations. But the theory also makes very strong predictions about the subject's responses to particular stimuli given his past sequence of stimuli, responses, and reinforcements. We have never examined these effects, yet we now consider them to be a fruitful focus for testing a learning theory. Indeed, preliminary analyses of this sort in concept identification (Dodd & Bourne, 1967; Falmagne, 1967; Levine, 1966) suggest a high information yield and anticipate rapid progress in altering possible theories about how this task is learned.

REPRESENTATION OF CUE SALIENCE

It is assumed that the stimulus pattern and its experimental context as perceived by the subject consists of an assemblage of N

attributes or stimulus dimensions (also called cues). Examples of attributes would be the color, size, position, orientation, and shape of geometrical figures shown on flashcards to the subject. Each effective attribute has two or more values; thus, red and blue would be the values of the color attribute.

Of these N attributes, the experimenter may recognize only a subset $k,$ which he has explicitly introduced, whereas the remaining $N - k$ attributes have been introduced or confabulated by the subject. These latter, incidental attributes presumably are based on unintentional cues, such as extraneous smudges on the flashcards, the tone of voice of the experimenter in delivering trial-by-trial feedback, traces from the past sequence of correct answers, and so on. Such incidental cues cannot be totally eliminated, and it is best to recognize explicitly their existence. One often has little other recourse to explain why learning is sometimes so much slower than what appears warranted by the explicit irrelevant cues that have been introduced.

To represent the salience or noticeability of an attribute (say, cue i), we will assign to it a weight, w_i, which is assumed to be a fixed parameter over the course of a single acquisition series. The N attributes then may be arranged in a hierarchy according to their weights. The weight is assumed to summarize the effects of all those factors that influence the noticeability or attention value of a cue.

To digress briefly, the factors affecting the weight of a cue may be classified roughly as innate, stimulus-bound, and past-training factors. The innate label simply covers an inability to explain species-specific differences in sensitivity to different cues and/or sense modalities. For example, in laboratory lore, pigeons are good on visual discriminations, rats on odors, dogs on pitch differences, and so on. The stimulus-bound factors refer to perceptual arrangements that make a cue stand out; included would be background-contrast arrangements, the physical difference between the several values of the attribute, the use of various emphasizers which themselves are not differential cues but which point to a differential cue (cf. Trabasso, 1963), the intensity or "vividness" of a particular stimulus component, and so forth. The past-training factor includes the discriminative history as well as instructions to human subjects to "look for" this and "ignore" that. Experiments by Lawrence (1949, 1950) and various others have established that animals can be trained to have a bias toward using particular attributes that have been successful in the past. The transfer work on intradimensional versus extradimensional shifts also points to rearrangements in the cue-weight hierarchy due to past training (Zeaman & House, 1963).

Although such factors as these are assumed to affect the weight of a cue, we must also add that the likelihood that a particular cue will be

51

selected or attended to must depend on the context of its presentation, or the alternative cues that are present and their weights. Such considerations lead us to postulate that the saliency or attention value of an attribute depends on its *relative weight* in the population of available cues. Letting a_i represent the attention value of cue i, we define the relative weight as

$$a_i = \frac{w_i}{\sum_{j=1}^{N} w_j} \tag{2.1}$$

This equation may be interpreted in the following way: if the subject were restricted by some means to representing the stimulus display by just one attribute, then a_i is the probability that he chooses the current value of attribute i to so represent it. Equivalently, a_i is the probability that the subject samples attribute i from the population of N attributes that he could notice.

Equation 2.1 has the same form as Luce's choice axiom (Luce, 1959), which relates choice probability of one from N responses to the strengths or v values of the N responses. Our w's are analogous to Luce's v's. Selection probabilities depend on the ratio of the w's, and such ratios can be estimated. By the nature of the case, if it is found that certain kinds of past training increase the ratio w_1/w_2, one cannot decide without further comparisons whether cue 1 has been enhanced in its importance, or cue 2 has been demoted, or both. Judicious comparisons with other, neutral cues not involved in previous problems may permit decisions among these types of changes.

A signal benefit of using Luce's axiom is that it tells one how to compute new sampling probabilities when several attributes are either added to or subtracted from a reference training set. One simply adds or subtracts the corresponding w's to the sum in the denominator of Equation 2.1. The implication is that the ratio of two sampling probabilities, a_i/a_j, is constant and independent of the other attributes that also may be present. This is a distinct advantage over the models of Lovejoy (1966) and Zeaman and House (1963) who define observing response probabilities directly for a particular stimulus situation, but then have no rule for calculating new probabilities when cues are added or subtracted from the base set.

THE SEARCH MODE

In learning a discrimination, the subject is assumed to operate alternately in the *search* mode, then in the *test* mode. While in the search

52

mode, the subject makes decisions about which attributes to select (or sample) from the array, and how to assign classificatory responses to the values of the attributes that have been so selected. It is assumed that the subject operates in this search mode for a brief time after he receives an error-feedback signal. At such moments the cue weights and the sampling process are brought into play. (Several alternative sampling schemes are discussed later.) To illustrate, suppose to the nth pattern of the series, the subject responds B and the experimenter gives the error signal, "No, the correct answer is A." The subject is viewed as immediately taking a fresh sample from the N attributes. Suppose he selects or decides to look at the size, color, and shape of the geometrical figure before him. To assign classificatory responses, he notes that the figure before him is a large blue square, and it was called A by the experimenter. The subject therefore assigns responses rationally consistent with this information, namely (large-A, small-B); (blue-A, red-B); and (square-A, circle-B). Each of these attribute-value-response assignments may be considered as a plausible hypothesis regarding the correct rule for classification. Restle (1962) speaks of this process as the sampling of hypotheses.

The result of the search operation is a selected number of attributes with associated responses assigned to their values. We will refer to this as the *focus sample*.

THE TEST MODE

Following selection of a focus sample, the subject is then viewed as switching over to the test mode for the next pattern shown in the training series (i.e., for trial $n + 1$). In the test mode the subject is viewed as testing out the correctness of the set of hypotheses in his current focus sample. This consists in classifying each subsequent stimulus pattern according to the hypotheses in the current focus sample, and evaluating the feedback or reinforcement obtained. When a response is correct or reinforced, hypotheses in the focus that dictated that response are retained whereas those that indicated the opposite (error) response are eliminated from the focus at that moment. (Implications of this are derived later.) When a response is in error, the sample focus is given up and the search mode is reactivated. A new sample focus is selected and the testing operations proceed on it. The alternation of search-sample-then-test goes on until an errorless solution is obtained. By hypothesis, a solution focus is defined as one that never reactivates the search procedure since it provides for errorless performance. While in the test mode, the weights or saliences of the various attributes have no bearing on the process. They enter only in determining the composition of the focus sample selected during the search operation. We have detailed our conception of this process to prevent misunderstandings which can arise when the details are merely insinuated. The assumptions employed here are essentially those proposed by Restle (1962).

OPERATIONS ON THE FOCUS SAMPLE

We now derive the probability that the subject will solve the discrimination problem after each error. Let c denote this solution probability per error. This probability is a function of two parts: first, the probability that the sample focus selected on an error (search) trial has particular compositions of relevant and irrelevant cues; and second, the likelihood that a sample focus of a particular composition will eventuate in a solution with no further errors. In the following, we derive the latter quantity, after which we turn to the former problem regarding sampling.

Suppose that a particular sample focus consists of s cues of which x are relevant and $s - x$ are irrelevant. The quantities x and s may be random variables with distributions implied by particular sampling schemes, but for the present, suppose that x and s are fixed numbers. We wish to know the probability that a focus of x relevant and $s - x$ irrelevant cues eventuates in a solution. Because of the random sequence of the stimulus patterns, each irrelevant cue will have an independent probability p on each trial of being allied with the correct, relevant cues. With probability $q = 1 - p$, an irrelevant cue will dictate the opposite or incorrect response on each trial. The response rule adopted for conflict trials is that of statistical learning theory, that is, the probability of the correct response is the proportion of cues in the focus sample that dictate that response.

To begin the derivation, suppose that an error has occurred on some arbitrary trial, call it 0 for a reference point. On the next trial, 1, the expected number of cues dictating a correct response is $x + p(s - x)$; that is, all the relevant cues plus a fraction p of the $s - x$ irrelevant cues. Thus the probability of a success on trial 1 (event S_1) given an error on trial 0 (event E_0) is

$$Pr(S_1 \mid E_0) = \frac{x + p(s - x)}{x + (s - x)}$$

The probability of an error on trial 1 is one minus the above, or

$$Pr(E_1 \mid E_0) = \frac{q(s - x)}{x + (s - x)}$$

Suppose that in fact the subject chooses correctly on trial 1. Thus he eliminates from his sample focus those irrelevant cues, $q(s - x)$ in average number, which dictated the opposite response on trial 1. His sample focus now consists of $x + p(s - x)$ cues. Given a success on trial 1, what is the likelihood of a success on trial 2 (event S_2)? Of the $x + p(s - x)$ cues in the current focus, an expected number $x + p^2(s - x)$ dictate the correct response. Hence this conditional probability is

$$Pr\,(S_2 \,|\, S_1 E_0) = \frac{x + p^2(s - x)}{x + p\,(s - x)}$$

and the probability of an error is

$$Pr\,(E_2 \,|\, S_1 E_0) = \frac{pq(s - x)}{x + p(s - x)}$$

Suppose that a correct response occurs on trial 2. This permits the subject to eliminate a further set of irrelevant cues, $pq(s - x)$ in average number, and thus the expected sample focus is reduced to a size of $x + p^2(s - x)$. By extending this elimination argument, it will be seen that the expected number of focus cues remaining after k consecutive successes is $x + p^k(s - x)$; and the conditional probability of yet another success is

$$Pr\,(S_{k+1} \,|\, S_k \ldots S_1 E_0) = \frac{x + (s - x)p^{k+1}}{x + (s - x)p^k}$$

and the probability of an error is

$$Pr\,(E_{k+1} \,|\, S_k \ldots S_1 E_0) = \frac{p^k q(s - x)}{x + (s - x)p^k}$$

At this point, we define a random variable, H', representing the number of successes before the next error. Once an expression for the probability distribution of H' is obtained, the solution probability (c) is easily derived from it. The distribution of H' may be obtained from the conditional probabilities calculated above. The derivations proceed as follows, where h_0 is used to abbreviate $q(s - x)/s$:

$$Pr\,(H' = 0) = Pr\,(E_1 \,|\, E_0) = \frac{q(s - x)}{x + (s - x)} = h_0$$

$$Pr\,(H' = 1) = Pr\,(E_2 S_1 \,|\, E_0) = Pr\,(E_2 \,|\, S_1 E_0) \cdot Pr\,(S_1 \,|\, E_0)$$

$$= \frac{pq(s - x)}{x + p(s - x)} \cdot \left[\frac{x + p(s - x)}{x + (s - x)} \right] = \frac{pq(s - x)}{x + (s - x)} = ph_0$$

$$Pr\,(H' = 2) = Pr\,(E_3 S_2 S_1 \,|\, E_0)$$

$$= Pr\,(E_3 \,|\, S_2 S_1 E_0) \cdot Pr\,(S_2 \,|\, S_1 E_0) \cdot Pr\,(S_1 \,|\, E_0)$$

$$= \frac{p^2 q(s - x)}{x + p^2(s - x)} \cdot \left[\frac{x + p^2(s - x)}{x + p(s - x)} \right] \cdot \frac{x + p(s - x)}{x + (s - x)} = p^2 h_0$$

It is clear that, as these chains of conditional probabilities are extended, the numerators are canceling the next denominators, leaving simple expressions. A conjecture that is easily proved is that the distribution of H' is given by

$$Pr\,(H' = n) = h_0 p^n = \frac{(s - x)}{s}\,qp^n \qquad \text{for } n = 0, 1, 2, \ldots$$

This is an improper distribution because it does not sum to one over all its values. What it sums to is the likelihood that there is another error sometime following the reference error with which we began. Call this sum $1 - c$, since c is the solution probability per error. The sum is

$$Pr\,(\text{another error}) = \sum_{n=0}^{\infty} \left(1 - \frac{x}{s}\right) qp^n = 1 - \frac{x}{s} = 1 - c \qquad (2.2)$$

Hence, the probability of no more errors following this reference error is $c = x/s$. This is the result we were seeking. The probability that a sample focus of x relevant and $s - x$ irrelevant cues eventuates in a solution is x/s, the proportion of relevant cues in the sample focus. Note that his solution probability is independent of p, the chance proportion correct when irrelevant cues are used for responding.

As noted already, the expression for the distribution of H' is improper because it does not sum to one (i.e., the next error is an *uncertain* recurrent event). However, by dividing that expression by $1 - (x/s)$, the likelihood of another error, one obtains the proper distribution of the length of success runs (between adjacent errors) conditional upon a next error occurring, namely,

$$Pr\,(H = n) = \frac{Pr\,(H' = n)}{\left(1 - \dfrac{x}{s}\right)} = qp^n$$

Thus success runs are expected to be geometrically distributed. This result was first derived by Restle (1962) and later by Bower and Trabasso (1964a). The latter have found it to be an accurate description of their data from simple concept-identification tasks. It is of interest that neither s nor x enters into the distribution of success runs between errors. This means that the data are expected to show the same run structure even though the size and constituency of the sample focus may vary between subjects or within one subject from one sample to the next.

The preceding discussion of elimination of cues from the sample focus can easily be extended to handle certain results on response latency and confidence ratings. Typically, it has been found (Erickson, Zajkowski, & Ehmann, 1966; Falmagne, 1967) that response latencies decrease for a number of trials following the last error and that the subject's confidence in the correctness of his response increases. Falmagne (1967) has shown that similar latency decreases are observed over a presolution sequence of successive correct responses, before the last error. A natural hypothesis is to suppose that response latency is proportional to the number of cues effective in the focus sample on a given trial; that is, each effective cue in the sample focus is scanned and a response determined for it, and each of these cue-scanning operations takes a randomly variable amount of time. If the x cues in the focus are scanned serially, each with a mean time of $\bar{t}$, then the mean time taken to produce a response will be linearly related to $\bar{t}x$. Since, by assumption, error-indicating cues are eliminated from the focus following correct responses, it follows that the mean size of the sample focus decreases during a run of correct responses (this is true before as well as after the last error). The unconditional mean size of the sample focus following k consecutive correct responses can be shown to be $sa + (s - sa)p^k$, where a is the sampling probability of relevant cues and p is the probability that an irrelevant cue is correct on any trial (usually one-half). This is a decreasing function of k, so this would explain the decreasing response latencies during a run of successes. The increasing confidence of the subject in the correctness of his response could be handled by supposing that his confidence rating is inversely related to his response latency. Two alternate bases may be suggested for his confidence judgment: first, confidence may simply be reciprocally related to the number of cues in the focus sample; and second, it may be directly related to the proportion of the focus sample cues that dictate the correct answer. As shown earlier, the conditional probability of a success following a run of k successes increases steadily with k, so this would account for the increasing confidence during a run of successes.

ALTERNATIVE SAMPLING SCHEMES

Recall that immediately following an error, the subject is assumed to give up his previous focus, reenter the search mode, and select a new sample focus to test. This selection of a new focus is assumed to occur by random sampling from the N attributes, where the sampling is restricted by certain rules. All the sampling schemes have simple urn representations, in which attributes correspond to different colored marbles that are drawn from an urn according to certain rules.

For this reason, a sampling scheme may be coordinated with its urn representation. It is at this point in our theorizing that the requirement for mathematical tractability weighs heavily. Several alternative sampling schemes are plausible, yet all but one of those considered lead to intractable mathematics. We mention briefly several alternative sampling schemes and indicate one or more of the analytic problems that thwarts their use.

1. *Independent sampling:* In this scheme each attribute i would have independent probability a_i of being sampled. The sample size would be a random variable, ranging in value from 0 to N. A problem with this scheme is that no simple closed expression can be derived for c, the solution probability per error (comparable to our Equation 2.4) so that not even additivity of learning rates can be tested. In order to simulate the system, all N parameters (a_i's) have to be known.

2. *Luce's ranking rule:* This scheme is to select a fixed number, s, of attributes using the w_i as per Luce's ranking rule (1959); that is, choose the most salient cue, set it aside from the choice set, then choose the next most salient cue, and so on until s cues have been selected. This leads to unwieldly equations for the probability that a particular (relevant) cue will appear in the sample, involving sums of s products of ratios of w_i's with changing denominators. To simulate the system, all N of the w_i need to be known.

3. *Fixed sample size, equal sampling probabilities:* In this scheme, the subject is assumed to sample s attributes without replacement, with each attribute having an equal likelihood (of s/N) of appearing in the sample (cf. Estes & Suppes, 1959). This scheme is tractable but it has no hope of accounting for the large differences we find in relative saliences of particular dimensions. For this reason it will not be pursued.

4. *Fixed sample size, multiple "elements" per attribute:* In order to bring in the notion of the saliency or weight of a dimension, this scheme first represents an attribute by a set of "elements," with the weight of the attribute coordinated with the measure or number of elements in the set. The ratio of the numbers n_i and n_j assigned to dimensions i and j is the same as their weight ratio, w_i/w_j. An appropriate urn scheme would represent the system by multiple varieties of colored marbles in an urn, with n_i marbles having color i. The rule is to sample s elements without replacement from this urn. The solution probability per error, c, has been worked out elsewhere (Bower & Trabasso, 1964c; Restle, 1962), and the scheme implies additive learning rates. However, it becomes intractable (cf. Bower &

Trabasso, 1964c) in carrying out derivations for the probability of various types of solution of a RRC problem, since these lead to factorial functions of parameters which cannot be estimated in an ordinary experiment.

A WORKABLE SAMPLING SCHEME

A tractable scheme, which we will use, is one differing only slightly from item 4 in the preceding list, and may be labeled "fixed sample size with independent selection probabilities." It has two representations that are equivalent so we state both. The first is that the subject takes a sample of size s with replacement, each time independently selecting from the N dimensions according to the same probabilities, the a_i. By the independence scheme, the subject could select a given dimension from 0 to s times on a trial; let x_i equal the number of times he selects attribute i. The weight of dimension i in the subject's sample focus is then x_i/s. The sample weight, x_i/s, is like an *amplifier* factor, reflecting the importance the subject is going to give to attribute i in determining his response. An alternate urn representation of this scheme is as in item 4 except that the n_i are presumed to be very large numbers, so that sampling of s elements with replacement gives essentially the same result as does independent sampling. Here x_i would represent the number of elements sampled from the n_i elements representing attribute i in the urn. This scheme implies that each random variable, x_i, is binomially distributed with parameters s and a_i, and that the joint distribution of all N random variables, the x_i's, is the N-level multinomial. This scheme is tractable, and some of its implications are shown in the following paragraphs.

The experimental case to which we wish to apply this scheme is that in which there are two redundant relevant cues, labeled simply 1 and 2, and a number of irrelevant cues. If one does not differentiate among the irrelevant cues that the subject is using at any moment, then these may be lumped together into a "single" irrelevant cue, 3, that has a combined weight equal to the sum of the separate weights of the irrelevant cues. In accordance with Equation 2.1, let a_1, a_2, a_3 denote the probabilities that an element selected represents attribute 1, 2, or 3. From Equation 2.1 and the definition of a_3, it follows that $a_1 + a_2 + a_3 = 1$.

The sample focus is described by the values of x_1, x_2, and $x_3 = s - x_1 - x_2$, that is, the number of sampled elements corresponding to attributes 1, 2, and 3. The sampling scheme implies that x_1, x_2, x_3 have the three-level *multinomial* distribution, namely,

$$Pr(x_1 = j + x_2 = k) = \frac{s!}{j!k!(s-j-k)!} a_1{}^j a_2{}^k a_3{}^{s-j-k} \qquad (2.3)$$

where j and k can vary from 0 to s, constrained by $(j+k) \leq s$. This multinomial form is easily generalized to accommodate as many relevant attributes as required by the experimental task. For example, with four redundant relevant attributes, there would correspond a five-level multinomial with probabilities a_1 through a_5 (summing to one), where a_5 denotes the combined probability of sampling from the pool of irrelevant cues. The a_i are always calculated according to Equation 2.1.

SOLUTION PROBABILITY

We now have the essential elements for calculating the probability of solving per error, c, which is the learning rate parameter of the learning model. Equation 2.3 gives the probability of drawing focus samples of particular compositions, and Equation 2.2 gives the likelihood of solution given a focus sample of a particular composition. These elements are combined in the following derivation:

$$c = Pr(\text{solution}) = \sum_j \sum_k Pr(\text{solution} \mid j, k) \cdot Pr(\text{sample with} \\ j + k \text{ relevant cues})$$

$$= \sum_j \sum_k \left[\frac{(j+k)}{s} \right] Pr(x_1 = j + x_2 = k)$$

The last expression shows that c is just $1/s$ times the sum of the average values of x_1 and x_2. For a multinomial, the average value of x_1 is sa_1, and of x_2 it is sa_2. Hence the final result is

$$c = \frac{1}{s} E(x_1 + x_2) = \frac{1}{s}(sa_1 + sa_2) = a_1 + a_2 \qquad (2.4)$$

The theory thus implies that the learning rate for a problem where cues 1 and 2 are redundant and relevant is the sum of their sampling probabilities, a_1 and a_2. The basic summation formula applies, of course, to any number of relevant cues. Surprisingly, this additivity result is independent of the sample size, s.

As indicated elsewhere (Bower & Trabasso, 1964a; Restle, 1962), this formula may be applied to predicting learning rate and error measures in cue-additivity experiments, of which there are several paradigms. The learning parameter is estimated by the reciprocal of the average total errors per subject for a particular condition. This follows from assuming that each subject begins in the presolution state, and may learn on each error trial with probability c. Under these assumptions, the average errors per subject before learning (call it T) should equal $1/c$. Hence the reciprocal of T is an estimate of c; it can be shown in fact to be a maximum likelihood estimate of c. If there are nonsolvers, that is, subjects who do not reach the learning criterion, then this estimation formula is altered in a minor way to take account of the nonsolvers (Trabasso & Bower, 1966).

In the introduction, we reviewed some of the effects on learning rate of adding relevant and irrelevant cues to the discrimination situation. There have been several designs used in such "cue additivity" experiments. We illustrate two briefly since the formulas are required for later use.

1. *Fixed attribute pool of size N:* In condition i, cue i is relevant and the remaining $N - 1$ cues are irrelevant. In condition $i + j$, cues i and j are redundant and relevant whereas the remaining $N - 2$ cues are irrelevant. From Equations 2.1 and 2.4 it may be shown that the learning rates should be related as:

$$c_{i+j} = c_i + c_j \qquad (2.5)$$

2. *Fixed pool of N − 1 irrelevant cues:* In condition i, cue i is added to the pool and it is relevant. In condition $i + j$, both cues i and j are added to the same irrelevant pool and they are redundant and relevant. The relationship implied by Equation 2.1 for this case is

$$c_{i+j} = \frac{c_i + c_j - c_i c_j}{1 - c_i c_j} \qquad (2.6)$$

The important feature of Equations 2.5 and 2.6 is that they permit prediction of the learning rate of the RRC group from prior assessment of the learning rates for control groups learning with each relevant cue singly. And, of course, with a good descriptive model, knowledge of the learning rate then permits predictions of all statistics regarding the course of acquisition of a group of subjects—the mean learning curve, the probability distribution of errors, of trials before the last error, and various sequential statistics of the data. Tests of Equations 2.5 and 2.6 have been reported elsewhere (Bower & Trabasso, 1964a; Restle, 1962) with uniformly confirmatory results. That is, the RRC group learns faster than the single-cue control groups, and by an amount about equal to that which the formulas imply. In Chapter 1, we said that additivity of learning rates would follow from one-look models because of increased probability of sampling a relevant cue in the RRC problem. In this section, we have shown that a multiple-look model can similarly accommodate the results on additive learning rates. The multiple-look model differs from the one-look models in allowing for, but not requiring,

61

multiple-cue learning in RRC problems. We now turn to derivations regarding this issue of what is learned in RRC problems.

THE NATURE OF THE SOLUTION FOCUS

Consider a RRC problem with cues 1 and 2. At the end of solving this problem, our subjects (cf. the following experiments) could be classified into one of three distinct categories: those subjects who learned the responses associated with cue 1 but not those correlated with cue 2; those who learned cue 2 but not cue 1; and those subjects who associated responses to both cues. Let p_1, p_2, and p_{12} (summing to one) denote the respective proportions of subjects falling into these three categories. We wish now to use our sampling theory to derive some prediction formula for these three probabilities. They are clearly *conditional* probabilities, that is, the likelihood that a subject enters one of these categories given that he has solved.

To illustrate what the model is calculating here, consider a search trial on which the subject samples two elements, possibly both from the same attribute. If both elements are irrelevant, then the subject cannot solve with this sample and it may be ignored for the present calculations. If one element is from attribute 1 and one from attribute 2, then the subject will solve on this sample and thus will have learned both attributes. However, he could solve knowing only attribute 1 either if both elements sampled were from attribute 1, or if one element were from attribute 1 and the other from an irrelevant attribute. From Equation 2.2 the latter sample has probability $1/2$ of eventuating in a solution.

We begin with the derivation of p_1, the likelihood that the subject learns cue 1 but not cue 2. In the sampling theory, p_1 is interpreted as the probability that a solving focus contains at least one element from the set representing attribute 1 and zero elements from the set representing attribute 2. The idea is that if attribute 2 is not represented in the solving sample, then it is not learned, so the subject will be unable to perform consistently correct on single-cue tests involving cue 2. A slightly more general rule would require some threshold number, r, of elements from a dimension to be in the solving focus in order to support transfer to single-cue tests involving that dimension. The equations below use $r = 1$ since this produces the simplest results.

The probability that a solution focus contains no elements from attribute 2 and one or more elements from attribute 1 may be written as

$$p_1 = \frac{Pr\,(\text{solution} + x_1 > 0 + x_2 = 0)}{Pr\,(\text{solution})}$$

Returning to Equation 2.4, the probability of solution in the denominator is $a_1 + a_2$. The numerator is obtained from Equation 2.3 by setting $k = 0$, multiplying by j/s, and summing over all j:

$$p_1 = \frac{1}{(a_1 + a_2)} \sum_{j=0}^{s} \left(\frac{j}{s}\right) \frac{s!}{j!(s-j)!} a_1^j a_3^{s-j}$$

This expression is similar to that for the mean of a binomial distribution. The difference is that a_1 and a_3 do not sum to one, but rather to $1 - a_2$. If we multiply top and bottom of the equation by $(1 - a_2)^s = (1 - a_2)^j (1 - a_2)^{s-j}$, we obtain

$$p_1 = \frac{(1 - a_2)^s}{(a_1 + a_2)} \sum_{j=0}^{s} \left(\frac{j}{s}\right) \frac{s!}{j!(s-j)!} \left(\frac{a_1}{1 - a_2}\right)^j \left(\frac{a_3}{1 - a_2}\right)^{s-j}$$

The summation terms now consist of $1/s$ times the mean of a binomial distribution which has parameters s and $a_1/(1 - a_2)$, and a mean of $sa_1/(1 - a_2)$. Thus,

$$p_1 = \frac{(1 - a_2)^s}{(a_1 + a_2)} \left(\frac{1}{s}\right) \cdot \frac{sa_1}{1 - a_2} = \frac{a_1}{a_1 + a_2} (1 - a_2)^{s-1} \qquad (2.7)$$

This is the expression we were seeking. We reserve comment on this result until p_2 and p_{12} have been derived.

The derivation of p_2 follows a similar line. In Equation 2.3, one sets $j = 0$, multiplies by k/s, and sums over all k. Using the same derivational procedure, the expression for p_2 is found to be symmetric to that for p_1 in Equation 2.7, namely,

$$p_2 = \frac{a_2}{a_1 + a_2} (1 - a_1)^{s-1} \qquad (2.8)$$

Equation 2.8 is the same as Equation 2.7 with an interchange of the subscripts 1 and 2.

Finally, to obtain p_{12}, the probability of learning both cues, we note that $p_1 + p_2 + p_{12} = 1$, since each solver must solve in one of these three ways. Hence, by subtraction one obtains:

$$p_{12} = 1 - p_1 - p_2$$
$$= 1 - \frac{a_1(1 - a_2)^{s-1} + a_2(1 - a_1)^{s-1}}{a_1 + a_2} \qquad (2.9)$$

We comment on these equations for the proportions of subjects who learn either cue 1 or cue 2 or both cues. A first important feature is that they are simple functions of a_1 and a_2, which are parameters that can be directly estimated from the average errors made by control subjects who learn with a single relevant cue, where either cue 1 or cue 2 is relevant. Thus the equations relate the proportions of various "solution types" in the RRC problem to the average errors made by different subjects trained on single-cue control problems. This nontrivial relation requires that the a_i parameters remain invariant across different experimental conditions; it affords a strong test of a mathematical theory. Second, the sample size parameter, s, enters explicitly for the first time into the prediction equations. As s is varied, the proportion of subjects who are expected to learn one or two attributes varies in a sensible way. For example, when $s = 1$ no subject should learn both cues, and Equation 2.9 gives $p_{12} = 0$ for this case. As s increases, p_1 and p_2 decrease, whereas the proportion of two-cue solutions, p_{12}, increases. That is, as the subject increases the breadth of his sample focus, he becomes more likely to learn both relevant cues in a RRC problem. The result is intuitively obvious, and one would want almost any sampling theory to imply something like it. Third, since s appears only in these equations, the observed values of p_1 and p_2 must be used along with Equations 2.7 and 2.8 to estimate the value of s. The predicted values of p_1 and p_2 ($p_{12} = 1 - p_1 - p_2$) depend on the three parameters a_1, a_2 and s. However, a quantitative test is possible if a_1 and a_2 are estimated from single-cue control groups, leaving only the free parameter s to be so chosen to fit the observed values of p_1 and p_2. And, of course, if the theory is incorrect, then possibly no value of s will suffice to fit the observed values of p_1 and p_2.

An alternative method of testing Equations 2.7 and 2.8 is to eliminate s and obtain a direct relationship between p_1 and p_2 which is independent of s. By taking logarithms of Equations 2.7 and 2.8 and carrying through some algebra, it is found that p_1 and p_2 should be related by a power function; that is,

$$p_1 = \frac{a_1}{a_1 + a_2} \left[\frac{p_2(a_1 + a_2)}{a_2} \right]^\alpha \qquad (2.10)$$

where $\alpha = \ln (1 - a_2) / \ln (1 - a_1)$. The converse relation of p_2 to p_1 may be obtained by interchanging subscripts in α and in Equation 2.10. If estimates of a_1 and a_2 are available from control groups, then Equation 2.10 permits a prediction of p_1 once p_2 is known (or vice versa). A plot of Equation 2.10 yields a two-parameter family of curves in the unit square (p_1 versus p_2), all falling within the convex space defined by the antidiagonal $p_1 + p_2 \leq 1$. The function lies on the main diagonal of the unit square when $a_1 = a_2$; otherwise the function is above or below the main diagonal accordingly as a_1 is larger or smaller than a_2.

In testing the relations in Equations 2.7–2.10, one must be mindful of the fact that a_1 and a_2 will be fallible estimates of true parameters obtained from control subjects. The variance of the estimate $a_i = c_i = 1/T_i$ may be shown to be

$$Var(a_i) = \frac{a_i^2(1 - a_i)}{N_i}$$

where N_i is the number of subjects in control condition i (Bower & Trabasso, 1964a). This variability in the estimates of a_1 and a_2 should be considered in assessing the accuracy of the p_i predictions, which suppose that the true values of the a_i are used in Equations 2.7–2.10.

IMPLICATIONS OF THE SOLUTION-TYPE EQUATIONS

At this point, it may be useful to indicate some of the implications of Equations 2.7–2.9 since much of the experimental work to be reported here is concerned with testing the implications of these equations. First, the formulas for p_1 and p_2 provide a succinct summary of the theory's predictions of "cue dominance." In particular, $1 - p_2$ is the likelihood that the subject learns at least cue 1, whereas p_1 is the likelihood that he learns only cue 1, so that cue 1 will dominate cue 2 in any subsequent transfer test. This prediction is tested in Chapters 3 and 4. If p_{12} is high, then the pattern of transfer results on single-cue tests will be essentially that predicted by the "mixed" model which assumes perfect pattern-to-component transfer. The relationship of p_1 and p_2 to the weights of these cues is found by using Equation 2.1 to substitute for a_1 and a_2 in Equations 2.7 and 2.8:

$$p_1 = \frac{w_1}{w_1 + w_2}\left(\frac{w_1 + w_3}{w_1 + w_2 + w_3}\right)^{s-1}$$

and

$$p_2 = \frac{w_2}{w_1 + w_2}\left(\frac{w_2 + w_3}{w_1 + w_2 + w_3}\right)^{s-1} \tag{2.11}$$

It is easy to show that if $w_1 > w_2$, then $p_1 > p_2$; that is, the more salient cue is more likely to dominate, and more so the greater the difference between the weights. If we fix w_2 and w_3 and increase w_1, then p_1 will increase and p_2 will decrease. Consider the result obtained when the combined weight of the two relevant cues is fixed, i.e., $w_1 + w_2 = K$. As w_1 varies from 0 to K, what happens to p_{12}, the likelihood of a two-cue solution? The prediction is that p_{12} increases from 0 through a maximum and then returns to 0 as w_1 approaches K (and w_2 approaches

65

0). The maximum of p_{12} can be shown in fact to occur when $w_1 = w_2 = K/2$—that is, when the cues are equally salient. This result means that when two cues are equally salient (learned at the same rate by single-cue control subjects), we expect more subjects in the RRC problem to learn both cues than in cases where one cue is more salient than another. This implication is tested in Chapter 6.

Consider now the expected outcome of varying the number and combined weight of the irrelevant cues (summarized by w_3 in Equation 2.11). Fixing w_1 and w_2, an increase in w_3 should lead to increases in p_1 and p_2, with a corresponding decrease in p_{12}, the proportion of subjects who learn both cues. Roughly speaking, the more noisy the stimuli, the more likely that the subject will learn only one of the two relevant cues. A further prediction is that if $w_1 > w_2$, then the relative dominance of cue 1 over cue 2 (p_1/p_2) will decrease as more noise (w_3) is added to the stimuli. That is, p_2 increases faster than p_1 as w_3 is increased. Implications such as these will be tested in Chapter 6.

EQUATIONS FOR THREE RELEVANT CUES

The techniques used to derive p_1, p_2, and p_{12} for two redundant relevant cues are general and may be applied to any number of relevant cues. In many respects, the test of the model becomes more severe as the number of relevant cues increases because the number of solution categories increases; thus the ratio of predictions to estimated parameters increases. For example, with three relevant cues, there are seven different types of solution foci: the three single cues, three different pairs of cues, and all three cues together.

In general, for a problem involving n redundant relevant cues there will correspond $2^n - 1$ different solution types—that is, different combinations of the relevant cues in the solution focus. The basic theory should predict the probabilities of the various combinations from knowledge of $n + 1$ parameters, namely, the a_i's for the n-relevant cues and s. The a_i's for the relevant cues could be estimated either from single-cue control groups or directly from the solution-type proportions. Since the $2^n - 1$ proportions must sum to one, there are $2^n - 2$ degrees of freedom in the data, and the theory would be testable from the solution proportions alone whenever $2^n - 2 > n + 1$, or when $n \geq 3$.

The equations for the three relevant-cues arrangement are presented here. Analogous to Equation 2.3, let a_1, a_2, and a_3 denote the respective sampling probabilities of the three relevant cues, and let $a_4 = 1 - (a_1 + a_2 + a_3)$ denote the likelihood of sampling from the combined set of irrelevant cues. Let i, j, k be arbitrary indices for the

66

three relevant cues; p_i is the likelihood of solving only on cue $i;$ p_{ij} is the likelihood of solving on cues i and j but not $k;$ and p_{123} is the likelihood of solving on all three cues. By methods analogous to those used before, general expressions for these probabilities are found to be

$$p_i = \frac{a_i(1 - a_j - a_k)^{s-1}}{(a_1 + a_2 + a_3)}$$

and

$$p_{ij} = \frac{(a_i + a_j)(1 - a_k)^{s-1}}{(a_1 + a_2 + a_3)} - p_i - p_j$$

The three-cue solution probability, p_{123}, may be obtained by subtracting the other six from unity. The consistency of these equations with Equations 2.7–2.9 may be checked by eliminating one of the relevant cues, say, by setting $a_3 = 0$; then the prior Equations 2.7–2.9 are obtained except for the altered label for the pool of irrelevant cues.

As of this writing, we have not done three-cue experiments because we had not previously thought of their significance for theory testing and therefore do not report such experiments here. The relevant prediction equations are included here for completeness of exposition and to make them available for a more stringent test of the theory. It is clear that a fairly large experiment (in subjects) is required for an adequate test of these predictions.

3
WHAT IS LEARNED

BACKGROUND AND PILOT WORK

In our first publication on concept identification (Bower & Trabasso, 1964a), a learning model was developed around the assumption that the subject was attending to or sampling only one attribute at a time. The data presented in that paper were concerned primarily with testing the all-or-none nature of the learning and not the details of the sampling assumptions. Later we became interested in testing the implications of this single-cue sampling idea with reference to what is learned. The most obvious implication is that when subjects solve a RRC problem they learn only one relevant cue.

We carried out two pilot studies to test this implication. In both studies college students learned to classify patterns with geometric figures wherein two different attributes were relevant and redundant. Following training to a criterion of ten successive correct responses, the subjects were tested for what they had learned. During testing (always carried out without feedback information) one of the relevant attributes was either removed or neutralized, and the subject classified the test patterns on the basis of the other, available, relevant attribute. The test series was of sufficient length and included patterns with only irrelevant dimensions so that it was unlikely that the subject could guess correctly on all the test trials with an attribute he had not learned.

The results of the pilot studies showed that the testing method was successful in identifying the mode of solution of individual subjects. Furthermore, the solution modes appeared as distinct "all-or-nothing" response patterns. For example, following learning of a problem in which the shape and color of geometrical figures were relevant and redundant, a typical subject might classify the sixteen test cards for color (with shape neutralized) correctly, whereas on the sixteen test cards for shape (with color neutralized) he would classify at the chance level,

68

eight correct and eight incorrect. Such individual data cause no equivocation in classifying this subject as having learned differential responses to color but not to shape.

An important feature of the pilot results was that a significant proportion of the subjects learned *both* relevant attributes, a clear contradiction of our prior assumption of single-attribute sampling. In order to modify the model to account for this, a rereading of Restle's (1962) theoretical paper was a distinct aid, since Restle had developed a similar model in which additive learning rates were implied *regardless* of the number of attributes the subject selects for his sample focus. Using Restle's ideas, we developed the particular theory elaborated in Chapter 2.

The advantage of that theory is that it identified the "solution type" as a manipulatable *dependent variable* and it provided definite predictions of how the solution type would be affected by variations in the experimental task. From that moment, the phenomenon of "two-cue solutions" became the primary dependent variable upon which much of our subsequent research was focused.

AN EXPERIMENT ON ADDITIVITY
OF CUES AND SELECTIVE ATTENTION

We began empirical testing of the particular model in the following experiment. It had two main purposes. The first was to test the numerical accuracy of the model's predictions about solution types with the attendant requirement of parameter invariance. In particular, the attribute sampling probabilities estimated from the total errors during learning of control groups should agree with the attribute-sampling probabilities required to fit the proportions of various solution types in the RRC problem. For these purposes three groups, two controls and one experimental, were used. The two control groups learned a problem with a single relevant attribute. For one group, the relevant attribute was the shape (triangle or circle) of the geometrical figure on the display cards. Call this cue S for shape. From this group's mean errors, one obtains an estimate of $a(S)$, the probability that the shape cue is sampled following an error. For the other control group, the relevant attribute was the location of a prominent dot above or below the central figure of the display. Call this cue D for dot location. From their mean errors, an estimate of $a(D)$ is obtained. The experimental group learned a RRC problem wherein the shape of the figure and the location of the dot were both relevant and redundant. The theory (cf. Equation 2.4) predicts that their learning rate will be $a(S) + a(D)$; but more importantly, depending on $a(S)$ and $a(D)$, it predicts via

Equations 2.7–2.9 the proportions of subjects who learn shape alone, dot alone, or both. A large number of subjects (90 college students) were run in this condition to provide reliable estimates of the probabilities of these three solution modes.

The second purpose of the experiment was to test an implication of the assumption that the subject does not add new cues to his sample focus on trials when he responds correctly. Consider the control group S wherein shape is initially relevant and the dot location cue is present but initially irrelevant. After a subject had learned this initial problem—as indicated by ten consecutive correct responses—half of the patterns were removed and thirty-two additional trials were given without interruption. For the remaining stimulus patterns the dot location was now redundant and relevant along with the initially relevant shape cue. In other words, during the post-criterion series the initially irrelevant dot cue was now made relevant and redundant along with the shape cue. Following this a subject was tested for learning of the dot location and shape singly.

For this test series, all subjects should respond correctly to the shape cue, since they must have learned that cue to meet the original criterion of acquisition. The important question is whether they have also learned to respond correctly according to the dot location, which was made relevant during the thirty-two post-criterion trials. The theory implies that subjects should not have acquired any knowledge about the dot cue; all subjects should classify the dot test patterns at the chance level.

This implication comes about as follows. If the subject eliminates irrelevant cues from his sample focus, then after ten consecutive correct responses the sample focus probably consists only of the relevant shape cue and no irrelevant cues (including the irrelevant dot cue). Upon entering the post-criterion series, there was no pause or break; the shape continues to be relevant but now the dot location is also relevant. The subject should continue responding correctly to the shape cue. Since by assumption he adds no new cues to his sample focus when he is correct, it follows that his sample focus will consist only of the shape cue at the end of the overtraining series. Therefore, during the test series that follows, he will treat dot location as an irrelevant cue and give chance classifications to the dot patterns. The general idea involved here has been tried in previous experiments with animals with a mixture of results. These will be discussed in Chapters 7 and 8.

To summarize, the second purpose of the experiment was to test for new learning of a redundant relevant cue following learning of a problem in which it was irrelevant. Both control groups S and D were used for this purpose. After learning with the one cue relevant and the second cue present but irrelevant, both received thirty-two trials on the $S + D$ redundant problem followed by the single-cue testing series. Two related control groups were also run with a similar purpose. Group S' was similar to group S in that shape was the relevant cue; however, it differed in that the dot cue was *absent* during acquisition for group S'. Similarly the conditions for group D' were like those for group D except the shape attribute was *constant* during acquisition. The subjects in group D' saw only squares (and neither triangles nor circles) during the acquisition series.

Following learning, groups S' and D' were shifted to the $S + D$ problem in which the other (previously absent) cue was introduced and its values correlated with the correct answer. For example, after ten correct, subjects in group S' now began to see cards on which a novel dot appeared, with the dot always located above a triangle and always located below a circle. Following thirty-two trials on this $S + D$ problem, the test series was given. The question again is whether the redundant cue is learned when it is introduced suddenly after the person has solved the problem on another initially relevant cue.

In its simplest form the theory implies that this novel, redundant cue would not be learned because the continued presence of the first-learned cue ensures correct responding during the $S + D$ series. However, it is known from the many studies of Sokolov (1963) and others (e.g., Thompson & Spencer, 1966) that novel changes in stimulation often will elicit an "orienting reflex" or will preempt attention. If the novel cue is noticed, then a few subjects may learn about it during the subsequent $S + D$ training series (see also Chapter 7 and Guy, Van-Fleet, & Bourne, 1966).

To summarize the experiment, Table 3.1 lists the groups, their designations, and their problems. The five groups differ in training, but

TABLE 3.1. SUMMARY OF THE EXPERIMENTAL DESIGN

Group	N	Training Shape (S)	Training Dot (D)	Post-criterion	Testing
$S + D$	90	Rel	Rel		
S	45	Rel	Irrel		
D	45	Irrel	Rel	(S Rel + D Rel)	Test S and
S'	45	Rel	Absent		Test D
D'	45	Absent	Rel		

71

have identical tasks during the post-criterion and testing series. The chief questions concern the learning rates of the five conditions and how these acquisition conditions affect performance on the single-cue tests at the end.

EXPERIMENT
Method

Subjects: The subjects were 270 undergraduate students at U.C.L.A. fulfilling a service requirement for their course in introductory psychology. They were run individually. Each set of six arriving subjects were assigned randomly to the five conditions, two to condition $S + D$ and one each to the other four groups. Nine subjects failed to meet the initial learning criterion—one in group $S + D$ and two in each of the other four groups. These nine subjects did not receive the post-criterion and testing series.

Procedure: Each subject was read the following instructions before beginning work on the training series:

"The purpose of this experiment is to find out how college students learn to make classifications. I have a deck of cards which may be divided into two classes, called Alpha and Beta. Each card belongs to only one category. Your job is to learn in which category a card belongs. I will show you one card at a time, and you are to classify the card as either an Alpha or a Beta. At first you must guess the category since you do not know the classification. After you classify the card, I will show you the correct answer. Then you will have a few seconds to study the card. I will then show you the next card to be classified. After awhile, you should learn a rule which will enable you to classify every card correctly as either an Alpha or a Beta.

"Before we begin, let me familiarize you with the nature of the cards. Here are two examples of cards which differ in several ways. (Two complementary patterns were shown.) The cards may differ in terms of (1) the shape of the figure, either a circle or a triangle (omitted for group D'); (2) the position of the dot, either above or below the figure (omitted for group S'); (3) the color, either red or blue; (4) the number of lines within the figure, either one or two lines; and (5) the position of an open gap on the side of the figure, either on the left or right. (These attributes were listed in different random orders for the various subjects.)

"The classification of the card will depend only on what appears on the card and nothing else. The cards are shuffled so that the order of the cards is not important. To review, I will show you one card at a time and you are to classify it as an Alpha or Beta. I will show you the correct classification and then we shall go on to the next card.

72

Guess on the first card. You can learn to classify the cards by a rule. Be accurate and avoid careless mistakes."

Following the instructions, the stimulus cards were presented one at a time on a cardholder. The subject gave his responses verbally at his own pace, and the correct classification was shown visually for four seconds on a card beside the stimulus card. A different order of stimulus presentation was shown to each subject by shuffling the deck of cards before training and after each run through the deck if the subject had not yet reached criterion. The learning criterion for the different groups is given below.

After the subject attained his learning criterion and had the post-criterion series, the experiment was interrupted while the following instructions were read before the test series:

"Okay. You have learned how to classify the cards correctly. Here is a deck of cards similar to the ones you just learned to classify. Would you sort this deck of cards into the categories, putting those cards you think are Alphas under this label and those you think are Betas under this label? I will not tell you whether you are right or wrong during this sort. You sort the cards *according to the rule you have just learned.*"

The subject had five minutes to sort the cards and all subjects complied with rapid sorting. After he had sorted the deck once, the test deck was reshuffled and the subject was asked to sort them again according to the rule he had just learned.

Questionnaire: After the sorting task, the subject was given a printed questionnaire and asked to complete it. At the top were listed two main questions:

"(1) Before you were asked to sort the cards, what was the rule you learned which enabled you to classify each card correctly?"

"(2) The rule that I used to sort the cards into Alphas and Betas was ———."

Then, fourteen statements followed wherein the subject was asked to check either Alpha or Beta or "Don't Know." These statements each asked a question about a particular value of a given dimension. For example, "If the dot was below a figure, the card was: an Alpha, a Beta, or Don't Know"; "If the figure was a triangle, the card was: an Alpha, a Beta, or Don't Know." The fourteen statements included reference to the two shape values alone, the two dot values alone, the two redundant pairs, the two opposed combinations of dots and shapes, and two irrelevant dimension values alone. The latter eight questions were included to test for cue preference and guessing on the sorting series. The subject has ten minutes in which to complete the questionnaire.

73

Stimulus Materials: Figure 3.1 shows examples of stimulus patterns used in training and testing. The stimuli were outlined geometric figures drawn in colored pencil from templates onto white 3×5-inch file cards. On each card was one value from each of the five binary attributes, as described in the instructions. The figures were approximately one square inch in area. The dot was .25 inch in diameter and was located .25 inch above or below the figure. For all problems, the color, number of interior lines, and position of open gap varied independently and were irrelevant. In training, the shape and dot dimensions were critical: when one was relevant and the other irrelevant (as in conditions S and D), there were $2^5 = 32$ patterns. When these two cues were relevant and redundant (condition $S + D$ and during overtraining), there were sixteen patterns. When one was relevant and the other absent there were sixteen patterns (as in conditions S' and D'). For group S', the dot was absent; for group D', the constant shape was a square.

The deck of test stimulus cards was composed of the same five attributes as used in training. There were forty-four test patterns in all. In each pattern, the color, number of interior lines, and location

Training

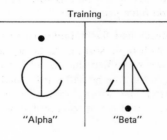

"Alpha"   "Beta"

Testing

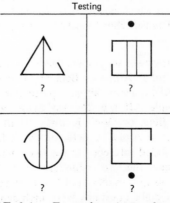

?   ?

?   ?

FIGURE 3.1.   *Examples of stimulus patterns used in training and testing.*

of open gap were present at one or another of their values. One subset of sixteen cards tested for learning of the shape cue; there were eight triangle cards, eight circle cards, and none of these cards contained a dot. A second subset of sixteen cards tested for learning of the dot cue (eight above and eight below). All these sixteen cards showed a square, thereby neutralizing the shape cue present during training. A third subset of eight cards had both the dot and shape cues removed (squares with no dot) and varied in the three irrelevant dimensions. This subset was used to reduce guessing on either the shape or dot during testing. A fourth subset of four "conflict" cards involved both relevant cues but they were opposed to one another; that is, the shape dictated one answer and the dot location dictated the opposite answer. This subset of cards occurred at the end of the sorting test and was used to assess preference or dominance of one over the other relevant cue particularly with reference to those $S + D$ subjects who learned both cues. The deck was gone through twice to check for the consistency of the subject's sorting rules.

Training Criteria: Subjects in group $S + D$ learned to a criterion of thirty-two consecutive correct responses and then were tested. Subjects in groups S, D, S', and D' learned their initial problem to a criterion of ten consecutive correct and then received thirty-two further trials on the $S + D$ problem. For example, for group D', at the transition point the shape of figures changed from all squares to either triangles (with dot above) or circles (with dot below). After thirty-two trials on the $S + D$ problem, the single-cue tests followed for all groups. The assignment of response classes to the values of the relevant dimensions was completely counterbalanced over the different subjects in each condition. A subject was considered to have not solved if he did not start his criterion run before trial 97.

RESULTS

Training

The speed of acquisition of the initial discrimination for the five different conditions will be discussed in terms of estimates of the learning-rate parameter of the Markov learning model. For condition i, let p_i denote the proportion of subjects who solve the problem, let $E(T_i)$ denote the average errors for all subjects combined in condition i, and let $a(i)$ denote the learning rate for condition i, which is assumed to equal the probability of sampling cue i. Then the maximum likelihood estimate of $a(i)$ may be shown to be

$$\hat{a}(i) = \frac{p_i}{E(T_i) - (1 - p_i)} \tag{3.1}$$

TABLE 3.2. ACQUISITION RESULTS: MEAN ERRORS AND SAMPLING PROBABILITY ESTIMATES FOR ALL CONDITIONS

Group	$E(T_i)$	p_i	$a(i)$ Estimate	Chi-square
$S + D$	4.14	89/90	.239	—
S	10.13	43/45	.094	31.3
D	5.87	43/45	.164	5.5
S'	8.40	43/45	.114	11.0
D'	5.55	43/45	.173	4.6

In case all N_i subjects in condition i solve their problem, this estimates $a(i)$ by the reciprocal of the average errors.

Table 3.2 displays the mean errors, number of solvers, and $a(i)$ estimates for the five acquisition conditions. The additive cue group, $S + D$, should learn their problem faster than the other four conditions and this appears true for the data in Table 3.2. To evaluate the reliability of these differences, the learning rate of group $S + D$ was compared separately to that of each of the other four conditions by means of a likelihood-ratio test (Bower & Trabasso, 1964a). Each comparison yields a chi-square value with one degree of freedom. These values are listed in the last column of Table 3.2. All are significant beyond the .05 level.

A further expectation of the theory is that the introduction of an irrelevant cue should reduce the learning rate to an extent depending upon the weight or salience of the added cue. Thus, groups S' and D' should learn slightly faster than their counterparts, groups S and D. This is true of the data in Table 3.2. The dot cue is apparently more salient than the shape cue (compare groups S versus D and groups S' versus D'). Therefore, adding the irrelevant dot cue to condition S' should degrade the learning rate more than will adding the irrelevant shape cue to condition D'. This is also true for the estimates in Table 3.2. When the added irrelevant cue is the salient dot, converting group S' into S, the learning rate is decreased 17 percent; when it is the weaker shape cue, converting group D' into D, the learning rate decreases by only 5 percent. These effects are small and statistically insignificant, but in this instance the theory predicts that the effects will be small.

Numerical Prediction of Learning Rates

The relationships among the five learning-rate estimates can be derived from the five following expressions. In these expressions, w_S and w_D are the weights of the shape and dot cues, and w_i summarizes the combined weights of all the irrelevant cues, including incidental cues introduced by the subjects.

$$a(S + D) = (w_S + w_D)(w_S + w_D + w_i)^{-1} \qquad (3.2a)$$
$$a(S) = w_S(w_S + w_D + w_i)^{-1} \qquad (3.2b)$$
$$a(D) = w_D(w_S + w_D + w_i)^{-1} \qquad (3.2c)$$
$$a(S') = w_S(w_S + w_i)^{-1} \qquad (3.2d)$$
$$a(D') = w_D(w_D + w_i)^{-1} \qquad (3.2e)$$

The reader will note that $a(S')$, when cue D is absent, differs from $a(S)$ by the absence of the factor w_D in the denominator, and similarly for the comparison of $a(D')$ with $a(D)$.

The first implication is that the right-hand side of Equation 3.2a is the sum of the right-hand sides of Equations 3.2b and c, so it follows that $a(S + D)$ should equal $a(S) + a(D)$. For the estimates in Table 3.2, the predicted value is $.094 + .164 = .258$, to be compared to the observed estimate of .239. A likelihood ratio test for equality of the observed and the predicted estimate of $a(S + D)$ yielded a nonsignificant chi-square ($X^2 = 0.62$, $df = 1$). Converting to average errors, the predicted mean is 3.88 compared to the 4.14 observed.

The relations between groups S' and D' and the other three are best expressed if we first transform Equations 3.2d and e according to

$$\phi(S') = a(S')[1 - a(S')]^{-1} = w_S w_i^{-1}$$
$$\phi(D') = a(D')[1 - a(D')]^{-1} = w_D w_i^{-1}$$

then define $Z = [1 + \Phi(S') + \Phi(D')]^{-1}$. The algebraic relations are as follows:

$$a(S) = \phi(S')Z$$
$$a(D) = \phi(D')Z$$
$$a(S + D) = [\phi(S') + \phi(D')]Z \qquad (3.3)$$

Using the estimates of $a(S')$ and $a(D')$ from Table 3.2, these expressions lead to the predictions listed in Table 3.3. The predictions are quite

TABLE 3.3. PREDICTED AND OBSERVED LEARNING RATES OF CONDITIONS S, D, AND $S + D$ USING DATA FROM CONDITIONS S' AND D'

Condition	Observed	Predicted	Chi-square
$S + D$	.239	.253	0.61
S	.094	.096	0.17
D	.164	.157	0.36

close in each instance. The nonsignificant chi-square values (each with one df) listed in the last column of Table 3.3 result from likelihood ratio comparisons of the pairs of observed and predicted parameter estimates.

To summarize this section, the estimate of the learning rate for the RRC condition, $S + D$, has agreed with predictions based on the theory, using either conditions S and D, or conditions S' and D', as "calibrating" control groups to assess the relative salience of the shape and dot cues. Also the numerical ordering of learning rates for conditions S versus S' and D versus D' are well accounted for by the theory.

WHAT IS LEARNED?

TESTING FOLLOWING $S + D$ ACQUISITION

The $S + D$ subjects were segregated into three distinct groups according to their stated solution hypothesis on the questionnaire: dot alone, shape alone, or both dot and shape. The sorting performance of these three classes of subjects is reported in Table 3.4 in terms of the group average proportions of correct sorts for the two single-cue subtests for the two sorts of the test deck. Sorts on the "conflict" test cards will be reported later.

A first feature to notice about the data in Table 3.4 is that more subjects stated their solution as involving the dot cue than the shape cue. Recalling that the comparative learning rates led to the inference that the dot cue was more salient than the shape cue, the relative dominance of dot over shape in the solution types agrees with expectations of the theory. A second feature to notice about Table 3.4 is that the patterns of

TABLE 3.4. MEAN AND STANDARD DEVIATION OF CORRECT PROPORTIONS OF SORTS ON THE SHAPE AND DOT SUBSETS ON TESTS 1 AND 2 FOR GROUP $S + D$, PARTITIONED IN TERMS OF THE VERBALIZED SOLUTION

| | | Test.1 | | | | Test 2 | | | |
| | | Shape | | Dot | | Shape | | Dot | |
Verbalized Solution	Number of Subjects	Mean	σ	Mean	σ	Mean	σ	Mean	σ
Shape	31	.99	.07	.50	.04	1.00	0	.51	.04
Dot	45	.52	.19	.99	.07	.52	.07	.99	.04
Both	13	.95	.06	.95	.06	.96	.11	1.00	0

78

sorting are stable from the first test to the second; that is, these are reliable and consistent sorting patterns.

Finally the results in Table 3.4 show a nearly perfect relationship between the sorting pattern and the solution verbalized on the questionnaire. Those subjects stating a solution involving only shape sorted the shape test cards nearly perfectly on both passes, whereas they sorted the dot test cards at the chance level (i.e., $p = .50$) on both passes. The performance pattern was similar for those subjects who stated "dot alone" as their solution focus. Finally, subjects stating that both cues were in their solution focus sorted nearly perfectly on both attributes. Of the eighty-nine subjects in group $S + D$ who learned and were tested, only four gave sorts that were discrepant in some way with their stated solution. Three subjects who stated only the dot solution also sorted correctly on the shape, and one subject who stated both cues as his solution made chance sorts on the shape. These subjects are responsible for the larger standard deviations of the percentages in the "dot alone" and "both" categories in Table 3.4. Later, following discussion of the sorting of the other four experimental groups, we shall take up the question of possible contaminants of this sorting test as a means for inferring the solution focus, and shall discuss the data in that light. For the moment, however, the sorting data is accepted on its face validity as indicating faithfully the composition of the solution focus for a subject.

To summarize these test data, the subjects in the RRC condition appear to have individually learned about one or the other or both attributes. The presence of an attribute in a subject's solution focus appeared to be an all-or-nothing affair: if a test cue was in his solution focus, he sorted it perfectly; if it was not in his solution focus, then in sorting he treated it as though it were an irrelevant cue. There was no evidence in these data to argue for partial, proportional, or "more-or-less" learning of each cue by individual subjects. Furthermore, the relative learning rate (indexing salience) of the single cues provided a good estimate of which cue would predominate in the solution focus for the RRC problem. Estimating salience from the learning rates in acquisition, groups D and D' learned approximately one and a half times faster than groups S and S', respectively; a similar ratio obtains for the number of subjects who learned only the dots to those who learned only the shapes in group $S + D$.

NUMERICAL PREDICTIONS OF SOLUTION-TYPE DISTRIBUTION

Equations 2.7–2.9 developed in Chapter 2 express the probability of various solution types as a function of three parameters: the saliences of the two relevant cues, $a(S)$ and $a(D)$, and the sample-size parameter, s. For the predictions that follow, the $a(S)$ and $a(D)$ values were estimated from the mean errors during acquisition of control groups S and D. Rounding the estimates to two significant decimals, they are $\hat{a}(S) = .10$ and $\hat{a}(D) = .16$.

The sample size, s, is a free parameter chosen to fit the observed distribution of solution types. This parameter must be greater than one here since some two-cue solutions occurred. By some trial-and-error checking, it was found that the best-fitting integer value of s was 2. The predictions with $\hat{s} = 2$ are compared to the observed frequencies of the solution types in Table 3.5. The fit of the predicted to the observed

TABLE 3.5. PREDICTED AND OBSERVED NUMBER OF SUBJECTS IN GROUP $S + D$ LEARNING SHAPE, DOT, OR BOTH CUES

Solution Type	Observed	Predicted
Shape	31	28.8
Dot	45	49.3
Both	13	10.9

frequencies is fairly close. A chi-square test for goodness of fit yielded a nonsignificant value (0.95, $df = 1$). The one degree of freedom for this test results from subtracting one, for the s parameter estimate, from the total of two for the frequency table.

These data have been fitted using the cue-salience estimates obtained from groups S and D. It is clear, however, that they would be predicted about equally well by appropriate transformations of the learning rates obtained from control groups S' and D'. This must be so, of course, since the results in Table 3.3 showed that the observed estimates of $a(S)$ and $a(D)$ were predicted quite well by the theory on the basis of the estimates of $a(S')$ and $a(D')$.

Table 3.5 shows the main comparison toward which this experiment was aimed. The solution focus of an RRC subject could be predicted from estimates of the cue saliences as measured by the learning rates of independent control groups. This is not a trivial prediction. There are many pitfalls in the chain of reasoning where the whole theoretical scheme could have failed; for example, the learning model could be wrong, the identification of salience with rate of learning could be erroneous, the salience estimates could be fallible, the theory of the solution focus could be wrong, and so on. Furthermore, in the absence of

80

a theory, there is no intuitively obvious relation between the mean errors of the control groups and the likelihood of the various solution types. Because of the low a priori probability that the numerical predictions would be successful, we consider the fact of their success as both remarkable and lending strong evidence to the type of theory that made this possible.

CONFLICT TESTS

Recall that the test deck contained four cards in which the dot and shape cues were opposed to one another. Sorting of these cards was a simple matter involving no conflict for those $S + D$ subjects who learned only one cue; they merely classified the conflict cards according to the value of the cue learned. Interest centers instead upon how these patterns were treated by the thirteen subjects in group $S + D$ who learned both cues. The question is whether on conflict trials they choose between the two learned cues according to the relative weights or saliences of these cues. If they were to do so, then in theory the probability that the subject responds according to the dot cue instead of the shape cue should be

$$Pr\,(\text{dot} \mid \text{2-cue solution}) = \frac{a(D)}{a(D) + a(S)}$$
$$= \frac{.164}{.164 + .094} = .64$$

where we have entered the learning-rate estimates of $a(D)$ and $a(S)$ taken from Table 3.2.

Turning to the conflict sorting data of the thirteen subjects who learned both cues, seven subjects always selected the dot cue, three always selected the shape cue, and three were random (50 percent) in their choices over the eight (four twice through) conflict tests. Averaging them together, the observed proportion of dot choices on the conflict tests for the two-cue solvers was

$$Pr\,(\text{dot} \mid \text{2-cue solution}) = \frac{7 + .5(3)}{13} = .65$$

which is practically the same as the .64 predicted by the theory.

Prediction of the conflict choices in this instance is an illustration of the "constant ratio rule," which is one version of Luce's choice axiom (Luce, 1959). This version supposes that the ratio of the choice probabilities of alternative A to alternative B should be constant and independent of the number and nature of the other alternatives in the choice set in which A and B appear. To translate that statement into our terms, the learning rate $a(D)$ may be thought of as the probability that cue D is chosen (on each error trial) when the choice set consists of the N alternative cues present during learning; a similar interpretation holds for the learning rate $a(S)$. On the other hand, conflict tests for two-cue solvers is analogous to restricting the choice set to just two members, D and S. The prediction formula says that the ratio of choosing cue D to cue S from N alternatives is the same as the ratio when these are the only two alternatives. For other evidence on the constant ratio rule, see Atkinson, Bower, and Crothers (1965, Ch. 4) and Luce (1959).

The disturbing feature in this case is that Luce's axiom fits the group average-choice proportion on the conflict tests, but not the individual-subject proportions, which were 1, .5, or 0. These reveal nonindependence of successive conflict choices (i.e., the subject sticks with his first conflict choice) and possibly different strategies, to be consistent or random. We will not pursue this issue further here, but the topic will appear again in Chapter 4 when we must deal with conflict choices by two-cue solvers.

PRIOR LEARNING THAT BLOCKS ATTENTION

We now discuss the test results of groups S and D. These subjects had the $S + D$ problem after learning one of the cues with the other irrelevant. *None* of these eighty-six subjects showed any evidence whatsoever of having learned the cue that was made relevant during overtraining. On the questionnaire, all of these subjects stated that the hypothesis used in sorting involved only the cue on which they had been initially trained. Their sorting behavior was perfectly consistent with their replies to the questionnaire. The average sorting proportions for these subjects are given in Table 3.6. Subjects in group S sorted perfectly on the shape tests and at chance on the dot tests. The complementary pattern occurred for subjects in group D. Two subjects in group D sorted incorrectly all the shape test cards, accounting for the variance in this group.

From these data we conclude that subjects do not learn a previously irrelevant cue when it is made relevant and redundant in an overtraining series during which their first-learned solution focus still "works" successfully. In other words, so long as no obvious changes in the stimulus sequence occur, subjects continue to focus on their first-learned cue to the relative exclusion of other concurrently reliable cues contained in the information display. We will return to this point after discussing the related results from groups S' and D'.

82

TABLE 3.6. MEANS AND STANDARD DEVIATIONS OF CORRECT SORTING PROPORTIONS FOR GROUPS *S* AND *D* IN TERMS OF VERBALIZED SOLUTION HYPOTHESIS

| | | | Test 1 | | | | Test 2 | | | |
| | | | Shape | | Dot | | Shape | | Dot | |
Group	Verbalized Solution	N	Mean	σ	Mean	σ	Mean	σ	Mean	σ
S	Shape	43	.99	.04	.50	0	1.00	0	.50	0
	Dot	0								
	Both	0								
D	Shape	0								
	Dot	43	.46	.11	.99	.02	.47	.11	.99	.02
	Both	0								

Recall that group *D'* saw only square figures during acquisition and learned to classify these according to whether a dot was above or below the square. After reaching criterion, there was a noticeable change in the stimulus patterns wherein squares no longer appeared but were replaced by triangles and circles that were correlated with the location of the dot. A similar description applies to group *S'* which first learned patterns without dots and then had the dot cue introduced at the start of the post-criterion series.

The card-sorting and questionnaire data for groups *S'* and *D'* are shown in Table 3.7. In Table 3.7, it is clear that only a small percentage of the subjects learned the correct response to the novel redundant cue: six of the forty-three subjects in group *S'* learned the added dot, whereas

TABLE 3.7. MEANS AND STANDARD DEVIATIONS OF CORRECT SORTING PROPORTIONS FOR GROUPS *S'* AND *D'* IN TERMS OF VERBALIZED SOLUTION HYPOTHESIS

| | | | Test 1 | | | | Test 2 | | | |
| | | | Shape | | Dot | | Shape | | Dot | |
Group	Verbalized Solution	N	Mean	σ	Mean	σ	Mean	σ	Mean	σ
S'	Shape	37	1.00	0	.50	.04	1.00	0	.51	.06
	Both	6	.98	.01	.92	.12	.98	.01	.92	.12
D'	Dot	42	.52	.03	1.00	0	.52	.10	1.00	0
	Both	1	1.00	0	1.00	0	1.00	0	1.00	0

only one of the forty-three in group D' learned the added shape cue. The percentages of subjects learning the novel dot cue as compared to the shape cue agree with the earlier estimates showing the greater salience of the dot cue.

In Table 3.7, all subjects in group S' who stated only the shape cue as their solution focus sorted perfectly on shape tests and at chance on dot tests; all subjects in group D' who stated only the dot cue sorted perfectly on dots and at chance on shape. For subjects stating both cues, six sorted perfectly on each test whereas one (in group S') sorted fourteen out of sixteen correct on shape and ten out of sixteen correct on dots. Thus only one subject (of 86) gave sorts that were discrepant in some degree from his stated solution focus.

In summary, when a novel cue was added and was redundant with a first-learned relevant cue, only a small percentage (8 percent here) of the subjects learned the relevance of this added novel cue. Moreover, the probability that the novel cue was learned increased with its salience. Comparing these results with those of groups S and D, in which no subject learned the redundant cue during overlearning, we emphasize the probable involvement of the orienting reflex to novel changes in the stimulus patterns. The stimulus change may cause the subject to sample the novel cue, and in some cases to incorporate it into his current solution focus. Physiological or behavioral indices of this postulated orienting reflex (OR) could be investigated in this context. Physiologically, the orienting reflex has been indicated by increases in conductance of the skin (GSR), or by vasodilation of the blood vessels of the forehead and vasoconstriction of those in the limbs (Maltzman & Raskin, 1965; Sokolov, 1963). In our situation, a good behavioral index of the OR probably would be an increased response latency (or stimulus-inspection time) just after the novel cue was introduced (cf. Kintsch, 1964, for evidence linking the OR to response latencies). Presumably groups S and D would show no OR during the overlearning whereas groups S' and D' would.

An interesting question for future research is whether introduction of a novel stimulus variable increases the likelihood that the subject attends again to all those dimensions of a stimulus pattern to which he has habituated, or whether attention is focused primarily on the novel cue itself. An indirect way to test this effect would be to see whether the proportion of two-cue solvers in the $S + D$ condition could be enhanced by introducing novel changes in an irrelevant cue during the post-criterion run on the $S + D$ problem. If the OR consists in a general scanning of all available cues, then a subject focused on one relevant cue

84

may thus be led to notice and incorporate other relevant cues into his solution focus.

NOTICING VERSUS USING A CUE

A small pilot study will be described since it helps clarify a conceptual distinction between noticing a cue versus the functional use of the cue in the solution focus. In the experiments discussed earlier, it could be argued that subjects failed to learn responses to the redundant cue simply because they were looking only at the cue in their solution focus and not noticing any of the other cues. In this pilot study, subjects were forced to "notice" all the available cues by requiring them to name aloud each stimulus value on the display before making their classificatory response. To simplify the naming, the stimuli were consonant letter clusters composed of four letters. The four attributes of the patterns were the four spatial positions (left to right) in the letter string. At each position, one of two letters occurred; these constituted the two values of a given attribute. The attribute-value pairs were (M,Z), (L,B), (Y,K), and (R,W), from which $2^4 = 16$ different strings were constructed (e.g., $MBKR$). During initial training to a criterion of ten consecutive correct responses, the correct classification depended on the letter in the second position (L in class 1, B in class 2). Following learning, subjects received thirty-two further trials, four passes through a subset of eight of the original sixteen cards. In these eight overtraining cards, the letter in the fourth position was redundant with the relevant letter in the second position (R always appeared with L, and W with B). During these overtraining trials—and only during these—the subject read aloud the letters on the card before he gave his classification (which was invariably correct). Following these trials, the subject was given tests on the individual relevant elements by removing the other. For example, on tests for the fourth letter, the second letter was replaced by a blank (e.g., $Z-KW$).

Only fifteen subjects (Stanford undergraduates) were run in this experiment. None of them showed any evidence of having acquired the terminal correlation between the fourth letter and the correct response. All second-letter sorts were consistently correct and all fourth-letter sorts were at the chance level.

These findings indicate that a subject may notice, name, and experience a cue in close temporal contiguity many times with the correct response, and still not learn the cue-response correlation. Noticing and using a cue for the auxiliary purpose of naming or identifying it is quite

85

different from noticing, learning, and using a cue for classfying the stimulus patterns. The sampling theory is concerned with the probability that a cue will be used in the second sense, that it becomes effective in the focus used for classification. In the first sense of "noticing," most of our subjects probably notice and identify most of the available cues on many trials throughout the acquisition series; they reveal this by being able to recall at the end of training the values of the attributes. In the second sense of "noticing," however, our results suggest that the subject is learning and using for classification only a small number of attributes at any one time.

These results are similar to those for associative learning reported by Thorndike (1928) under the heading of "belongingness." Thorndike's experiments purported to show that two verbal items became associated only if the subject organized them as belonging together, as a pair to be rehearsed and stored as a unit; temporal contiguity of elements without "belonging" produced little if any association between them.

POSSIBLE CONTAMINANTS OF THE TESTS

Throughout the preceding discussion, the sorting results have been treated as valid for inferring a subject's solution focus. A cue was said to be in his solution focus if he sorted correctly on almost all tests with that cue, and not if he sorted at the chance level.

Consider now some possible factors that could reduce the validity of these inferences. As in statistical tests, there are two kinds of errors possible in such inferences: an inferential error of the first kind occurs if a subject sorted incorrectly even though the corresponding cue had been in his solution focus at the end of training; an error of the second kind occurs if a subject sorted correctly even though the corresponding cue was not in his solution focus at the end of training.

Errors of the first kind could occur if the subject forgets the correct assignments of the two values of the relevant cue ("Did triangles go in class 1 and circles in class 2, or vice versa?"). This forgetting could occur between the end of the training and the beginning of the test series, or during the test series itself. Since no information feedback was given during the test series, there was no opportunity to relearn the value-response assignments. Forgetting of this kind appeared infrequently in our experiments. The correct response assignments involved one bit of information; if the subject recalled the response to one value, he could infer the response to the other value. In addition, the subject had received a large number of criterion trials (32–42) on which these assignments were used correctly.

86

In the data only two of the 261 subjects showed evidence of this kind of forgetting. One subject in group $S + D$ stated that he had solved on both the shape and dots, and yet, although his dot sorts were correct, his shape sorts were at chance. The second subject, in group S', stated that he had used both the shape and dots for classification but he sorted 14/16 correct on shape and 10/16 correct on dots.

Errors of the second kind—inferring from a subject's correct sorting that he had learned that cue—appear to us to be somewhat more likely. Consider the strategies a subject might employ on, say, the dot tests given that he had learned only the shape. For the dot test cards, the shapes available in training were replaced by a square, with the dot location and other irrelevant cues still available. Since shape was not available, the subject might follow one of several alternative strategies:

1. Sort all dot cards at random.
2. Sort all dot cards into a single class.
3. Select some other attribute and sort all nonshape cards consistently according to the variations in that attribute.

Strategies 1 and 2 lead to 50 percent correct sorts with respect to the dot cue. Strategies of type 3 lead to 100, 50, or 0 percent correct depending on the cue selected and the class assignments used. If the cue selected is irrelevant (e.g., the number of interior lines), then 50 percent will be correct regardless of the response assignments. However, if the dot location is selected, then the sorts would be 100 percent correct provided the subject guessed the correct response assignments (upper dot is sorted into Alpha, lower dot into Beta) but would be 0 percent correct if he guessed the reverse.

If subjects choose strategy 3 with appreciable frequency, then a particularly worrisome question is whether, by reviewing what they remember from the training series, they have a bias toward selecting the redundant relevant attribute with its correct response assignments. Recall that the results from the pilot study have already forced the distinction between noticing a cue (possibly even storing information about it) versus using a cue for classification. If from this storage the person could later recall and infer intercue correlations or redundancies between cues (e.g., "I remember now—the upper dot always went with circles.") that he had not used previously, then such a bias would be explained. If it occurred in substantial degree, then the model would have to be elaborated to distinguish between these two senses of "learning a cue": using a cue-response hypothesis in the solution focus versus having stored the basic data for inferring a cue-response relation when later conditions induce a memory search for such relations. At the moment, however, this is a rather ill-defined distinction.

Judging from our previous research on memory in concept-identification types of tasks (Trabasso & Bower, 1964b), this conjectured bias due to searching through stored material may be considered small and unlikely. It was found that college students remembered only small fractions of either the interattribute correlations or the attribute-response correlations to which they had been exposed in a short series of patterns. What they remembered was approximately what one might suppose they were "carrying along" in their current solution focus.

Concerning present data relevant to these conjectures, it is difficult to determine exactly how often these events occurred. There was fairly clear evidence of it for five of the 261 subjects. Three subjects in group $S + D$ stated that they had solved only on the dot cue and yet they sorted all the shape cards correctly. And two subjects in group D (who stated D alone as their focus) sorted *incorrectly* on all their shape cards, that is, they reversed associations for the shape values.

Overall, then, these data give one little cause for refuting the validity of the sorting data for inferring the solution focus. Judging from these data, errors of type 1 occurred in about 0.8 percent of the cases, and errors of type 2 in about 1.9 percent of the cases. These error frequencies are sufficiently low so that one may feel justified in continuing to treat the sorting tests as valid. Accordingly, in later experiments, this issue will not be raised again.

SUMMARY

This experiment was designed to find out what people learn in a RRC problem. The primary data came from single-cue tests that followed learning of a RRC problem. The tests assessed whether the subject had learned to classify stimuli on the basis of one or another or both of the relevant cues.

It was found that subjects typically displayed "all-or-none" patterns of responding on the tests: that is, with a given attribute, the subject responded either consistently correct or at chance. Such response patterns permitted an unambiguous classification of what a subject had learned.

Four control groups were run to assess the theory's predictions of the data of the RRC group, $S + D$. Two groups learned a shape discrimination, one with (S) and one without (S') an irrelevant dot attribute. Two groups learned a dot-location discrimination, one with (D) and one without (D') an irrelevant shape attribute. Adding an irrelevant cue retarded learning, and the amount of this retardation was predictable: learning rates for conditions S and D were predicted by those of groups S' and D'. Group $S + D$ learned the fastest and their learning rate was predicted equally well by the learning rates of either groups S and D or groups S' and D'.

Of primary interest was the fact that the probability distribution of solution types in group $S + D$ was independently predicted from the learning rates estimated from the control groups. The solution-type distribution showed more dot learners than shape learners, a result in line with the faster learning of groups D and D'. The best estimate of the size of the sample, taken by a subject following an error, was two elements.

The four control groups received post-criterion training on the $S + D$ problem to determine whether these subjects would learn about the redundant cue after initial training had ensured their focusing on the first-learned relevant cue. For groups S' and D', the introduction of the novel cue at the beginning of overtraining caused a small percentage (8 percent) of these subjects to learn the relevance of the added cue. For groups S and D, overtraining involved no obvious changes in the stimulus sequence, and none of these subjects learned the relevance of the cue made redundant with the first-learned cue. These results support the theoretical assumption that subjects do not add new cues to their solution focus so long as the present focus enables them to respond correctly. The chief alteration of this general assumption is that abrupt introduction of a novel stimulus variable may evoke an orienting reflex, causing this cue to be incorporated into the solution focus. A pilot study was described which forces a distinction between noticing a cue versus using a cue for classification.

The experimental results gave overall support for the theoretical model presented in Chapter 2. The theory successfully related learning rates to relative cue saliences or attention values, and also related these saliences to the probability of solving RRC problems in various ways.

4

TRANSFER FOLLOWING
REDUNDANT CUE TRAINING

Several alternative methods exist for assessing what a subject has learned in an RRC problem. One method is simply to ask him what classfication rule he used. Another is to give him a number of single-cue sorting tests without knowledge of results, thus requiring him to classify according to one or another cue separately. Finally, he can be given some kind of "transfer-learning" task wherein the problem is altered slightly from the first one learned.

Several transfer tasks are plausible for assessing what was learned in RRC training. Generally speaking, the transfer tasks are such that one of the redundant training cues is retained as relevant with the same response assignments as in original training, whereas the other redundant cue either is removed (or is made constant) or is made irrelevant in the transfer problem. An alternative transfer task utilizes an "intradimensional shift" similar to the foregoing case except that the specific values of some or all dimensions are changed in the transfer problem (e.g., the values of the color attribute might be changed from the red-blue of training to yellow-brown). However the transfer task may be constructed, the subject typically is trained until he masters it. The common presumption is that the more a subject originally learned about the cue retained as relevant in the transfer problem, the faster he will master the transfer problem.

Such transfer tasks have been used widely to infer what was learned in some initial problem. For example, transfer learning is the predominant method used with lower animals; this is preferred to, say, single-cue tests because of the difficulty in devising blank or null trial outcomes that do not alter the animal's behavior over a series of such trials. That is, whether one reinforces all, some, or none of the test responses, the response dispositions of the animal may change over a long test series,

90

thus complicating inferences about what he knew at the start of the series.

Because of the frequent use of transfer designs, we asked how the proposed theory makes contact with such results. The following experiment therefore was concerned with predictions of transfer performance following RRC training. In the present experiment, one of the RRC cues was made irrelevant during transfer. This seems to be a simpler task to handle than the alternate procedure of removing a cue or replacing its two prior values by a constant, third value—for example, circles or triangles replaced by all squares. Pilot work on the latter procedure indicated that a significant proportion of subjects interpreted the abrupt shift in stimulus patterns as a signal for a shift in the entire problem, and hence they performed as though the transfer problem were completely new. Rather than explore these possible complications, we decided to confine ourselves to the "irrelevancy" transfer procedure.

In our theory, a group-average index of transfer (e.g., errors in transfer learning) represents an average over three heterogeneous subgroups. The group average performance in transfer will depend upon (a) the proportions of subjects solving the initial redundant problem on the retained cue, the currently irrelevant cue, and on both cues, and (b) the transfer performance obtained from each of these subgroups. Thus for a theory to handle transfer results it not only must predict the proportions of various solution types but also it must contain accurate assumptions concerning how the transfer task is learned by subjects who solved the RRC problem in the three different ways. The first issue, predicting proportions of various solution types, was discussed in Chapter 2. The second, assumptions about transfer learning, is considered here.

The general working assumption is that transfer is an all-or-nothing process in the circumstances to be considered: that is, a subject should transfer perfectly or not at all, learning the transfer problem at the same rate as an appropriate control subject. In particular, subjects who originally solved only on the retained cue should show perfect transfer, whereas subjects who originally solved on the irrelevant cue should show no positive transfer. A similar hypothesis, and evidence to support it, was offered by Greeno and Scandura (1966) to account for transfer in a verbal concept-learning situation of the type developed by Underwood and Richardson (1956a, b). However, that task, which depends upon overlap in the associative hierarchies to different words, differs considerably from the one under present consideration.

An additional assumption is needed to handle transfer for those subjects who initially learned both cues in the RRC problem. When one

91

cue is made irrelevant during transfer learning, these subjects will soon encounter a "conflict trial," when the two attributes dictate different responses. To illustrate, suppose in initial training all circles are red and called A, whereas all triangles are blue and called B. During transfer, a new pairing of the values—for example, a blue circle—would produce conflict since circle dictates response A but blue dictates response B.

The questions are: how does the subject behave on the first conflict trial in transfer, and how does he react to this trial's outcome? It will be assumed that on a conflict trial the subject chooses among the learned cues with a probability determined by their respective weights or sampling probabilities. Evidence for this was reported in Chapter 3. In general, we will let d denote the probability that on a conflict trial the subject chooses the cue retained as relevant in the transfer problem. If the subject chooses the retained attribute, he responds correctly on the conflict trial. It is assumed that at this point he will discard the irrelevant cue from his sample focus, will continue to use the retained cue (since it leads to correct responses), and thus will solve the transfer problem with no errors. Suppose, however, that he chooses the irrelevant cue on the conflict trial and thus makes an error. What then ensues? We shall consider two hypotheses. The first hypothesis is that the error leads the subject to reject the selected irrelevant cue and revert to the alternate (retained) cue of his focus. By this hypothesis, he should make only that one error before solving. The alternative hypothesis is that the error reactivates the search mode, causing the subject to discard his previous focus and to start afresh on the transfer problem. In this case, his expected errors before solving the transfer problem are the same as for a control subject. For convenience in the following, these two assumptions will be referred to as the "rational" and "irrational" hypotheses. The reader may note that the irrational hypothesis uses the same rules for treating conflict trials during transfer and during initial acquisition.

These are substantive hypotheses about transfer. They could possibly be wrong and they are worth testing in some detail, as we do in the following experiment. It is doubtful whether these assumptions will have very wide applicability—for example, it appears that lower animals do not give the all-or-none transfer pattern. The assumptions are plausible, however, for the experimental arrangements used here. Taken jointly, our hypotheses about initial solution types and their subsequent transfer performances imply several laws about *group-average* transfer results, which to our knowledge have not been contradicted by experimental findings. For example, some positive transfer is expected to any retained cue following RRC learning. With several initially redundant cues, the amount of positive transfer will increase with the proportion of retained to nonretained relevant cues in transfer. More positive transfer should be obtained when the retained cue is the more salient one of the initial redundant cues. Relative to control subjects, the amount of positive transfer should be amplified by decreasing the numbers or weights of the irrelevant cues present both in the original and the transfer problems. These and similar implications follow primarily because the variable in question affects the probability that the RRC subject initially learns a retained cue, thus giving perfect transfer.

A question that has been postponed in the foregoing discussion regards the appropriate control condition to be compared to the RRC condition in transfer. For example, we have stated that a subject who solved initially on the irrelevant cue will show no positive transfer in comparison to an "appropriate control" subject. But what is an appropriate control condition? There is no single, simple answer to this question, since the answer depends on one's ideas about what variables affect transfer performance. We will enumerate a few possible controls for a particular comparison. Suppose subjects learn an initial problem with shape and dot location as RRC's, and are transferred to shape relevant and dot irrelevant. We are concerned with those subjects who solved initially on the dot and now must learn shape.

One possible control is group S of Chapter 3; those subjects learned an initial problem with shape relevant and dot present but irrelevant. Then the initial learning of group S would be compared with the transfer performance of the RRC group. One could object that this is inappropriate if there is a nonspecific practice effect, since second learning of the RRC transfer subjects is being compared to first learning of group S. So a second control that might be proposed is to have subjects learn a similar problem (not involving stimuli used in transfer) for practice before the S problem. The difficulty here is in deciding what is a "similar" practice problem, whether specific ones really aid learning of the S problem, whether the practice task alters the relative cue saliences of the S problem, and so forth. Clearly one needs more information about the practice effect before one can be assured of the information provided by this controlled comparison. A third possible control would have subjects learn an initial problem with cue D relevant and cue S irrelevant, and then transfer to the S problem, with S relevant and D irrelevant. This is a "nonreversal shift" problem which has been treated extensively (e.g., Kendler & Kendler, 1962). Subjects in this condition would simulate in some respects those $S + D$ subjects who initially learned only cue D and then were transferred to cue S. Both kinds of subjects would begin transfer focused on cue D and have to discard it eventually and pick up cue S. A possible objection to this comparison is that for control subjects, cue S is initially irrelevant and hence it may be tried and rejected during initial training, thus lowering its probability of being selected in transfer. With this objection in mind, consider a fourth comparison in which the control group initially has cue D relevant and cue S absent (the D' condition of Chapter 3), then transfer is to the S problem, with S novel and relevant whereas D is now irrelevant. This condition possibly simulates the $S + D$ subjects who solved on D but not S since it could be argued that they did not "notice" the S cue, and it could have just as well been absent for them. There are several objections to this control comparison. First, if the novel S cue for the controls elicits an orienting reflex (as argued in Chapter 3), then the controls may solve the S problem faster. Second, it could be argued that all cues are noticed but not used by $S + D$ subjects, and cues not used are demoted in their weights, thus retarding learning of cue S.

This enumeration illustrates the difficulty in specifying an appropriate control comparison when one is uncertain of the many factors determining transfer performance. The possible factors mentioned— practice effects, "adaptation" of irrelevant cues, orienting reflex to novel changes, and so on—are *not* formalized within our theory, but they are possible factors that are uncontrolled in one or another of the contrasts illustrated. Perhaps the point to be learned from this discussion is that an adequately controlled contrast can be contrived only after one already understands a great deal about the phenomenon under consideration. In the following, two of these above-mentioned controls, the first and the third, are used. Subjects trained on problem $S + D$ and transferred to S are compared first with subjects from Chapter 3 who learned problem S from scratch, and second with subjects who first learned problem D (with S irrelevant), and then learned problem S (with D irrelevant). The design of the experiment was symmetric, some $S + D$ subjects were transferred to the S problem and some to the D problem, with controls first learning the S or D problem before transfer to the alternate problem.

EXPERIMENT
Method

Subjects: The subjects were 208 volunteers from introductory psychology classes at the University of California, Los Angeles. One hundred twenty subjects initially learned the $S + D$ problem, sixty were transferred to the S problem (group $S + D \rightarrow S$), and sixty to the D problem (group $S + D \rightarrow D$). Forty-six subjects initially learned the S problem and then were transferred to the D problem (group $S \rightarrow D$), whereas forty-two subjects had the D problem followed by the S problem (group $D \rightarrow S$).

94

Procedure: The training instructions, problems, stimuli, apparatus, and procedure were identical to those used in the main experiment of Chapter 3 with the following exceptions: (1) the response categories were the nonsense syllables "mib" and "dax"; (2) instead of a sorting test following initial learning, subjects were transferred without interruption to their second problem; (3) the learning criterion for both the original and transfer problem was ten consecutively correct responses; and (4) subjects who failed to reach the learning criterion within sixty-four trials on the initial problem were dismissed and were not transferred; transferred subjects continued training either until reaching criterion or until sixty-four transfer trials had ensued.

RESULTS

The acquisition results were similar in pattern to those obtained previously: problem D was learned faster than problem S, and problem $S + D$ was learned faster than either single-cue problem. Only three subjects, all from group $S \rightarrow D$, failed to learn their initial problem and were not transferred, thus reducing the number of transferred subjects to thirty-nine in group $S \rightarrow D$.

In transfer following $S + D$ training, fewer errors were made by subjects transferred to problem D than by those transferred to problem S. Average transfer errors were 2.78 for group $S + D \rightarrow D$ and 6.62 for group $S + D \rightarrow S$. These means differed significantly ($t = 2.59$, $df = 118$, $p < .05$).

Groups $S + D \rightarrow D$ and $S + D \rightarrow S$ showed substantial positive transfer when compared to their respective control groups. The 2.78 mean errors of group $S + D \rightarrow D$ may be compared to the 6.10 errors of group D of Chapter 3 or the 7.18 transfer errors of group $S \rightarrow D$ of the present experiment. Similarly, the 6.62 mean errors of group $S + D \rightarrow S$ may be compared to the 10.65 errors of group S of Chapter 3 or the 11.74 errors of group $D \rightarrow S$ of the present experiment.

The main reason for the lower average errors made by groups $S + D \rightarrow D$ and $S + D \rightarrow S$ was a high frequency of subjects making zero or one error before reaching the transfer criterion. Combining groups $S + D \rightarrow D$ and $S + D \rightarrow S$, 57.5 percent of the subjects had either zero or one error, whereas for subjects in groups $S \rightarrow D$ and $D \rightarrow S$, none made zero and only 1.2 percent made one error. Alternatively, the former percentage may be compared to that of groups S and D from Chapter 3: during their initial learning 23.3 percent of those subjects solved with zero or one error. Thus RRC training increased the probability that the subject tranfers nearly perfectly to the retained cue.

TABLE 4.1. CONDITIONAL MEAN TRANSFER ERRORS FOR
THOSE SUBJECTS WHO MAKE ONE OR MORE, OR
TWO OR MORE ERRORS DURING TRANSFER

	Transfer Problems			
	One or More Errors		Two or More Errors	
Prior Training [a]	S	D	S	D
None	10.65	6.28	11.29	8.16
Other cue	11.74	7.18	11.74	7.35
Redundant	11.31	6.18	13.06	7.67

[a] The column headings, S and D, denote the problem from which the scores derive. The meanings of the row headings are: "none" is initial acquisition of groups S and D from Chapter 3; "other cue" refers to groups $D \rightarrow S$ and $S \rightarrow D$; "redundant" refers to groups $S + D \rightarrow S$ and $S + D \rightarrow D$.

The data also show that if an RRC subject did not show perfect transfer, then his subsequent errors in learning the transfer problem were nearly the same as controls who did not have the prior RRC training. This similarity of transfer performance may be seen by computing the conditional mean transfer errors for those subjects who did not transfer perfectly. Recalling the prior discussion on how to treat subjects who make one error, Table 4.1 presents conditional mean transfer errors with the one-error subjects included or excluded.

The claim is that the three conditional means in each column are essentially the same. This is apparent by inspection and the null hypotheses of equality of means within any column cannot be rejected by F tests. In fact, all four F's are less than one, so there is no suggestion of any reliable differences among the prior training conditions. There are no consistent orderings of the row conditions over the four columns. The data support the contention that RRC subjects who fail to transfer perfectly show no faster transfer learning than do suitable controls. In turn, this conclusion supports the all-or-nothing view of transfer in this situation.

THEORETICAL PREDICTIONS OF TRANSFER

The model will now be used to predict the transfer results in detail. Ideally, the predictions can be made without estimating any parameters from the transfer results being predicted. We shall concentrate mainly upon the distribution of transfer errors by subjects in groups $S + D \rightarrow S$ and $S + D \rightarrow D$.

To cover both cases in our theoretical expressions, let p_r, p_n, and $p_{r,n}$ denote the proportions of subjects solving the RRC problem on the retained cue, the nonretained (now irrelevant) cue, or both, respectively. Let c denote the probability of learning the transfer problem on each error made by a subject who solved on the nonretained cue. The "rational" and "irrational" hypotheses may be translated into quantitative terms by introducing a parameter y, which denotes the probability that a two-cue solver reacts "rationally" to the first conflict error in transfer. The rational hypothesis supposes that the subject solves the problem on this error trial whereas the irrational hypothesis supposes that the error causes him to start over on the transfer problem. The first or second hypothesis is equivalent to setting y equal to one or zero, respectively.

The probability that a RRC-trained subject makes k errors during transfer is written as follows:

$$Pr\,(T = k) = \begin{cases} p_r + dp_{r,n} & \text{for } k = 0 \\ (1 - d)yp_{r,n} + [p_n + (1 - d)(1 - y)p_{r,n}]c & \text{for } k = 1 \\ [p_n + (1 - d)(1 - y)p_{r,n}]c(1 - c)^{k-1} & \text{for } k \geq 2 \end{cases}$$

(4.1)

To explain the reasoning involved here, first consider the two terms expressing the probability of zero errors. The first term, p_r, is the likelihood of a retained-cue solution; such subjects should not be disturbed when the unlearned cue is made irrelevant, and hence they should make no errors. The second term, $dp_{r,n}$, is the probability that a subject solves on both cues, guesses correctly on his first conflict trial, and thus solves the transfer problem without errors.

Consider next the terms for one error. The first, $(1 - d)yp_{r,n}$, is the likelihood that a subject solves on both cues, chooses incorrectly on a conflict trial, but then solves rationally with probability y. The second term expresses the assumption that all the remaining subjects not mentioned above, a proportion $p_n + (1 - d)(1 - y)p_{r,n}$, have probability c of solving the transfer problem on their first error. The remaining terms, for $k \geq 2$, apply to this remaining proportion of subjects the geometric learning rule, that is, following each error there is probability c of solving the problem. The reader may verify that all the probabilities sum to one since p_r, p_n, and $p_{r,n}$ add to one. As mentioned earlier, the distribution of T for the rational and irrational hypotheses are obtained by setting y in Equation 4.1 equal to one or zero, respectively. Obviously, the value of y will be pertinent only when $dp_{r,n}$, a fraction of the proportion of two-cue solvers, is appreciable.

The average or expected value of T according to Equation 4.1 is

$$E(T) = (1 - d)yp_{r,n} + [p_n + (1 - d)(1 - y)p_{r,n}]c^{-1}$$

where c is the controls' learning rate. The reciprocal of the control errors should equal c, or c^{-1} can be replaced by the average control errors, $E(T_c)$, thus yielding

$$E(T) = (1 - d)yp_{r,n} + [p_n + (1 - d)(1 - y)p_{r,n}]E(T_c) \qquad (4.2)$$

A further statistic we shall examine is the mean errors conditional upon one or more errors occurring. The expression for this statistic is

$$E[T \mid T \geq 1] = \frac{E(T)}{1 - Pr(T = 0)} = \frac{E(T)}{1 - p_r - dp_{r,n}} \qquad (4.3)$$

A few features of these equations are worth noting here. First, when $y = 0$, the conditional mean errors in Equation 4.3 equal the control errors, $E(T_c)$. Second, the mean errors in Equation 4.2 is always less for $y = 1$ than for $y = 0$ whenever $E(T_c) > 1$ (as it invariably is). Third, the mean transfer errors increase monotonically with p_n, the proportion of subjects initially solving the RRC problem on the nonretained cue.

The transfer data will be predicted by Equations 4.1–4.3, using parameters obtained from independent groups, not from groups $S + D \to S$ and $S + D \to D$. For these purposes, there are three independent choices of parameters. First, for the solution-type probabilities, either the observed or theoretical proportions from the experiment in Chapter 3 may be used. These two distributions are reproduced in Table 4.2 for convenient reference. The theoretical proportions displayed a

TABLE 4.2. PARAMETER VALUES USED IN PREDICTIONS OF TRANSFER PERFORMANCE OF THE REDUNDANT-CUE GROUPS

Solution-Type Proportions [a]			Control Mean Errors [a]		
Type	Empirical	Predicted	Condition	S Problem	D Problem
Dot	.505	.553	Shifted	11.74	7.18
Shape	.349	.323			
Both	.146	.124	Nonshifted	10.65	6.10

[a] Empirical and nonshifted control data are from the experiment reported in Chapter 3.

TABLE 4.3. Observed and Predicted Proportions of Zero, Mean, and Conditional Mean Errors (One or More) during Transfer

Parameter Combination	Transfer Groups					
	$S + D \to S$			$S + D \to D$		
	$Pr(T = 0)$	$E(T)$	$E[T\|T \geq 1]$	$Pr(T = 0)$	$E(T)$	$E[T\|T \geq 1]$
Observed	.42	6.62	11.31	.55	2.78	6.18
I. Empirical p_i						
A. Shift controls						
$y = 0$	.40	7.05	11.74	.60	2.87	7.18
$y = 1$	.40	6.02	10.02	.60	2.55	6.38
B. Nonshift controls						
$y = 0$	.40	6.40	10.65	.60	2.44	6.10
$y = 1$	.40	5.47	9.14	.60	2.18	5.33
II. Theoretical p_i						
A. Shift controls						
$y = 0$	.37	7.41	11.74	.63	2.66	7.18
$y = 1$	.37	6.58	10.42	.63	2.36	6.38
B. Nonshift controls						
$y = 0$	.37	6.71	10.65	.63	2.26	6.10
$y = 1$	.37	5.98	9.50	.63	2.02	5.45

stronger dominance of the dot cue over the shape cue than did the observed proportions. Second, and independently, for the control errors, $E(T_c)$, in Equation 4.2, one may use either the shifted groups, $D \to S$ and $S \to D$, from the present experiment or the nonshifted groups, S and D, from Chapter 3. Estimates of c^{-1}, or $E(T_c)$, from these four groups are also given in Table 4.2. Finally, the parameter y may be set equal to one or zero, representing the hypothesis that a two-cue solver reacts either rationally or irrationally to his first transfer error. In all, there are eight combinations of the three parametric decisions, and there are no arguments for choosing among them a priori. Predictions based on all eight parameter combinations are shown in Table 4.3 so that the reader may compare their relative merits. The data are in the first row and the eight prediction sets follow in the next eight rows. For all of these predictions, the parameter d, the probability of choosing the retained cue on the first conflict trial, was calculated theoretically from the $a(D)$ and

$a(S)$ values obtained in Chapter 3. Thus, for transfer group $S + D \rightarrow D$, d was .164/.258 or .64; for transfer group $S + D \rightarrow S$, d was .094/.258 or .36.

In Table 4.3, the proportions of subjects showing errorless transfer are predicted with tolerable accuracy, with the prediction based on the empirical p_i's being better. These predictions would be more accurate (.42 and .58, respectively) if the conflict-choice parameter, d, were set at the chance level of one-half. In theory, the proportions of subjects showing errorless transfer in groups $S + D \rightarrow S$ and $S + D \rightarrow D$ should always add to unity. For the data, these add to $(25 + 33)/60 = .97$. Second, considering the mean errors and conditional mean errors for the eight parameter combinations, all the predicted values fall within one standard error of the observed mean values (standard errors were 1.27 and 0.75 for groups $S + D \rightarrow S$ and $S + D \rightarrow D$, respectively). In this sense then, none of the theoretical combinations can be rejected by these data. By the same token, the experiment was not sufficiently powerful to differentiate among the slightly varying combinations. This was true in part because the proportion of two-cue solvers in this problem is small, thus providing too little leverage for deciding questions regarding transfer of two-cue solvers.

Although it is difficult to obtain an overall impression of the best fitting combination of parameters, a few marginal comparisons of variables are possible. That is, one may examine goodness of fit of $E (T)$ when one parameter is varied while the others are fixed. By such comparisons, the following are found: (1) the shift controls always lead to higher predictions of $E (T)$ than do the nonshift controls; in seven of eight cases the nonshift predictions are lower than the data, whereas three of the shift predictions are above and five below the observed $E (T)$; (2) predicted errors for $y = 1$ are always below the observed errors, whereas predictions for $y = 0$ are equally often above and below the observed $E (T)$; (3) comparing predictions of $E (T)$ based on the empirical versus the theoretical p_i's, the former are always higher for group $S + D \rightarrow D$ and always lower for group $S + D \rightarrow S$, but neither dominates the other in being consistently closer to the data. These marginal comparisons are informative, but in combination they do not single out the best rows. In terms of average absolute discrepancies from $E (T)$, the best combinations occur in lines I-A-0 and II-A-1 of Table 4.3, whereas the largest discrepancies occur in rows I-B-1 and II-B-1.

By use of Equation 4.1 one may predict the complete probability distribution of transfer errors. Some illustrations of the cumulative error distributions—the frequency of k or fewer errors—are shown in Figures 4.1 and 4.2. The predictions in Figure 4.1 come from the combination in

100

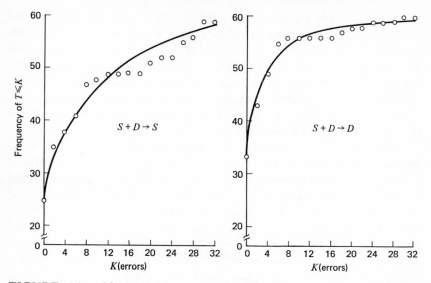

FIGURE 4.1. *Observed (dots) and predicted (smooth curve) cumulative error distributions in transfer for groups trained on S and D as RRC's. Predicted values are based on Equation 4.1 using theoretical p_i's, shift controls, and $y = 1$.*

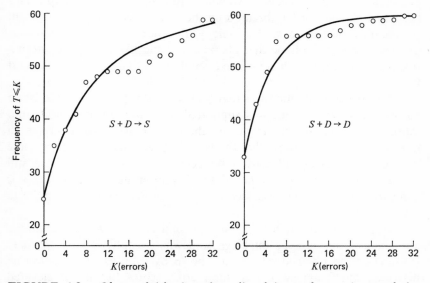

FIGURE 4.2. *Observed (dots) and predicted (smooth curve) cumulative error distributions in transfer for groups trained on S and D as RRC's. Predicted values are based on Equation 4.1, empirical p_i's, nonshift controls, and $y = 0$.*

101

line II-A-1; that is, theoretical p_i's, shift controls, $y = 1$. The predictions in Figure 4.2 derive from line I-B-0; that is, empirical p_i's, nonshift controls, $y = 0$. The fit of predicted to observed cumulative frequencies was compared using a Kolmogorov-Smirnov one-sample test, which depends on the maximal discrepancy between the two cumulative distributions. The largest discrepancy among the four cases shown in Figures 4.1 and 4.2 was .09 ($p < .20$). Thus one cannot reject the fit of these theories to the error distributions in transfer.

Another statistic that one can examine is the average trial of the last error in transfer. For $y = 0$ or 1, the expected trial of last error is just twice the mean transfer errors predicted by the theory. The observed trial of last error averaged 5.30 for group $S + D \rightarrow D$ and 14.15 for group $S + D \rightarrow S$. These values are consistently underpredicted by $y = 1$ for any combinations of the other parameters, whereas they are better predicted by $y = 0$. For example, line II-A-0 (theoretical p_i's, shift controls, $y = 0$) yielded predictions of 5.74 and 14.10, respectively, for mean trial of last error for groups $S + D \rightarrow D$ and $S + D \rightarrow S$. This flaw of underprediction by $y = 1$ relates to its consistent underprediction of transfer errors. (See Table 4.2.)

In summary, the general premises of the model have been supported by the RRC transfer data. The error distribution in transfer was predictable using parameters estimated from independent groups. This basic fact should not be obscured by the simultaneous juggling of eight parametric combinations. The sole justification for the simultaneous presentation was the hope that the reader would like to see the alternative predictions rather than only the one that was judged to give the best fit.

Our basic assumption was that transfer in this problem would be an all-or-nothing affair. This was supported by a division of subjects into those who made no errors versus those who made some errors in transfer, and then showing that the latter subjects made about the same number of errors as did control subjects. Of course, the question still remains whether we have chosen the "appropriate" controls for this comparison. But having discussed this point earlier, we have no more to say on it here.

A possible objection to the use of total error scores to decide the all-or-none transfer issue might go somewhat as follows: the "partial" learning of the retained cue, to be shown by subjects not transferring perfectly, might appear not in total error scores but in an elevated probability of responding correctly prior to meeting the criterion of transfer learning. In other words, the partial transfer might appear in a "correct-response" bias but not in total errors. The transfer data were analyzed regarding this conjecture, and the evidence fails to support it. The most relevant statistic is the proportion of correct responses before the "imperfect" transfer subjects met their criterion of transfer learning. Combining groups $S + D \rightarrow S$ and $S + D \rightarrow D$, this observed proportion was .505, which is very close to the chance level of .500 predicted by the all-or-none transfer idea. For groups $S \rightarrow D$ and $D \rightarrow S$, these values were .488 and .513, respectively. Thus, in this sense, subjects did not demonstrate partial learning in their correct response probabilities prior to solving the transfer problem. Transfer performance appears from these data to be two-valued, the chance level and then perfect responding. The RRC training induces positive transfer by causing more subjects to begin the second problem in the "perfect responding" state.

ALL-OR-NONE TRANSFER
IN VERBAL CONCEPT LEARNING

The all-or-none transfer reported here is not restricted to learning classifications of geometric stimuli since Greeno and Scandura (1966) and Polson (1967) have reported similar results for verbal concept learning. In verbal concept learning, the subject learns to group together a set of words that possess a common preestablished associate. In a normative study by Underwood and Richardson (1956a), subjects were asked to give "sensory impression" associations to a large set of common nouns. Using the associative norms so obtained, other subjects may be required to learn a common identifying response to (or to group together) a set of words each of which evokes a common "sensory impression" mediator with appreciable frequency. Thus the subject might have to learn the identifying response "dax" to the words eye, head, barrel, and button, each of which evokes the mediator "round"; and a different response "mib" to the words paste, ivory, sheep, teeth, which evoke the mediator "white." Underwood and Richardson (1956b) showed (a) that such groupings did occur during learning, as indicated by similar points of learning of the various items within a set; and (b) that learning of a group proceeded faster the more items within a set and the higher the probability of the common-associate mediator to the items within a set.

Greeno and Scandura (1966) trained their subjects on the initial list (shown in Table 4.4) which involved three concepts—the mediators small, white, and round—with varying numbers of instances of the three concepts: four, two, or one. Following initial learning, subjects were shifted to the six-item transfer list shown in Table 4.4. The transfer list consisted of one new instance of the former three concepts, paired with

103

TABLE 4.4. TRAINING AND TRANSFER LISTS IN THE VERBAL CONCEPT-LEARNING
EXPERIMENT

	Training List			Transfer List	
Concept	Stimulus Item	Response	Concept	Stimulus Item	Response
Small	Freckle	Pel	Small	Atom	Pel
	Earthworm	Pel	(Control	Sulfur	Pel)
	Tweezer	Pel			
	Grasshopper	Pel			
White	Paste	Mur	White	Ivory	Mur
	Sheep	Mur	(Control	Alley	Mur)
Round	Knuckle	Dix	Round	Globe	Dix
			(Control	Beak	Dix)

(From Greeno & Scandura, 1966.)

the same identifying response, and three new control items that elicited
none of the concept associates (small, white, or round) with appreciable
frequency.

Qualitatively, the Greeno and Scandura results showed high positive transfer to the concept items relative to the control items, and more
transfer the greater the number of concept representatives in initial
learning. They reasoned that transfer of, say, the response "mur" to the
stimulus "ivory" would occur (a) if the initial items (paste, sheep) in
the white concept set were originally learned by using the white mediator, so that the association white-"mur" was formed, and (b) if the test
item, ivory, evoked the sensory associate, white, thus producing the
response "mur" to ivory. Greeno and Scandura argued that the number
of instances per concept affected transfer via the first factor, the probability that the sensory mediator was learned.

Of interest in the present context is the fact that Greeno and
Scandura found evidence for all-or-none transfer in this task. Their
evidence was similar to ours, namely, those concept items having at least
one error in transfer were learned no faster than were control items
having at least one error. The differential degrees of transfer for the
three kinds of concepts, having one, two, or four original instances, was
solely attributable to the proportion of zero-error cases in transfer.

Polson (1967) reported similar all-or-none transfer in an extension
of the Greeno and Scandura study using "sense impression" concepts
and also "supraordinate" verbal concepts. Subjects in the supraordinate

concept condition learned five successive paired-associate lists similar to those shown in Table 4.5. Items in successive lists evoking a common category label (e.g., animal) were assigned the same response. When compared to "learning-to-learn" controls who mastered five unrelated lists in succession, subjects learning the concept lists in Table 4.5 showed progressively greater positive transfer over the last four lists. Presumably, having learned, say, horse-8 and cat-8 in the first two lists, the subject develops the hypothesis that animal words are assigned to re-

TABLE 4.5. VERBAL STIMULI IN THE FIVE SUCCESSIVE LISTS IN POLSON'S EXPERIMENT

Category	Response	Learning Stimuli [a]				
		List 1	List 2	List 3	List 4	List 5
Furniture	1	Couch	Bed	Table	Desk	Lamp
Body parts	2	Leg	Head	Foot	Neck	Arm
Insect	3	Ant	Flea	Bee	Wasp	Fly
Fruit	4	Orange	Apple	Plum	Peach	Banana
Clothing	5	Pants	Skirt	Dress	Hat	Coat
Geologic term	6	Valley	Rock	Cliff	Lake	Hill
Vehicle	7	Car	Truck	Boat	Bus	Wagon
Animal	8	Horse	Cat	Lion	Bear	Dog

[a] Each row represents members of one supraordinate category.

sponse 8, and so responds with 8 to the lion, bear, and dog items in lists 3, 4, and 5, provided he realizes that these belong to the animal category. For immediate purposes, the relevant point was that Polson found that the all-or-none transfer hypothesis was always upheld; that is, concept items on which at least one error occurred were learned no faster than were control items at that stage of the experiment. The progressively greater positive transfer over lists for the concept items was attributable almost entirely to the increasing percentage of zero-error (perfect transfer) items. Thus these results of Greeno and Scandura, and Polson illustrate the same feature of transfer that we have emphasized in our own data from concept identification.

LEARNING DURING NONREVERSAL SHIFT

Up to this point, we have ignored the question of transfer learning raised by comparing the $D \to S$ and $S \to D$ groups with the S

and D groups. The former subjects are undergoing a nonreversal shift (NRS) and it is apparent that our model for initial learning must be modified to handle NRS data. The NRS subject begins his transfer problem already focused on a particular attribute which has been successful, whereas in initial learning no systematic starting bias exists.

Without wishing to become involved too deeply into this topic here, we will sketch a tentative model for use in the analysis of NRS data. We suppose that an NRS subject during transfer learning can be characterized as being in one of three states on any trial: (1) state P—the subject is perseverating on his former solution hypothesis, which is now irrelevant; (2) state S—he has given up his former hypothesis and is "searching" for the new relevant cue; and (3) state L—he has found the new relevant cue and has solved the transfer problem. In states P and S, he has probability q (usually .50) of making an error, and in state L he makes no errors. While in state P, after each error the subject has probability r of rejecting his old hypothesis (leaving state P) and $1 - r$ of perseverating with it despite the error; if he has rejected his old hypothesis, he has probability c of learning the correct hypothesis after each error. The latter assumption is the same as that for initial learning; the former assumption is added to handle NRS transfer.

The Markov matrix appropriate to these assumptions is as follows:

State on trial $n + 1$

		L	S	P	
State on trial n	L	1	0	0	
	S	qc	$1 - qc$	0	(4.4)
	P	qrc	$qr(1 - c)$	$1 - qr$	

The NRS subject usually begins in state P on trial 1 of the transfer series (assuming he has learned an initial problem to a criterion). A change in state from P to S does not improve the performance probabilities (it is q in both states) but it does increase the probability of learning on any given error. The parameter c should be sensitive primarily to the stimulus structure of the problem (discussed in Chapter 2), whereas the newly introduced parameter, r, summarizes the effects of variables influencing the extent to which the subject perseverates with an old hypothesis in the face of disconfirming evidence. Thus r should depend on such factors as the length of the criterion run (e.g., overlearning) before transfer, the subject's confidence in the correctness of his hypothesis, the discriminability of error-feedback signals and of the change from the acquisition to the transfer series, the cost of errors, whether or not acquisition provided occasional misinformation or partial reinforcement for the correct hypothesis, and so on.

Techniques of derivation for such Markov learning processes can be found in Atkinson, Bower, and Crothers (1965). Only a few properties of this NRS model will be noted here. First, the parameters r and c can be estimated separately since c should just be the rate of learning this problem initially, without the prior training. The expression for mean errors is

$$E(T) = \frac{1-r}{r} + \frac{1}{c} = \frac{1-r}{r} + E(T_c) \tag{4.5}$$

where $E(T_c)$ is the expected errors for a group learning the problem initially. An alternative way to view Equation 4.5 is to say that the errors the NRS subjects make in excess of their initial-learning controls should be a constant, $(1-r)/r$. In Table 4.2, we see that the excess errors for group $D \rightarrow S$ over group S is 1.09, and the excess for group $S \rightarrow D$ over group D is 1.08. So this appears to support that feature of the model. The estimate of r based on these differences is .48, which means that subjects in the NRS conditions required an average of about two disconfirmations before they gave up their former solution hypothesis. The near equality of these two numbers could be purely fortuitous, of course, and we should require more data before placing much confidence in the model.

The model in Equation 4.4 also yields a predicted error distribution which is the convolution of two geometric distributions, the first (t_0) describing the errors required before leaving state P, and the second (t_1) the errors before leaving state S if it is entered. These state-specific error distributions are:

$$Pr(t_0 = k) = r(1-r)^{k-1} \qquad \text{for } k = 1, 2, 3, \ldots$$
$$Pr(t_1 = x) = c(1-c)^x \qquad \text{for } x = 0, 1, 2, \ldots$$

Letting $T = t_0 + t_1$ be the total errors before reaching state L, it is distributed according to

$$Pr(T = n) = \sum_{k=1}^{n} Pr(t_0 = k) \cdot Pr(t_1 = n - k)$$

$$= \frac{rc}{(r-c)} [(1-c)^n - (1-r)^n] \tag{4.6}$$

A few features of this error distribution may be noted. First, in comparison to a geometric distribution having the same mean, the distribution in Equation 4.6 is "hump-shaped" with a mode occurring at some $T > 1$, whereas the geometric distribution has its mode at $T = 1$. In the observed error distributions, the modes for groups S and D were

107

at $T = 1$ as expected by the geometric distribution, whereas the modes for groups $D \rightarrow S$ and $S \rightarrow D$ were each at $T = 3$. Using the estimate $r = .48$ obtained above, then Equation 4.6 predicts that the mode for group $S \rightarrow D$ (with control $c = .164$) will occur at 3 and the mode for group $D \rightarrow S$ (with $c = .094$) will also occur at 3.

Using $r = .48$ and the c's estimated from the nonshift control subjects, the cumulative error distribution may be predicted by summing the terms of Equation 4.6. The fits of the predicted to the observed cumulative-error distributions are shown in Figure 4.3. The fit is good

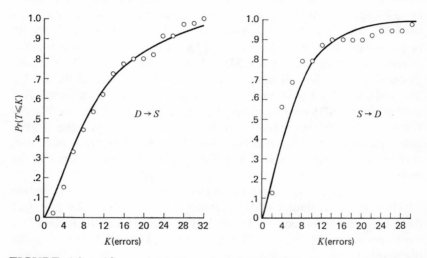

FIGURE 4.3. *Observed (dots) and predicted (smooth curve) cumulative error distributions in transfer for single-cue groups. Predictions are based on Equation 4.6 using independent estimates of the rates of learning.*

for group $S + D \rightarrow S$ but somewhat poorer for group $S + D \rightarrow D$. According to a Kolmogorov-Smirnov one-sample test, the null hypothesis cannot be rejected in either group ($p > .20$ in both cases). Thus the error distributions of the shift groups are predictable from the three-state model and parameters estimated from the nonshift control groups. We do not carry this topic further since it diverts from our main interest, which concerns transfer of the RRC groups. One can attach the NRS model in Equation 4.4 onto our assumptions about transfer of RRC learners. That is, a proportion $p_r + dp_{r,n}$ of the transfer subjects begin in state L whereas the remaining proportion, $p_n + (1 - d)p_{r,n}$, begin in state P of the Markov process. This corresponds to using the shift controls for the $E(T_c)$ of Equation 4.2. All the predictions about transfer (the proportion of zero errors, mean errors, conditional mean errors, and trial of last error) are the same as previously calculated for the case where $y = 0$ and the shift controls are used. Recall too that these cases generally led to the more accurate predictions of the transfer data for groups $S + D \rightarrow S$ and $S + D \rightarrow D$.

SUMMARY

In this chapter, we have been concerned with transfer to a new problem following RRC learning. In the transfer experiment both cues that were relevant and redundant during initial training remained available but one became irrelevant in the transfer task. It was argued that the transfer performance of an RRC subject could be characterized in different ways, depending upon how he had solved the initial redundant problem. The hypothesis was that transfer in such circumstances would be an all-or-nothing process for an individual subject. Subjects who had solved the RRC problem on the cue retained as relevant in transfer should make no errors. Subjects who had initially solved on the cue made irrelevant in transfer should show no positive transfer compared to appropriate control subjects. Subjects solving initially on both cues were assumed to choose between the cues when the first conflict trial occurred and to solve if a correct choice was made, and react either "rationally" or "irrationally" if an error was made.

In the experiment, subjects were trained on the $S + D$ problem and then transferred either to the S or D problem. Both groups showed significant positive transfer compared to controls. In agreement with the higher estimated salience of cue D, there was more transfer going from $S + D$ to problem D than to problem S.

The main, and possibly the only, locus of this positive transfer following $S + D$ learning was an increase, relative to controls, of subjects making zero errors. For those subjects failing to transfer perfectly, the average transfer errors were nearly the same as control subjects. Moreover, there was no evidence for partial transfer in correct responding by those subjects making one or more errors. Their overall proportion of correct responses prior to criterion on the transfer problem was at the chance level of .50. Such data support the hypothesis of all-or-none transfer in this context.

Using parameters estimated from independent groups, the theory successfully predicted the transfer error distributions for groups $S + D \rightarrow S$ and $S + D \rightarrow D$. Predictions of eight different parameter combinations were examined. Generally, predictions tended to be more accurate when (a) the control learning was identified with shift controls

109

$(D \rightarrow S$ or $S \rightarrow D)$ rather than the nonshift controls $(S$ or $D)$; (b) a two-cue solver was assumed to react "irrationally" to a conflict error; and (c) the empirical rather than theoretical proportions of solution types from Chapter 3 were used. These orderings are tentative, however, because the predictions of the various parameter combinations did not differ very much and none was significantly off from the data.

Finally, some discussion was given to the "nonreversal shift" problem (e.g., $D \rightarrow S$ versus S) and a tentative model was sketched to aid in analysis of such data. This differed from the model for original learning by assuming that the NRS subject may persevere with his former, solution hypothesis for several error trials before abandoning it to search for a new, correct hypothesis. Comparisons of this model to the shift data of groups $D \rightarrow S$ and $S \rightarrow D$ were generally favorable. For example, error distributions of the NRS subjects were predicted fairly well using parameters estimated from independent nonshift control subjects. In general, the theoretical analysis of the entire experiment, as in Chapter 3, demonstrated the point of "parameter invariance," which is essential in testing a theory. That is, parameters which in theory should have the same value were shown in several instances to have indeed nearly the same value.

5
PAIRED-ASSOCIATE LEARNING

In the preceding chapters, the notions of cue salience and cue selection were developed and tested with concept-identification (CI) tasks. The present chapter attempts to extend these notions to handle similar observations from paired-associate learning (PAL). The main experiment to be reported uses a particularly simplified form of PAL.

Perhaps before proceeding further, it is worth asking whether there are sufficient commonalities in CI and PAL to warrant any optimism about the probable success of extending to PAL a model developed for CI. Although both tasks would be broadly classified as involving "discrimination learning," they differ in multiple ways, some of which are:

1. The construction of the stimuli. Typically in CI the patterns arise by combining all possible value of N binary attributes, yielding patterns with maximal overlap of components. In PAL, the stimulus items (typically compounds) can be constructed to overlap to any desired degree. Often one is interested in minimizing the number of common elements among patterns.
2. The number of response alternatives. In CI the number of responses is far less than the number of stimulus patterns; for example, in our experiments with N binary attributes, there were 2^x stimulus patterns but only two responses. In PAL the number of responses often equals the number of stimulus patterns, usually with a one-to-one correspondence.
3. A rule for S-R assignments. In CI there is a systematic and simple rule describing the assignment of stimuli to responses. In PAL there usually is no systematic rule; the one-to-one mapping of stimuli onto responses is usually random and arbitrary.
4. Distinctions concerning cue validity. In CI the rule for S-R assignments imposes a natural classification of attributes into those that are either relevant or irrelevant. In PAL most nominal components are

111

unique, redundant, relevant cues for their associated response. The only irrelevant cues are, possibly, shared common elements of patterns requiring different responses, and incidental extraneous cues.

5. The theoretical unit of analysis. In CI one typically does not distinguish and record separately the responses to each of the 2^x stimuli. The unit of analysis is the string of successes and errors the subject gives to all the patterns considered as a single unit. In PAL one distinguishes and records separately the responses to each stimulus; the individual item is the unit of analysis. From a CI subject working on 2^x stimuli, one learning protocol is obtained; from a PAL subject, 2^x separate protocols are obtained.

This list is not meant to be exhaustive; possibly readers familiar with both research areas can supply many further differences. However, we believe the list includes the more important procedural differences between the typical CI and PAL tasks.

Some of these factors appear to us to be unessential differences, at least judging from the way experimenters apply the CI and PAL labels in practice. Paired-associates studies of high intralist similarity, with complete sharing of components among list compound patterns, suggest that stimulus construction is not that essential to the distinction. Similarly, the number of responses in PAL can be reduced to two or three, well below the number of stimulus items, and yet investigators still apply the PAL label to the procedure. The essential difference, we believe, is the presence or absence of a systematic rule describing the S-R assignments. In CI a simple rule characterizes the assignments; in PAL they have to be enumerated and no simple rule suffices. The conspicuous presence of rules in CI determines in large measure the behavior of experimenters in treating their data: first, in identifying the unit of analysis as the subject's pattern of responses to the entire population of stimuli; and second, in assuming theoretically that the subject is sampling and testing out hypotheses or simple classificatory rules. Learning of a rule transcends the specific instances from which it was inferred; that is, the rule will *mediate* transfer of differential responses to similar but new stimuli not yet seen in the experiment. Subjects in a CI task frequently "solve" the problem before they have been exposed to a substantial fraction of the population of stimulus patterns. In PAL with its arbitrary enumeration of S-R assignments, such mediated transfer from one to another similar item is typically of no help; indeed, it is assumed to be a major source of interference in making progress toward mastery of the learning task.

With this point in mind, one can construct experimental hybrids that lie between CI and PAL, depending upon the relative contribution of rules versus enumeration to learning the correct answers. For example, starting from the binary CI task with, say, color as the relevant attribute, one can approach conceptually the PAL task by (a) decreasing the number of irrelevant cues, (b) increasing the number of different colors (say, from two to eight), and (c) assigning a uniquely different response to each color, thus requiring some lengthy enumeration. Starting from a conventional PAL task, one moves toward a CI task by imposing some kind of rule for the S-R assignments. Such rules can vary in their degree of constraint. For example, suppose that the list of stimulus items consists of one-half nonsense syllables and one-half three-digit numbers, and similarly for the response members. Then a restricting assignment rule would be that nonsense syllable stimuli have digit response members, and digit stimuli have nonsense syllable responses. Such a rule would aid in learning the list of pairs because it permits the subject to confine his responses to the class appropriate to the stimulus. Postman and Riley (1957) have reported research showing the facilitative effect of such rules, and have used this fact to reinterpret some of Köhler's (1941) earlier data on more rapid learning of "perceptually organized" pairs in PAL. If the responses were restricted to just two—a nonsense syllable and a number—then the transition to a CI task would be reasonably complete; the rule would then specify a unique response (rather than a class of responses) for each instance of a stimulus class (rather than for each unique stimulus).

REVIEW OF PRIOR RESEARCH

As already noted, in the typical PAL situation most of the components of the stimulus compounds are RRC's. To the extent that this is so, some kind of stimulus selection would be anticipated to occur during learning. That is, many cases should arise in which one or another component of the compound could become the sole effective component in the compound.

There have been several recent experiments on PAL which have set out to analyze possible cue selection. In a cogent article analyzing differences between the *nominal* (compound) stimulus and the *functional* (effective component) stimulus, Underwood (1963) reviews the main evidence up to that date. There are two types of indirect evidence of cue selection. The first type is based on subjects' reports of the strategies they used in learning PA items. In an experiment by Mattocks (cited in Underwood, 1963, p. 35), which involved learning eight nonsense trigrams as stimuli and common words as responses, subjects

113

reported that a large proportion of the pairs (62 percent) were learned using only the first letter of the trigrams. When two items shared a common first letter, then a different, distinguishing letter would be used as the functional stimulus. The second line of indirect evidence comes from an experiment by Yum (1931) in which, following PAL with nonsense trigrams as stimuli, subjects were tested for generalization of responses to new trigrams constructed by changing one or more letters of the original trigrams. Not surprisingly, the more letters changed in the original trigram, the less probable was the original response, since by changing more letters it was more likely that the effective component was removed. Of more interest is the fact that among changes of one letter only, generalization decrements were greatest when the first letter of the trigram was changed. This evidence suggests that the first letter was most frequently the functional cue for the response. This is indirect evidence, however, because it does not require such an interpretation. Conceivably, the entire trigram was effective but a first letter was necessary for the subject to reintegrate the compound with any certainty.

More direct evidence for cue selection comes from a series of experiments on what had been called the "context effect" in PAL. The term was introduced in the first experiment, by Weiss and Margolius (1954), and its rationale will be described shortly. The Weiss and Margolius experiment was very similar to the experiment in Chapter 3; that is, subjects were trained on a list of PA items, each stimulus involving two RRC's, and then were tested for what they had learned about each cue. Adopting a procedure first introduced in verbal learning by Dulsky (1935), Weiss and Margolius used nonsense syllables presented on a different colored background for each of the nine nonsense syllables. They referred to the nonsense syllable as the "primary" stimulus and its colored background as the "context" in which the primary stimulus appeared. The linguistic distinction appears an anachronism, based as it was upon a prejudgment of which component would become the functional cue.

Three learning groups were run. Group *SC* learned with nonsense syllables and colors as redundant and relevant stimuli. Group *S* learned with syllables alone on a constant gray background. Group *C* learned with colors alone and no syllables. Learning rates for these three conditions came out in the order *SC, C,* then *S* from fastest to slowest. Mean trials to a list criterion of one perfect recitation were 4.93 for *SC,* 5.37 for *C,* and 6.62 for *S.* Thus the acquisition results were qualitatively in line with additivity of learning rates.

Twenty-four hours later the subjects in group *SC* received a recall test and relearning series under one of four conditions: (1) the stimulus compounds were the same as in learning, or *SC;* (2) the color was removed and only the syllable was shown, or *S* alone; (3) the color was the same but the syllable was slightly altered, or *S'C;* or (4) the color was removed and the syllable was slightly altered, or *S'*. The mean recall scores (out of nine possible) for these four conditions were 7.37, 3.25, 5.50, and 1.37, respectively. Trials to relearn the transfer list were in full accord with these first-trial recall scores, that is, faster relearning with better recall. From these scores one may conclude that recall was best when both the color and syllable components were reinstated, and a decrement was produced either by removing the colored background component or by altering or removing the nonsense syllable. The colored background appeared to have been a more effective cue than was the syllable. This accords with the facts of acquisition wherein group *C* learned faster than group *S*.

Although these results are sufficient to show general average differences in the effectiveness of the *C* and *S* cues, the testing method was not sufficient to reveal the sort of patterns of "solution types" that we obtained in Chapter 3. The procedure of averaging over subjects receiving only a single transfer condition yields results not permitting distinctions between partial or proportional learning of the two cues by each subject versus all-or-none learning of one or both cues by a single subject for a single item. Further, it is clear now that an important transfer condition (viz., *C* alone with *S* absent) is missing for the *SC* subjects.

Two later experiments, one by Underwood, Ham, and Ekstrand (1962) and one by Sundland and Wickens (1962), employed similar procedures, except transfer tests occurred immediately after training rather than twenty-four hours later as in the Weiss and Margolius (1954) experiment. In both these later experiments the nominal stimulus was a compound of a colored background and a printed verbal unit; the responses were seven single digits in the Underwood, Ham, and Ekstrand study and nine words in the Sundland and Wickens study. In both experiments an attempt was made to manipulate the relative effectiveness of the verbal unit by making it a low meaningful nonsense trigram in one case (actually a unique pair of trigrams in the Sundland and Wickens study) and a highly meaningful word in the other. In each study the supposition was that the word would be a more effective cue than the nonsense trigram.

In the Underwood, Ham, and Ekstrand experiment, group *WC* learned with word and color as RRC's and group *TC* learned with trigram and color as RRC's. Upon reaching a list criterion of one perfect recitation, subjects were shifted to a transfer learning task, with *C* alone,

TABLE 5.1. MEAN NUMBER OF CORRECT RECALLS (OF SEVEN) ON THE FIRST TRANSFER TEST IN THE UNDERWOOD, HAM, AND EKSTRAND EXPERIMENT

Group	Testing	Number Correct
WC	*WC*	6.3
	W	5.0
	C	3.8
TC	*TC*	5.5
	T	2.6
	C	5.4

(From Underwood, Ham, & Ekstrand, 1962.)

with the verbal unit alone (*W* or *T*), or with both together (as a control for the post-criterion drop in performance). The mean correct responses on the first transfer trial are shown in Table 5.1; these were estimated from the graphs in the Underwood, Ham, and Ekstrand paper.

From the data one may infer that the word dominated the color in the *WC* compound whereas the color dominated the trigram in the *TC* compound. The relative saliences of the words and trigrams is reflected too in the fact that initial acquisition was faster in the *WC* condition than in the *TC* condition. Mean trials to the list criterion were 8.67 for *WC* and 10.52 for *TC*. A minor discrepancy turned up in a subsidiary experiment run to assess learning rates on words alone, trigrams alone, or colors alone. Although both words and colors were learned faster than trigrams alone, the first two did not differ significantly. Thus the slight advantage of words over colors displayed in the transfer data was not confirmed in their respective learning rates. The data were not reported in a form suitable for assessing the prediction of faster learning for groups *WC* and *TC* compared to groups *W, T,* and *C*.

Underwood, Ham, and Ekstrand (1962) recognized that their average transfer data were not in a form required to distinguish alternative discriptions of what was learned. The possibilities they mentioned, for example, in the *WC* transfer to *W* alone or *C* alone, were (1) a given subject used either *W* alone or *C* alone for learning all seven of his paired associates, with *W* alone used by more subjects; (2) each subject learned some items using *W* alone, and some items using *C* alone, with the former mode being more frequent; or (3) each subject showed partial learning on each component, with the *W* component being some-

116

what stronger than the C component. By inspection of the recall numbers, these investigators also inferred that at least some of the subjects were learning at least some of the items by using both components in the compound. However, there was no way to infer the frequency of this joint learning from their data.

Underwood, Ham, and Ekstrand interpreted the relative dominance of words over colors (in a WC compound) as resulting from the words being more "meaningful" than color. Meaningfulness presumably is to be measured by Noble's (1952) method, as the number of verbal associates elicited within a brief time by the stimulus component. The idea was that such meaningfulness would correlate with the relative speed with which a stimulus component would enter into an association with the response to be learned. Thus this approach also expects a correlation between learning rate on a cue and its relative dominance in a redundant cue compound.

Our own view is that dominance relations in RRC problems are best viewed as due to selective attention to components, according to their saliences. In Chapter 2 we listed some of the multiple determinants of the salience of a particular cue; and for verbal stimuli, we would have no quarrel with accepting meaningfulness as a correlate of the salience of this class of stimuli. However, we are less sure—presumably as also would be Underwood, Ham, and Ekstrand—whether meaningfulness would be a generally valid index of salience for nonverbal stimuli. However, that possibility cannot be rejected out of hand, and it would be useful to see some research on the issue.

In fairness to Underwood, Ham, and Ekstrand, it may be pointed out that they recognized that their results did not prove that meaningfulness was the factor determining cue dominance. For example, in ascribing the dominance of words over colors to the higher meaningfulness of words, they say:

> We have no independent evidence for this and it may not be valid. The Ss, being much more practiced in dealing with word stimuli than with patches of color as stimuli, may be biased toward the selection of the verbal stimuli. (Underwood, Ham, & Ekstrand, 1962, p. 408.)

The Sundland and Wickens (1962) study was similar in many respects to the Underwood, Ham, and Ekstrand study. Five groups received fifteen acquisition trials with nonsense syllables only (S), or colors (C), or words (W), or syllables plus colors (SC), or words plus colors (WC) as redundant cues.

After the fifteen acquisition trials, each subject in groups WC and SC received one test trial on color alone and one test on symbol alone

117

TABLE 5.2. MEAN PERCENTAGE CORRECT RESPONSES TO TEST COMPONENTS FOR EXPERIMENTS I AND II BY SUNDLAND AND WICKENS

Learning Compound	Test Component	Experiment I	Experiment II
WC	W	97.8	91.5
	C	10.8	9.5
SC	S	72.8	78.2
	C	47.2	37.9

(From Sundland & Wickens, 1962.)

(either W or S), half the subjects getting the color test first and half getting it second. Pooling the two test orders, the mean percentage correct responses for the two components are shown in Table 5.2, under Experiment I. The additional results in Table 5.2 from Experiment II by Sundland and Wickens come from other groups of subjects trained on condition WC and SC, then tested for components, and then asked to fill out a questionnaire on their methods for learning the pairs.

The results in Table 5.2 show fairly close agreement across the two experiments. In condition WC the word dominated the compound to a high degree with very little learning of the color. The 10.8 and 9.5 percent scores for the C test may be compared to the $1/9 = 11$ percent achievable by guessing among the nine response alternatives (of course, the actual scores included an unknown frequency of failures to respond with any associate). In condition SC the nonsense syllable still dominated the color, but to a lesser degree than in the WC condition. As expected, as transfer to the symbol alone declined, transfer to the color alone increased.

The reader may rightly wonder why the color cue is so weak in this experiment in contrast to the Weiss and Margolius and the Underwood, Ham, and Ekstrand experiments reviewed earlier. This presumably is due to variations in the actual physical presentation procedures used in the experiments. Whereas Weiss and Margolius presented their syllables typed on a large colored card (size not reported), the stimuli in the Sundland and Wickens were projections of transparencies onto a screen in the front of a classroom before a group of subjects. It is not implausible to suppose that the vividness (saturation) of the colored background would be different under these circumstances.

The subjects in Experiment II by Sundland and Wickens were

118

asked to indicate what cue they used to learn the list of pairs. Apparently they made only one judgment about how they had learned all nine pairs, rather than being queried about each pair separately. The alternatives available for their checking were: used colors only, symbols only (i.e., S or W), symbols and colors together, or symbols sometimes and colors sometimes. Table 5.3 gives analyses of the transfer data partitioned according to the component the subjects claimed to have used.

TABLE 5.3. PERCENTAGE CORRECT RESPONSES TO TEST COMPONENTS RELATED TO STATED METHOD OF LEARNING

Group	Stated Method	Number of Subjects	Percentage Correct	
			Symbol	Color
WC:	W only	26	90.6	6.8
	"Sometimes"	2	100.0	44.5
SC:	S only	10	100.0	1.7
	S + C together	6	89.5	54.3
	"Sometimes"	8	77.3	49.9
	C only	4	5.5	79.0

(Data from Experiment II of Sundland & Wickens, 1962.)

In the WC condition, the overwhelming majority of subjects used only the salient W cue and learned nothing about C. This is consistent with the average test results in Table 5.2. In the SC condition, where S was nearer in salience to C, only 36 percent of the subjects used S only whereas 64 percent used the color cue in some way some of the time. The percentage corrects are generally in line with expectations from the stated methods, except the "together" and "sometimes" subjects still show better transfer to S alone than to C alone. Perhaps these two discrepancies would have disappeared had the subject been permitted to state his learning method for each item separately rather than being required to state the predominant method used with all nine items.

Sundland and Wickens discussed their results in terms of "discriminability" of variations within a particular class of cues (colors, words, syllables). A class of cues is either high or low in discriminability depending upon the ease with which one can distinguish variations within the class. Presumably, the more easily members of a class are distinguished, the quicker differential responses can be attached to these members. The difference (or discriminability) between the values of a dimension may be taken to be one of the factors influencing its salience

119

and sampling probability. For example, in a concept-identification problem in which geometrical figures vary in size between two values, the likelihood that the subject samples or notices the size difference depends upon how large that difference is (cf. experiments in Chapter 6). Accordingly, the discriminability of the two sizes is assumed to be reflected in the weight and relative salience of the size attribute (Archer, 1962; Shepp & Zeaman, 1966).

Although not in basic disagreement with the discriminability hypothesis of Sundland and Wickens, we would point out that some problems attend attempts to find a common measure for comparing the relative discriminability of colors and nonsense syllables. Without independent, comparative measurements, post hoc pronouncements that words are more discriminable than colors are viewed as merely a reformulation of the dominance relations in the data that are to be explained.

Recent experiments by Houston (1967) have further advanced our knowledge of stimulus selection in PAL. In a first study, Houston replicated the Underwood, Ham, and Ekstrand (1962) experiment with colors and trigrams as RRC's, adding the further finding that overtraining did not increase the learning of the nondominant (trigram) component of the RRC. In a second study, Houston showed that when a trigram had already been used as a cue in a first PAL task, it was predominantly selected in a second PAL task when it was an RRC along with a novel trigram. That is, prior experience at discriminating and using trigram *A* biased the subject toward use of *A* in the next PAL task when *A* and a novel trigram, *B,* were RRC's. In a third study, Houston showed that in a color and trigram RRC task, the amount of learning of the weak (trigram) component was affected by instructing subjects before training that they would later be tested only on the colors, or on the trigrams only, or on both cues. Subjects learned more about the component on which they expected to be tested, and less about the one on which they did not expect to be tested. These factors—prior discriminative use and instructions—seem amenable to interpretation in our terms as modifying the sampling probabilities of the cues involved.

This section will be concluded with a review of a PAL study by Hill and Wickens (1962) which demonstrated additivity of cues both in learning rate and in a compound test situation. Five groups of subjects received ten training trials on a list of nine PA items. The stimulus components were nonsense syllables (*S*) or background colors (*C*), and the five groups differed in the training stimuli. Three groups learned the list for ten trials with *S* alone, *C* alone, or *S* + *C* as redundant cues. On a test trial that followed, mean correct responses (out of nine) for group *S* + *C* was 8.05, for group *S* was 6.68, and for group *C* was 6.54. This shows faster learning for the $S + C$ group, as expected in theory. New and interesting data were provided by the other two groups; group SC learned syllables alone for the first five trials and colors alone for the next five trials, whereas group CS had the reverse order of training. These subjects then received tests on compounds of syllables plus colors. Here, the same response had been separately associated to the syllable and the color which were later presented together on the compound test. As in the Hara and Warren (1961) study reviewed in Chapter 1, the question in the Hill and Wickens' study was whether subjects would perform better when two partly learned cues were added together. As would be expected, percentage correct responses on the $S + C$ tests for groups SC and CS were higher than percentages correct to either component alone.

Further analyses of these data by Hill and Wickens showed that the "summation" effect was more apparent than real. Responses to the $S + C$ test compound occurred only when prior tests on either the S or C component had shown that one or both had been learned. If neither had been learned, then responses to the $S + C$ compound were no more frequent than were control, "nonsummation" items. Thus there was no evidence in these data that subthreshold habit strengths of the components were being summated to produce suprathreshold correct responses to the stimulus compound. Rather it appeared that the response occurred to the compound only if one of the individual components had been learned independently.

DESIGN OF THE PRESENT EXPERIMENT

The following experiment is similar to the Weiss and Margolius study with slight alterations. The test procedure was arranged to find out whether a given item for a given subject was learned on the basis of color (C) alone, nonsense syllable (S) alone, or both. Thus problems concerned with averaging over items or subjects with heterogeneous learning was avoided. Other alterations were designed to afford a clearer test than heretofore of the additivity of learning rates during acquisition in PAL. An experimental restriction to only two responses was adopted in order to analyze the results in terms of a mathematical model—the so-called "all-or-none" or "one-element" model—which has been successfully applied in PAL when two responses are involved (cf. Bower, 1961, 1964).

Three groups of subjects learned different lists of eight PA items. For subjects in group CS the nonsense syllable and its distinctive color were the RRC's for the associated PA response. For group S the syllable

121

was relevant (e.g., "dap" was always correlated with response 1), whereas the colors of the syllable varied randomly over trials and were irrelevant. For group *C* the color was relevant (e.g., red was always correlated with response 1), whereas syllables appeared with a given color randomly over trials and were irrelevant. These single-cue control groups differed from those typically used in PAL studies. The control subjects have the other cue introduced as a deliberately misleading, irrelevant cue. However, the three conditions are directly comparable to conditions *S + D, S,* and *D* of our experiment in Chapter 3.

Immediately after reaching criterion, the subjects in group *CS* received tests (without feedback) on color alone and on syllable alone. Each component of each item was tested four times, totaling eight tests on the separate components of each *CS* item. The response patterns on these test trials provide evidence for cue dominance and "solution type" which we hoped to predict from the learning rates estimated from independent control groups, *C* and *S.*

EXPERIMENT
Method

Subjects: The subjects were forty-eight students from the introductory psychology classes at the University of California, Los Angeles. The subjects were assigned irregularly to one of three groups of sixteen, each composed of eight males and eight females. The subjects were run individually by the same experimenter.

Stimulus Materials and Lists: The stimuli were compounds consisting of a nonsense syllable with its letter made from colored construction paper, mounted on white 5×8-inch display cards. The responses were the numerals 1 and 2. There were eight nonsense syllables of 80 percent association value (Hilgard, 1951) having no consonants in common. The syllables were "dap," "mik," "wes," "gor," "lav," "yeh," "fij," and "noz." The eight colors, chosen for high discriminability among those commercially available, were red, light green, brown, yellow, blue, pink, purple, and dark green. There were $8^2 = 64$ stimulus compounds in all, composed by cutting out the letters for each syllable from each of the eight colored construction papers. Each letter of a syllable was drawn 2×1.5 inches in size from a template. On reinforced trials, the correct response (1 or 2) was shown visually.

The sixty-four patterns were divided into eight separate "lists" within which each syllable and color appeared exactly once. Across the eight lists the syllable-color combinations varied so that overall each syllable occurred once in each color. For the test trials that followed original learning, two additional lists were constructed. To test for color learning, the syllable was replaced by three X's and eight cards were made by constructing the X's from the eight different colors. To test for syllable learning, eight cards were made by constructing the eight different syllables in black letters (not used before).

Procedure and Groups: Group *C* learned paired associates for which the color of the stimulus compound was relevant (i.e., consistently paired with the same numeral response) while the syllable was irrelevant (i.e., randomly paired with the two numbers over trials). Group *S* learned a task for which the syllable was relevant while the color of the syllable was irrelevant. For these groups all eight different training lists were used over successive trials. Half of the items had response 1 as correct and half had response 2 as correct. Group *CS* learned a single list in which color and syllable were RRC's (i.e., the same color-syllable combination was always paired with the same response). Two subjects of the sixteen in group *CS* were assigned to each of the eight color-syllable lists described above.

Training was by the "study trial-test trial" procedure. On a study trial, the eight stimulus-response pairs were separately presented, each pair for two seconds. On the test trial that immediately followed, each stimulus was presented alone for two seconds during which time the subject responded. No feedback was given on test trials. For groups *S* and *C*, the test list differed randomly from the immediately preceding study list, that is, different color-syllable combinations from those just studied. The order of presentation of the items within each trial and the trial orders of the various lists for groups *S* and *C* were randomly determined for each subject. Similarly, the particular assignment of correct responses to the relevant stimuli was varied randomly over subjects, with the restriction that responses 1 and 2 were each correct to four items.

The following instructions were read to all subjects:

"In this experiment, you are to learn to make associations. I will show you a card and a number together. Your job is to learn to associate the number with the stimuli on the card. Then I will test you for your association by showing you only the stimulus card. This is how we shall proceed. I will show you a card and a number for a short time. Look at both the card and number and try to associate them. The number will be either a one or a two. Each card will differ. After I show you all the cards and numbers, I will then show you only the cards and you have to tell me the number you think is associated with it. After you can give the correct numbers to all cards a certain number of times, we shall stop."

Each subject was then trained until he met a learning criterion of three consecutive errorless test trials on the list of eight items. At this point, subjects in groups *S* and *C* were dismissed from the experiment, whereas subjects in group *CS* received a series of single-cue tests. Before these tests the following instructions were read to *CS* subjects:

"Good, you have learned to give correctly the associations to the cards. Now I am going to show you a series of cards on which either the syllable or colored X's will appear. Try to give the number you think was correctly associated with each syllable and color in the lists you have just learned. I will repeat these cards a number of times and then we shall stop."

Following these instructions, the two test lists (for syllables and colors, respectively) were presented four times. Each test item was presented for two seconds and the order of presentation was randomized each time by shuffling the decks of cards. There was no feedback to indicate whether the subject's response was right or wrong.

RESULTS

Acquisition

The acquisition results were analyzed in terms of the total errors a subject made on each item since this measure bears a reciprocal relation to the theoretical learning-rate parameter. The three groups and eight items were compared on this measure by an analysis of variance. Table 5.4 summarizes the results of this analysis.

The only significant source of variation was that due to the different groups. Differences between items and the group by item interaction were small and statistically insignificant.

The mean numbers of errors per item per subject were 3.04 for group *C*, 0.82 for group *S*, and 0.30 for group *CS*. Specific comparisons

TABLE 5.4. ANALYSIS OF VARIANCE OF ERROR SCORES DURING ACQUISITION

Source	df	SS	MS	F
Between				
Mean	1	796.37	796.37	
Groups	2	608.52	304.26	23.36 [a]
Error (B)	45	585.73	13.02	
Within				
Items	7	4.86	0.69	0.61
Groups vs items	14	5.93	0.42	0.37
Error (W)	315	355.59	1.13	

[a] $p < .01$.

124

TABLE 5.5. COMPARISON OF MEAN ERRORS FOR GROUPS $C, S,$ AND CS DURING ACQUISITION

Source	df	MS	F
Group comparisons			
S vs C	1	45.36	28.17 [a]
C vs CS	1	66.99	41.60 [a]
S vs CS	1	2.10	1.30
Error	45	1.61	

[a] $p < .01$.

by F tests were carried out on these group means with the results summarized in Table 5.5. Group C learned significantly slower than either group S or group CS, but the difference between the latter two groups was not statistically significant. These results indicate that color was much less salient than the syllable. Adding color as a RRC with the syllable produced only a small, insignificant reduction in errors.

Prediction of Acquisition Results

A simple learning model is now applied to the acquisition results. Assume that the subject selects, independently for each item, a subset of cues to associate to the reinforced response. Let $a(S)$ and $a(C)$ denote the probability that the syllable and the color cues, respectively, are selected, and $1 - a(S) - a(C)$ is the probability that some other, irrelevant aspects of the patterns or background situation are selected for association.

To develop the model, consider group S for whom the syllable is relevant while the color and other possible aspects of the situation are irrelevant. Starting on the first study trial, with probability $a(S)$ the syllable cue is selected for association, whereas with probability $1 - a(S)$ the syllable is not selected but some other, irrelevant cue is selected. If the syllable cue were selected for association, then all subsequent reinforcements to that syllable will agree with this learned association, and hence there would be no cause for the subject to change this association. In other words, when the subject first selects the relevant cue, that item is learned for the remainder for the experiment.

Suppose, however, that on the first study trial (or any later one), the subject selects an irrelevant cue (color) instead of the syllable to associate to the correct response. Since no feedback occurs on test trials, the next opportunity for the subject to learn that he has selected an inappropriate cue occurs on the following study trial, when the correct

125

answers are shown. The probability that the irrelevant color will be reinforced by the same correct response (i.e., same as previously learned to this color) on the next study trial is one-half, whereas with probability one-half the response will be changed, thus indicating an "error" in the prior-learned color association. Assume that the color-response association is maintained when it is confirmed by the next study trial. However, if the next study trial disconfirms the color association (probability $1/2$), then the subject resamples from the available cues. With probability $a(S)$ in this resampling he selects the relevant syllable cue, forms the correct association, and learns the item.

It is recognized that there is a certain "grossness" about some of these assumptions, and some details of all the possible happenings have been ignored (e.g., competition between paired S and C units that were connected to different responses). The assumptions, however, lead to a mathematical model that accounts fairly well for our data.

These assumptions can be represented by a two-state Markov model. Let state R be the state of an item when the association is keyed to the relevant component; let state I be the state when the association is not yet keyed to the relevant component, but rather to an irrelevant component. While in state R the subject always responds correctly to the relevant component; while in state I, he responds correctly only half the time.

The matrix of transition probabilities for a single item for a subject in group S is as follows:

		State on test trial $n + 1$	Start vector	Probability of correct response
		R $\qquad$ I		
State on	R	1 $\qquad$ 0	$a(S)$	1
test trial n	I	$.5\,a(S)$ $\quad$ $1 - .5\,a(S)$	$1 - a(S)$	$.5$

$$(5.1)$$

This matrix is consistent with the preceding discussion of learning by group S. With probability $a(S)$ on the first study trial, the subject selects the syllable, and hence enters the first test trial on this item in state R. With probability $1 - a(S)$, he selects an irrelevant cue (enters state I); from state I he can transit to state R by having an inconsistency (probability $.5$) on the next study trial and then selecting the syllable cue with probability $a(S)$. Hence, from test n to test $n + 1$, the net transition probability from state I to state R is $.5a(S)$.

The transition matrix for group C, with color relevant, is the same as Equation 5.1 except $a(S)$ is replaced by $a(C)$, the sampling probability of the color cue. By the same reasoning, the matrix for group CS, with color and syllable redundant and relevant, is identical in form to Equation 5.1 except $a(S)$ is replaced by $a(CS)$.

Additivity of Learning Rates

The learning rate for group CS, denoted $a(CS)$, should be equal to the sum of the learning rates for groups C and S, or $a(S) + a(C)$. Estimates of these learning-rate parameters are obtained from the average errors per subject per item. Let T_S, T_C and T_{CS} denote the average errors for the three conditions. The expected value of T_S is calculated from the matrix of Equation 5.1. With probability $a(S)$, the subject begins in state R on an item on trial 1 and hence makes no errors on it. With probability $1 - a(S)$, he begins in state I on this item on trial 1 and may make some errors. The average number of test-reinforcement cycles required before moving from state I into state R is $1/.5a(S)$, since the transition occurs with probability $.5a(S)$ on each trial. During these trials in state I for this item, the subject has probability $.5$ of making an error on the test trials. Thus, starting in state I on trial 1, the subject will average $.5[1/.5a(S)] = 1/a(S)$ errors on such an item. Since the item starts in state I with probability $1 - a(S)$, the expected total errors on it is therefore

$$E(T_S) = \frac{1 - a(S)}{a(S)} \tag{5.2}$$

Equation 5.2 relates the average errors to the learning-rate parameter. An estimate of $a(S)$ is obtained by solving $a(S)$ in terms of $E(T_S)$:

$$\hat{a}(S) = \frac{1}{1 + E(T_S)} \tag{5.3}$$

Since the formal model for groups C and CS is the same as for group S (interchanging learning rates), equations similar to Equations 5.2 and 5.3 can be used to estimate $a(C)$ and $a(CS)$.

The observed values of mean errors were $T_S = 0.82$, $T_C = 3.04$, and $T_{CS} = 0.30$. Substitution of these for the theoretical expected values in Equation 5.3 and its counterparts for the other groups leads to the following estimates:

$$\hat{a}(S) = \frac{1}{1.82} = 0.550$$

$$\hat{a}(C) = \frac{1}{4.04} = 0.248$$

$$\hat{a}(CS) = \frac{1}{1.30} = 0.769$$

The additive prediction is that $a(CS)$ will equal the sum of the first two, or 0.798. This comes suitably close to the obtained estimate of 0.769.

Converting to mean errors for further comparison, the prediction is 0.25 errors versus 0.30 observed errors per subject per item in group CS.

These data therefore provide evidence supporting the prediction of additivity of learning rates, at least as they have been evaluated by this particular model. The weak part of the demonstration is that the syllable was so much more salient than the color in this experiment that adding the two cues together produced only a small, statistically insignificant reduction in errors.

Analyses of Acquisition Data

The acquisition data will be further analyzed for comparisons with the learning model. A first important implication of the all-or-none model is that there should be no improvement in performance prior to the learning of a given item. Technically speaking, the sequence of correct and incorrect responses before the last error should form a stationary and independent series of Bernoulli observations. Moreover, the proportion of correct responses during these precriterion trials should be constant at the chance level of .50. For mathematical reasons, it is important to note that in Equation 5.1 the transition probability $.5a(S)$ applies between each test trial and the next test, independently of whether the subject responded correctly or incorrectly on the test trial. This point follows from the assumption that learning can occur only on study trials with this study-test method. The term $.5a(S)$ does *not* result from averaging correct and error test responses with respective learning rates of 0 and $a(S)$, because by assumption no learning occurs at all on test trials. Rather, the $.5a(S)$ term results from averaging confirming and disconfirming component-response pairings on the intervening study trial, these events having respective learning rates of 0 and $a(S)$. This subtle, interpretative distinction is important because it affects the predicted proportion of correct responses before the last error to an item, the so-called "stationarity value." The latter, intended interpretation, that $.5a(S)$ applies on each test-study trial cycle, implies a stationarity value of .50; the former, unintended interpretation implies a stationarity value of $.5/[1 - .5a(S)]$, which is considerably above .50 for most of our conditions (cf. Atkinson, Bower, & Crothers, 1965, p. 254; Greeno & Steiner, 1964).

Since these precriterion predictions are the same for all acquisition conditions, the analyses are based on such data pooled over precriterion data of the three groups. The analyses performed are explained in detail by Atkinson, Bower, and Crothers (1965, Chap. 2). To assess stationarity of the proportion of correct responses, the trials before the last error in each protocol were divided into a first and second half, discarding any

128

odd trial in the middle if necessary, and the numbers of successes in each half were compared. If the true proportions of successes are equal for the two halves, then the number of protocols having more successes in the first than second half of trials should be balanced by an equal number having more successes in the second half.

Of the 115 protocols for which this comparison was possible (i.e., last error on trial 3 or later), there were thirty-nine cases with second-half successes less than their first-half successes, thirty-eight cases with the opposite relation, and thirty-eight cases of equality of successes in the two halves. The mean proportion of successes in the first half of trials was .502 and in the second half was .496, averaging to .499. Thus these data support the hypothesis of a constant proportion of correct responses at the chance level of .50 over those trials prior to the last error on a given item.

To assess the independence of successive responses during the precriterion trials, the conditional probabilities of an error following an error and following a success were calculated for trials before and inclusive of the last error for an item. Approximate equality of these two conditional probabilities would indicate independence of successive pre-criterion responses. The observed probability of an error on the trial following an error was .622 and on the trial following a success was .597. These do not differ significantly ($X^2(1) = 0.45$). Thus the hypothesis of precriterion independence of responses is supported.

These precriterion data, then, give general support to the "two-state" representation of performance. To assess the constancy of the transition (learning) parameter of the two-state Markov chain, one must examine statistics which are, in theory, a function of this parameter. Accordingly, two distributional statistics are examined, total errors per item and the trial of an item's last error, and one sequential statistic, the conditional probability of an error following an error. Let c denote the learning rate for the three cases: it will be replaced by $a(S)$, $a(C)$, or $a(CS)$ depending on which condition is being considered.

Consider first the conditional probability of an error on the trial following an error. Since errors can occur only while the item is in the unlearned state (state I), the error indicates that the item was in state I on that trial. To make an error on the next trial, the intervening reinforced trial must be ineffective, which has probability $1 - .5c$ from Equation 5.1; and on the next test trial, with the item still in state I, the response is incorrect (probability .5). Hence the joint probability of not leaving state I and guessing incorrectly is $.5(1 - .5c)$.

Next consider the probability that the last error occurs on trial n, written as $Pr(L = n)$. For the last error to occur on trial n, the

129

following three events must be jointly realized: (1) the item is in state I on trial n, with probability $I(n)$; (2) an error occurs on trial n, with probability .5; and (3) no more errors occur after this trial, with probability θ. The probability that $L = n$ is the joint likelihood of these three events, or $.5\theta I(n)$.

Now $I(n)$ and θ must be derived. $I(n)$ is the probability that an item is in state I on the nth test trial. The process starts in state I on trial 1 with probability $1 - c$, so $I(1) = 1 - c$. $I(2)$ is equal to $I(1)(1 - .5c)$ since $1 - .5c$ is the likelihood of remaining in state I from one trial to the next. The general relation for $I(n)$ is

$$I(n) = I(n - 1)(1 - .5c)$$

and the solution to this difference equation is

$$I(n) = I(1)(1 - .5c)^{n-1} = (1 - c)(1 - .5c)^{n-1}$$

Now θ has been defined as the likelihood that no errors follow a test response made while in state I. The probability θ can be expressed in terms of the following series, where the jth term is the probability of j consecutive correct guesses and failures to learn, then successful learning:

$$\theta = .5c + [.5(1 - .5c)].5c + [.5(1 - .5c)]^2.5c + \cdots$$
$$= .5c \sum_{j=0}^{\infty} [.5(1 - .5c)]^j$$
$$= \frac{.5c}{1 - .5(1 - .5c)} = \frac{c}{1 + .5c}$$

The first term of the series, $.5c$, is the probability that learning occurs on the next reinforced trial; the second term is the likelihood that learning fails on that trial, another correct guess occurs, and then learning occurs; and so on.

The random variable, L, is well defined for sequences having at least one error. If there are no errors, set $L = 0$. The probability that an item has no errors is $c + (1 - c).5\theta$. That is, with probability c the initial reinforcement produces learning, whereas with probability $1 - c$ the first reinforcement was ineffective, a correct guess occurs on trial 1 (probability .5) and no errors follow that trial (probability θ).

These derivations are summarized as follows:

$$Pr\,(L = n) = \begin{cases} c + .5\theta(1 - c) & \text{for } n = 0 \\ .5\theta(1 - c)(1 - .5c)^{n-1} & \text{for } n \geq 1 \end{cases}$$

130

The average value of the trial of last error is

$$E(L) = \frac{2(1 - c)}{c(1 + .5c)} = \frac{2E(T)}{1 + .5c}$$

where $E(T)$ is the average total errors per item (Equation 5.2).

Finally, consider the probability distribution of the total errors per item, denoted by T. The likelihood that $T = 0$ was calculated above as $Pr(L = 0)$. The likelihood of $T = 1$ is the product of two event probabilities: (1) the subject makes at least a first error, which has probability $1 - Pr(T = 0)$, and (2) following this first error, there are no further errors, an event having probability θ. Thus, $Pr(T = 1)$ is equal to $[1 - Pr(T = 0)]\theta$. The likelihood of $T = 2$ is obtained from (1) a first error occurs, with probability $1 - Pr(T = 0)$, (2) after this first error, another error occurs, with probability $1 - \theta$, and (3) after the second error there are no further errors, which has probability θ. So the terms for $Pr(T = 2)$ are $[1 - Pr(T = 0)](1 - \theta)\theta$. The general expression for n errors is

$$Pr(T = n) = Pr(T = n - 1)(1 - \theta)$$

The solution to this recursion is

$$Pr(T = n) = \begin{cases} c + .5\theta(1 - c) & \text{for } n = 0 \\ [1 - Pr(T = 0)]\theta(1 - \theta)^{n-1} & \text{for } n \geq 1 \end{cases}$$

The mean value and standard deviation are

$$E(T) = \frac{1 - Pr(T = 0)}{\theta} = \frac{1 - c}{c}$$

$$\sigma(T) = E(T)\sqrt{\frac{1 + c}{1 - c}}$$

To apply these equations to the data, c was estimated by the above mean-errors equation. The model was then tested by its predictions of the probability of an error following an error, the mean and standard deviation of the trial of the last error, L, the standard deviation of total errors, T, and the probability distribution of T. Because learning was so fast in groups S and CS, only a few items have many errors. Accordingly, the T distribution was segmented into two parts: those protocols having zero or one error, and those having two or more errors.

The comparisons of observed and predicted statistics for the three groups are shown in Table 5.6. Inspection of Table 5.6 reveals that the model accurately predicts the major sequential statistic—the likelihood of an error following an error—and generally is respectably close to the statistics for the two fast-learning groups, CS and S. There is a consistent

131

TABLE 5.6. Observed and Predicted Statistics for the Three
Acquisition Conditions with Mean Errors Used to
Estimate the Learning Rate

Statistic	CS		S		C	
	Obs.	Pred.	Obs.	Pred.	Obs.	Pred.
Pr. err after an error	.308	.308	.334	.362	.436	.438
Mean errors	.304	.304	.820	.820	3.040	3.040
Standard deviation	.696	.841	1.315	1.520	2.383	3.910
$Pr\ (T \leq 1)$	.932	.932	.804	.800	.313	.462
$Pr\ (T \geq 2)$	.068	.068	.196	.200	.687	.538
Trial of last error	.391	.438	1.490	1.294	5.091	5.400
Standard deviation	.903	1.330	2.482	2.711	3.872	8.500

overprediction of standard deviations of T and L for all three groups, and the discrepancies are quite large for group C, the slower learners.

The distributions of errors or trial of last error in group C are not well predicted by the model. The model expects a nearly geometric distribution for both random variables, whereas the observed distributions tended toward uniform distributions in group C. Examination of the group C data clearly showed that the assumption of "independently learned" items is wrong in this case. Roughly speaking, a subject tended to learn all eight of his items on very nearly the same trial, as though he had suddenly noticed the weak color cue and used it thenceforth on all items. This effect is the same as that one would obtain if the separate stimuli in a concept identification task were to be treated as though they were distinct paired associate items. However, the predictions are based on the assumption that the color cue is selected independently and on randomly different trials for different items being learned by the same subject. It would be possible to modify the model to handle this "list-dependent" learning in group C, for example, all items have $c = 0$ until some "insight" occurs at a random trial, whereafter $c > 0$ (Batchelder, 1967; Falmagne, 1965). However, the additional complexities seem not important enough to pursue in this instance. An appropriate summary of this section is that the all-or-none learning model predicted accurately the data of groups S and CS but failed on group C because of strong interitem dependencies, in contradistinction to the item independence assumed by the model.

Single-Cue Tests following CS Learning

Each item for each subject in group CS received four test trials on the color component and four on the syllable component. The overall proportion of correct responses was .93 to the syllables and .68 for the colors (versus .50 by chance). The difference in percentage correct responses to the two components was statistically significant (matched $t(15) = 11.40$, $p < .01$). These data indicate that the original learning rate and subsequent recall on the color and syllable components were closely related. Group S learned much faster than group C, and group CS learned responses to the syllables much better than to the colors on the component test trials.

To estimate the proportions of items-by-subjects falling within each "solution type," each item for each subject was classified according to its correct responses on the eight test trials, four on the color and four on the syllable. An item was classified as a "color" type if the four test responses to its color component were correct but one or more errors occurred among the four tests to its syllable component. It was classified as a "syllable" type if all tests with its syllable were correct, but there were one or more errors to its color component. If responses to both components were all correct, it was classified as a "both" type. The "both" category may include a few items which, in fact, were learned only on one component, yet the subject guessed correctly on the four tests with the unlearned component. This possibility is taken into account in predictions of these data.

Of the $8 \times 16 = 128$ item-by-subject protocols, all but nine fell into the three categories above. These nine cases had at least one error within the four tests on both components. This could have occurred because the item was not learned or there was momentary forgetting of the associate of a learned component, or because the entire color-syllable compound was acting as the functional stimulus in these cases, with generalization decrement issuing upon removal of one component of the functional pattern. Four of these nine odd items were contributed by one subject.

The overall frequencies of subject items in the various categories are shown in Table 5.7. The majority of items were learned on both components, with "syllable only" being nearly as frequent as the "both" category. The strong dominance of the "syllable only" category over the "color only" category is in good agreement with the faster learning rate of cue S compared with cue C.

A relevant datum of interest concerns the ways in which individual subjects learned their eight items. For example, it might be supposed that a given subject would learn all eight of his items in the same way. The individual data given in Table 5.8 shows that this was a very infrequent event, shown by only one subject (No. 11, who learned all items on both components). Fifteen of the sixteen subjects distributed at least some of their items over two or more solution categories. With a

TABLE 5.7. FREQUENCY OF SOLUTION
TYPES SHOWN IN SINGLE-
CUE TESTS WITH GROUP *CS*

Type	Frequency
Syllable	52
Color	10
Both	57
Neither	9
Total	128

few exceptions, most subjects tend to distribute their items over categories roughly in proportions similar to the mean frequencies. What is needed is some index to assess the agreement of individual subjects' distributions with the mean distribution. For this purpose we used Kendall's "coefficient of concordance" which measures the agreement among many subjects in their ranking of N categories. The frequencies of items

TABLE 5.8. SOLUTION TYPES SHOWN FOR THE EIGHT ITEMS FOR
EACH OF THE SIXTEEN SUBJECTS IN GROUP *CS* [a]

Subject	Syllable (S)	Color (C)	Both (B)	Neither
1	5	0	3	0
2	3	0	4	1
3	6	0	2	0
4	1	0	7	0
5	3	2	2	1
6	3	0	4	1
7	4	0	4	0
8	1	0	7	0
9	0	4	3	1
10	5	0	3	0
11	0	0	8	0
12	4	0	4	0
13	5	0	3	0
14	7	0	1	0
15	3	2	2	1
16	2	2	0	4
Totals	52	10	57	9

[a] Entries are number of items for that subject showing particular solution types.

in the three main categories—both, syllable, and color—were ranked for each individual and correlated with the ranking of the mean frequencies (which is *B, S, C*). The coefficient of concordance was $+.50$ ($p < .001$), indicating good overall agreement of individual subjects' rankings with the mean ranking of the three solution types. The coefficient was lowered by many inversions of the *B* and *S* categories which are nearly equally frequent overall.

Prediction of Solution Types

Although the learning model developed above was cast in terms of the sampling of single cues, the arguments can be formulated (as in Chapter 2) so that a number of cues, *s*, can be selected in the sample focus, and yet this does not affect the learning-rate characteristics of the model. So we may apply to the solution data in Table 5.7 the equations developed in Chapter 2 for the probability of various solution types. The theoretical expressions must be corrected, however, to allow for the subject guessing correctly on the four test trials with an unlearned dimension.

Let N_S, N_C, and N_B represent the number of item subjects classified as syllable, color, and both. Let F_S, F_C, and F_B represent their respective proportions, corrected for guessing, and let P_S, P_C, and P_B represent the theoretical probabilities of a solution on syllable, color, or both. The prediction equations are:

$$N_S = NF_S = NP_S(1 - .5^4) = \frac{15N}{16} \frac{a(S)[1 - a(C)]^{s-1}}{a(S) + a(C)}$$

$$N_C = NF_C = NP_C(1 - .5^4) = \frac{15N}{16} \frac{a(C)[1 - a(S)]^{s-1}}{a(S) + a(C)}$$

$$N_B = N - N_S - N_C$$

For these equations, N is the total number of cases in the three categories, which is 119 for our case.

To fit these equations to the data in Table 5.7, the theoretical saliences of the syllable and color cues, estimated from the learning rates of the controls, are used. These estimates were $\hat{a}(S) = .550$ and $\hat{a}(C) = .248$. Predictions of the observed frequencies using these estimates are shown in Table 5.9 where the sample-size parameter is set equal to 2, 2.45, and 3. For $\hat{s} = 2$, the calculated frequencies show too many single-cue solvers; for $\hat{s} = 3$, too few single-cue solvers. The weighted average of these two calculated frequencies (weights .55 and .45) is entered under the last column labeled $\hat{s} = 2.45$, and these correspond closely to the observed frequencies.

TABLE 5.9. COMPARISON OF OBSERVED AND CALCULATED FREQUENCIES OF SOLUTION TYPES IN GROUP CS

Type	Observed	$\hat{s} = 2$	$\hat{s} = 3$	$\hat{s} = 2.45$
Syllable	52	57.6	43.4	51.1
Color	10	15.4	6.9	11.5
Both	57	46.0	68.7	56.4

Although s is conceived as an integer-valued random variable, fractional estimates of it (like 2.45) could arise from fitting group data. The theory supposes that s may vary between subjects, and even from one sample to the next for the same subject. The learning rate predictions follow regardless of such variations in s; in particular, the probability of solving after an error is independent of s, the size of sample taken. The parameter s appearing in the solution-type probabilities refers to the size of the last sample taken (on the last error trial) before solution. But in pooling results over subjects and items having possibly different s values on their solution trial (e.g., half with $s = 2$ and half with $s = 3$), overall results are obtained that are best fit by fractional s estimates.

We conclude that the frequencies of the component learning patterns are well accounted for by the sampling model. The dominance of the syllable over the color cue appeared in relative learning rates and also in the frequency of solution types in the RRC problem. The model was accurate in predicting the solution-type distribution from parameters estimated from the acquisition speed of independent control groups.

DISCUSSION

The issue investigated here concerns the transfer to components of responses learned to redundant-cue compounds. For the present list structures, subjects may be expected to learn responses to one or another or both components. In the former case, the unlearned component acquires no associative strength with respect to its response. This last conclusion requires some discussion since it appears to conflict with other evidence reported by Binder and Estes (1966), Binder and Feldman (1960), Friedman (1966), and Friedman, Trabasso, and Mosberg (1967).

These latter investigators were concerned with the general "overlap" question, that is, how to characterize how and what a subject learns

136

when he comes to discriminate among patterns that share common (overlapping) components. For example, a task wherein the paired letters ab are to be associated with response R_1 and the paired letter bc with R_2 is a simple prototype of an overlap task. Another prototype arises when the single letters a and b are to be associated to R_1 and R_2, respectively, whereas the pair ab is to be associated with R_3. The two aspects of the data relevant to models about this process are (1) the pattern of confusion errors among stimuli during learning and the overall speed of learning, and (2) the pattern of transfer resulting when the elements used during training are tested singly or in novel combinations with other elements. Depending upon the particular structure of the list of training items and the transfer items, many interesting questions can be raised and the pattern of training and transfer results can become quite complex. In the cases cited, particular mathematical models have been used to try to understand the patterns of results.

A common working assumption of the models used in the papers cited is that the subject conditions entire patterns of stimulus elements as single units, and whenever a pattern becomes conditioned to a response, all components of the pattern also become conditioned to that response. Further assumptions are added to account for transfer to novel recombinations of the elements; but the success of the models for their particular data lends support to this common assumption of conditioning patterns as units and all components becoming conditioned along with the pattern. This assumption is completely counter to our model and data regarding cue selection. In our task, subjects do not learn entire patterns of elements, nor even compounds of RRC's; the evidence instead indicates appreciable learning of single components with no learning of another, redundant component.

So what is the matter? Which assumptions are correct? One answer is that both sets of assumptions could be correct within their own experimental domain (i.e.. for different structures of the list of items to be learned), but that subjects can adopt different sampling strategies depending upon the requirement of the learning task with which they must deal. In this regard, there are many differences between our tasks and those studied by the investigators cited.

To illustrate some differences, consider the experiment by Friedman, Trabasso, and Mosberg (1967). In their paired-associate experiment, the subjects learned one of three responses to nine different pairs of Greek letters. Using the letters $a, b, c, \ldots$ to stand for Greek letters, and 1, 2, and 3 for the color names used as responses, the structure of the nine-item list was as follows:

S	R
ab	1
ac	1
bc	2
bd	2
cd	3
ef	3
fg	1
hi	3
jk	2

The ordering of the two letters within a pair was varied and was irrelevant. The structure of this list may be contrasted with our "list" in Chapter 3, where shape of figure and dot location were relevant cues, and color, number of interior lines, and location of an open gap in the figure were irrelevant cues.

First, the concept of an attribute or dimension is inapplicable to the stimuli of the Friedman, Trabasso, and Mosberg experiment. In our terminology, there is really only one dimension or attribute involved, that is, Greek letters, since each presumably is not further analyzed by college students. The list is then composed of eleven different "values" of this single dimension, arranged in pairs with varying overlapping elements. But this difference already puts the experiment outside the domain of the present sampling theory. Recall that the present theory presupposes stimuli composed of combinations of different attributes (like color, shape, size, etc.); and it supposes that the subject switches in analyzers or encoding responses appropriate to only a few of these dimensions at any one time. For this reason the subject might learn dimension A but not the redundant dimension B because the model supposes that the switching in of the A and B analyzers are independent events (one can occur while the other does not). But in the Friedman, Trabasso, and Mosberg list, there is only one dimension, and consequently only one analyzer is always switched in. In this sense, then, our model of analyzer selection is inapplicable.

This does not mean, of course, that some selection of elements (i.e., values as opposed to dimensions) cannot occur in such cases. The Mattocks and Yum studies reviewed at the outset imply quite the contrary. The degree of element selection would be related to the stimulus structure of the list, and the sampling strategy that a list structure induces the subject to adopt during learning. If all elements in every compound were relevant and redundant (e.g., all stimuli were different pairs of letters), then some selection of elements would occur since

138

either element would support correct responding, and this would be true for all items in the list. But consider the control items, *hi* and *jk,* in the Friedman, Trabasso, and Mosberg list. Here *h* and *i,* and *j* and *k,* are redundant and both relevant, yet the researchers reported that subjects transferred the correct response nearly perfectly to either element tested alone. In this case we may suppose that the overall structure of the list promoted strategies of pattern learning. Many of the items of the list cannot be learned by selecting a single element, and these force the subject to sample and associate responses to entire patterns. This strategy would tend, of course, to produce double-cue learning of the *hi* and *jk* control items of the list.

In the list of the Friedman, Trabasso, and Mosberg experiment, the reader may note that the structure suggests a classification of single elements according to their "validity." An element is valid to the extent that its presence in a compound identifies a unique correct response. On this basis, the Greek letters corresponding to *a, e, g, h, i, j, k* are completely valid, those by *c, d, f* are completely invalid, whereas the *b* element is partially valid (since it appears with response 2 twice and with response 1 once). The validity notion is directly related to the notions of relevant and irrelevant dimensions in concept identification experiments. A relevant dimension is one for which *all* of its values are completely valid; similarly, an irrelevant dimension has all its values invalid. Transfer to novel combinations of elements in the Friedman, Trabasso, and Mosberg experiment was largely determined by the relative validities of the components in the test pattern. That element having the higher validity in the test compound was more likely to be selected and determine the transfer response to the novel compound. This result is similar to ours on transfer with relevant versus irrelevant dimensions; in a test compound following learning, the response was controlled by the relevant dimension irrespective of the number of irrelevant cues present on the test.

The list structure of the Friedman, Trabasso, and Mosberg study brings out a limitation of our sampling model not previously discussed. The limitation is that the sampling model is not formulated to allow for patterned learning. For example, the model would not learn a conjunctive concept. Only simple, one-dimensional hypotheses have been treated, whereas conjunctions are, by definition, two-dimensional hypotheses. The sampling model reflects this one-dimensional aspect perfectly. If, say, color and shape are effective cues in the current sample focus, there is a one-dimensional hypothesis about each attribute, and the two combine additively in determining the response to any pattern. But conjunctive concepts or pattern discriminations simply cannot be

139

solved by addition of one-dimensional hypotheses. What is required is some "and" operation on cues in the sample focus (e.g., set intersection or multiplication). A theory to handle certain cases of this type has been reported elsewhere (Trabasso & Bower, 1964a). We outline it here to show how our cue-sampling theory makes contact with results on configural learning.

The four-category problem requires a configural, or conditional, discrimination. In this problem the classificatory responses depend upon the joint values of two *independent,* binary, relevant attributes. An example using geometric figures would be that all attributes are irrelevant except color and form, and the four response assignments are red circle-1, red triangle-2, blue circle-3, and blue triangle-4.

In our previous paper, the subjects' learning of this task was represented as involving the learning of two independent subproblems, that is, the form subproblem with the assignments circle-1 or 3, triangle-2 or 4, and the color subproblem with the assignments red-1 or 2, blue-3 or 4. Letting $p_{1,n}$ and $p_{2,n}$ denote the probabilities of a correct response to the first and second subproblems on trial n, the probability of a correct compound response, p_n, was assumed to equal the product, $p_{1,n}p_{2,n}$ (cf. Bourne & Restle, 1959). The experiments reported in the Trabasso and Bower (1964a) paper tested this proposal in several ways with favorable results.

This combination rule will be used, along with our assumptions about cue sampling, to fit results on learning rate and additivity of cues in the four-category situation. The four-category problem involves two independent relevant dimensions and I irrelevant dimensions. To simplify the following, we shall assume that the attributes are approximately equal in salience. This is a good assumption for the specific results to be discussed below (from Bourne & Pendleton, 1958) since in that experiment the specific attributes of the $2 + I$ which were relevant varied from one subject to the next within a given condition.

Assuming equal salience for the relevant attributes means that $p_{1,n} = p_{2,n}$, so that $p_n = (p_{i,n})^2$. The learning model assumes that each subproblem is learned independently according to the equation $p_{i,n} = 1 - .5(1 - c_i)^{n-1}$. Hence, for $c_1 = c_2 = c$,

$$p_n = (p_{i,n})^2 = [1 - .5(1 - c)^{n-1}]^2$$
$$= 1 - (1 - c)^{n-1} + .25(1 - c)^{2(n-1)}$$

140

The statistic to be considered is the average total errors during learning. Its expected value is given by the summation of $1 - p_n$, that is:

$$E(T) = \sum_{n=1}^{\infty} (1 - p_n) = \frac{1}{c} - \frac{.25}{2c - c^2}$$

If c is small, then the c^2 term on the right can be ignored, yielding the approximation

$$E(T) \simeq \frac{.875}{c}$$

The sampling theory implies a relation between the subproblem learning rate, c, and the number of irrelevant cues, I. The simplest assumption is this: for each subproblem dimension, ignore the presence of the alternate relevant dimension and assume that the subject samples randomly from among the target relevant dimension and I irrelevant dimensions. Thus his probability of selecting the target relevant cue each trial is proportional to the reciprocal of $1 + I$, thus:

$$c = \frac{k}{1 + I}$$

where k is a proportionality constant depending upon the presolution error rate, the percentage of feedback information, and like variables.

Substituting this equation for c into the earlier approximation equation for mean errors, one obtains

$$E(T) \simeq \frac{.875}{k}(1 + I) = K(1 + I)$$

where $K = .875/k$. Thus the subproblem-learning analysis, in conjunction with random sampling among the relevant and irrelevant cues, implies that errors to solution in the four-category problem will increase linearly (or nearly so) with the number of irrelevant attributes.

This derivation fits the facts: errors to solution in the four-category problem vary approximately linearly with I (cf. Bourne & Restle, 1959). To illustrate, Table 5.10 displays the data from twelve groups of subjects run by Bourne and Pendleton (1958). There were four percentages of feedback information following the subjects' responses, 100, 90, 80, and 70 percent, the remaining trials being "blanks" with no information. Within each feedback condition, three groups were trained with one, three, or five irrelevant cues. In Table 5.10 a different value of K was estimated (by least squares) for each of the four feedback conditions.

141

TABLE 5.10. OBSERVED AND PREDICTED AVERAGE ERRORS RELATED TO NUMBER
OF IRRELEVANT CUES AND PERCENTAGE FEEDBACK TRIALS

Percent Feedback		Number of Irrelevant Cues			
		1	3	5	K Estimate
100%	Obs.	22.6	42.6	66.9	
	Pred.	22.0	44.0	66.0	11.00
90%	Obs.	26.8	52.0	80.0	
	Pred.	26.5	53.0	79.5	13.23
80%	Obs.	31.0	67.9	97.7	
	Pred.	32.8	65.6	98.4	16.40
70%	Obs.	39.2	77.2	120.8	
	Pred.	39.2	78.4	117.6	19.60

(Data from Bourne & Pendleton, 1958.)

As would be expected, the K estimates increase with increasing proportions of blank trials. Comparison of observed to predicted errors in Table 5.10 leaves little to be desired; the discrepancies are small and unsystematic. Similar good fits can be provided for other four-category results reported in the Bourne and Restle (1959) paper.

Current tests of this sampling theory for four-category learning must rely on data regarding additivity of irrelevant cues because no further cue manipulations have yet been tried with this paradigm. However, it is clear that redundant-cue four-category problems could be set up and data collected regarding solution types, as in our two-category experiments. An example would be the following assignments: large red circles-1, small red circles-2, large blue triangles-3, and small blue triangles-4. In this example, size, color, and form are relevant cues; however, color and form are redundant whereas size varies independently of the other two. To solve the problem the subject must use the size cue, and also either the color cue or the form cue, or both. While expecting an increase in learning rate, this problem also seems appropriate for obtaining a tripartite division of solvers: those who learn color but not form, those who learn form but not color, and those who learn form and color. Of course, all subjects must learn size, of necessity, if they are to solve the problem. The single-cue tests would proceed analogously to those for the two-category problems —for example, on the tests for color learning, a new form (a square) would be used to remove any influence of form learning, and one would assess whether the subject classified large red squares as 1's, small red squares as 2's, large blue squares as 3's, and small blue squares as 4's; if so, he would be termed a "color" solver, and so on.

The supposition is that one would again obtain evidence of selective attention in this four-category context, and that the cue selection would vary according to similar sorts of variables that we have investigated for the two-category case. This analysis readily suggests several interesting comparisons between the distribution of solution modes (color, form, or both) obtained when the color plus form problem appears alone in a two-category context (as in Chapter 3) versus when it appears as one subproblem of a four-category problem like that mentioned above. For example, if the two subproblems are learned independently, then the distribution of solvers in the four-category problem should be the same as that obtained in a two-category problem involving the same population of stimuli except that the size cue is removed. Alternatively, and more plausibly, the size cue in the four-category problem would require one "slot" in the fixed-capacity sample focus, thus reducing the effective sample size for the concurrent color plus form subproblem to $s - 1$. If so, then fewer two-cue solvers would be expected when color plus form appears as a subproblem of a four-category problem than when it appears alone in a RRC two-category problem.

SUMMARY

This chapter reported an extension of the sampling theory to investigate cue additivity and cue selection in a modified paired-associate learning task. The main differences between the paired-associate and concept-identification tasks were discussed; it was argued that the most important difference concerns the presence or absence of a systematic rule which characterizes uniquely the correct response assigned to each stimulus pattern. Moreover, paired-associate tasks typically involve stimulus compounds consisting of several RRC's which would allow for selection among cues. Evidence was reviewed which showed such selectivity, that is, the functional stimulus was often less than the nominal stimulus.

The new experiment on paired-associate learning involved three groups, two (C and S) learned with either the color or the syllable as the relevant cue with the alternate cue present but irrelevant. A third group (CS) learned with color and syllable as RRC's and then were tested for transfer to the color cue and to the syllable cue. The syllable cue was learned much faster than the color cue, and when these cues were redundant, learning was facilitated only slightly. A model formulated for acquisition handled the learning data with fair success, including prediction of the learning rate of group *CS* by addition of the learning rates of groups *C* and *S*.

In testing, 93 percent of the items for the *CS* subjects were classified as learned on color, syllable, or both cues. The subjects were homogeneous in how they distributed their eight items into these categories. Most items were learned on both components, next most on the syllable only, and fewest on the color only. The frequencies of the solution types were consonant with the relative rates of learning the syllable and color cues by the control groups. Moreover, the frequencies were predicted on the basis of the component-cue saliences estimated from the learning of the control subjects. Overall, the extension of the sampling theory to this particular paired-associate task may be judged as successful.

6
CUE SALIENCE AND WHAT IS LEARNED

The sampling theory of Chapter 2 implies that any factor which affects the attention value or weight of a cue also affects how fast that cue is selectively learned. Consequently, these same factors should affect what is learned in relevant and redundant cue (RRC) problems. In extending our work to cue salience, we first review general methods by which one can vary the discriminability of attributes and thus affect both their salience and speed of learning. Our focus is on concept-identification experiments; three studies in particular have investigated cue salience with human subjects and are reviewed in detail. Following this, we describe an experiment on RRC discrimination training with variation in the salience of one of the relevant cues and indicate how the sampling theory of Chapter 2 makes contact with these data. The implications of the model for what is learned in RRC problems when cue salience is varied are then discussed. Then two new experiments are reported in which we attempted to direct the subject's attention to cues in RRC problems via alterations in stimulus patterns. Following the presentation of the experiments, we discuss the general notion of cue salience in terms of a noticing order of cues or hierarchy of attending responses, and how one might obtain independent assessments of this hierarchy.

THE MANIPULATION OF CUE SALIENCE

There are several procedures by which one may enhance the salience of environmental features. Most of these methods are probably common lore among advertisers as well as experimenters in discrimination learning, but their systematic listing would appear to be useful as a guide to possible research on those factors that affect attention in learning. Therefore some brief descriptions on how the discriminability

145

of a cue might be manipulated along with various examples found in the literature will be given.

The relative salience of a cue may be increased by removing irrelevant cues or decreased by adding irrelevant cues. In general, we may say that the effect of irrelevant cues is additive in the sense that the speed of learning or the probability of selecting a relevant cue decreases as more irrelevant cues are added to the stimulus populations. In concept identification, we may cite studies by Archer, Bourne, and Brown (1955) and Bourne and Haygood (1959) which have systematically shown both effects. This feature, it will be recalled, was discussed extensively in Chapter 1 where we indicated how the theory fit existing data on additivity of both relevant and irrelevant cues.

An alternative and powerful way of affecting the relative salience of an attribute is to change the discriminable difference between the values of the attribute. For example, a brightness discrimination may be made easier by using as values black versus white rather than light-gray versus dark-gray for the discriminanda. In human concept identification, three studies (which we shall review in more detail later) have systematically manipulated this variable and all have shown that as one increases the difference between values (e.g., large versus small figures) the speed of learning also increases (Archer, 1962; Imai & Garner, 1965; Trabasso, 1963).

A third general way of increasing the salience of a stimulus variable is to make it "stand out" from other background cues. Specifically, this has been accomplished in a number of ways. In classical conditioning, where the subject must discriminate the presence or absence of a stimulus, the rate of conditioning is faster with a physically more *intense* stimulus (e.g., a brighter light or a louder tone). Furthermore, in compound conditioning, the more intense stimulus usually becomes the one that dominates responding (Miles & Jenkins, 1965; Pavlov, 1927). Thus both speed of learning and cue dominance in RRC learning are influenced by making a stimulus more intense, providing a higher signal-to-noise ratio. Similarly, in discrimination learning, the salience of a cue, relative to the background in which it is embedded, can be increased by simply adding more of that cue to the stimulus pattern. For example, when one uses three-dimensional objects rather than two-dimensional patterns, the discrimination is easier to learn (Harlow, 1945; House & Zeaman, 1960). One may also "add more" of a given attribute by increasing the area it occupies in a two-dimensional pattern. For example, Blazek and Harlow (1955) made color discriminations easier for monkeys by increasing the colored area of each pattern (e.g., using completely filled versus half-filled red and green squares).

146

A third way to make an attribute value "stand out" is to use some device that literally directs the subject's attention, such as having an arrow point at the critical cue. These devices have been termed stimulus "emphasizers" and have been studied by Trabasso (1963). To illustrate an early and well-known usage, Hull (1920) produced faster learning of Chinese characters by coloring the relevant radical in red, thereby providing a contrast of that cue with the black and white background in which it was embedded.

The relative salience of a cue also depends on its spatial location in relation to where the subject responds and where the reinforcement is delivered. For example, with monkeys practically no learning occurs if the critical stimuli are separated by six or more inches from the response (Murphy & Miller, 1955). Stollnitz (1965), in a review of this literature, interprets these failures to learn as a result of the monkey's restricted attention to only those cues in the immediate vicinity of what its hand is touching. Similar effects have been reported for young children (Jeffrey & Cohen, 1964).

Finally, prior successful use of a cue facilitates the selection and learning of that cue in new discrimination tasks. Lawrence's (1949, 1950) classical studies on the acquired distinctiveness of cues, and transfer of an easy to a hard brightness discrimination (1952) are examples of such effects. The converse may also hold, namely, that prior failures of responses to a cue may lead to that cue being set aside and "ignored" in transfer. For example, Levine (1962) randomly reinforced cues prior to their becoming relevant in a subsequent concept-identification problem. With as few as four random reinforcements, subsequent learning was retarded. However, this "ignoring" may be problem specific and occur only while the problem remains unchanged. Hammer (1955) found no transfer between problems where irrelevant cues remained the same but the relevant ones changed; likewise, Trabasso and Staudenmayer (1967) found that subjects would "ignore" cues having a history of random reinforcement only if they were from the same dimension or where the problems were otherwise unchanged. Thus the relative salience of irrelevant cues may decrease within a problem but this change may not endure across problems.

EXPERIMENTS ON CUE SALIENCE IN CONCEPT IDENTIFICATION

One of the first direct manipulations of cue salience in concept identification was conducted by Archer (1962). Archer called this variable "obviousness," and he used size and form cues that could be varied on a continuum of differences between the respective attribute values.

147

Subjects learned to classify stimuli in a four-category concept-identification problem. One of the manipulated cues was either relevant (with another cue such as number of figures or the presence of a dot) or irrelevant (along with one or three other irrelevant cues). To reduce the salience of the size attribute, Archer decreased the difference in length of the sides of the figures from one-fourth to one-eighth inch; similarly, form was reduced in salience by using a square as one of the figures and varying the opposite, acute angles of the other, parallelogram figure from 87 to 84 degrees. The result of interest is the obtained interaction between the degree of cue discriminability and cue function. When a highly discriminable cue was relevant, learning was the fastest; when it was irrelevant, learning was slowest. Let H and L stand for high and low salience, and R and I stand for either relevant or irrelevant cue function. Combinations of these letters yield the four conditions in Archer's study and the mean times (in minutes) to criterion were HR, 12.7; LR, 15.6; HI, 16.5; and LI, 11.7. These data are consistent with the expectations of the sampling theory. Equation 2.1 predicts learning rate to increase if one increases the weight of the relevant cues or to decrease if one increases the weight of the irrelevant cues. Archer's study supports the general assumption that the rate of learning is directly proportional to the number and weights of relevant cues in the problem.

We mention one other result reported by Archer. In his main experiment, an interaction among attribute, sex, and cue relevance was observed. In this interaction, male subjects performed better but female subjects performed worse when form was the relevant cue; both sexes did equally well when size was relevant. From this, form would appear to be more salient for males than for females. After completing the main experiment, Archer asked a group of eighty subjects to describe the stimuli that he had used in his HR and HI conditions. Unfortunately, he did not report the recall order of the attributes, which might have indicated an order of noticing these cues; but he reported that the men described the stimulus figures appropriately as either squares or parallelograms whereas females described them as either "squares and non-squares" or "tippy squares." This differential labeling of form cues by male and female college students suggests that past experience (e.g., the study of plane geometry) altered the relative salience of form cues within the subject population.

Several of the procedures just described were used by Trabasso (1963) to enhance the attention values of cues in concept identification. This investigation studied the effect of various stimulus "emphasizers" or "counteremphasizers" which directed the subject's attention to or away from a particular attribute. The stimuli were flower designs that varied in

148

the number of attributes such as the angle of the leaves to the stem, the color of the flower, the color of the angle, the type of flower, and the number and serrations of leaves. The subjects were required to learn to classify these patterns into two categories.

In all conditions the angle of the leaves to the stem was a critical relevant attribute. Trabasso used three different manipulations that emphasized this angle cue and served to increase substantially learning speed. In one condition the angle variable was emphasized by the simple operation of removing or holding constant all irrelevant attributes. In another the angle was emphasized by making it "obvious" in Archer's terms: the discriminability of the angle was increased by doubling the difference between angles from 30 to 60 degrees. In a third condition the angle was made more salient by coloring it. In one case the color was constant throughout the problem, whereas in another it varied and was irrelevant (e.g., red or green).

The success of the first manipulation indicates that irrelevant stimuli "compete" for the subject's attention and interfere with the selection of the relevant attribute as a basis for solution. The second demonstration replicates Archer's (1962) finding and shows that emphasis directly affects the weight of the relevant cue. The third is analogous to Hull's (1920) procedure of making the relevant radical stand out from its background. Of interest is the emphasis effect obtained in the last condition where the addition of an irrelevant color cue actually facilitated learning when it was placed in physical contiguity with the relevant angle.

Trabasso used Restle's (1962) strategy selection model (which is similar to that underlying the sampling theory of Chapter 2) and was able to account for these results quantitatively. An equation identical to Equation 2.1 was employed, and emphasis was assumed to increase the weight of a cue by a multiplicative factor. An application of the present sampling theory to Trabasso's data may be found in Bower and Trabasso (1964a, pp. 47–48).

Trabasso was also able to decrease a subject's attention to the relevant angle cue by "counteremphasis" when color was added to the flower rather than to the angle. Two transfer conditions testing this were run. In one condition the angle was emphasized by placing color on it but the color was also a relevant and redundant cue; in another condition the color was a RRC but it was placed on the flowers. Transfer in both conditions was to an identical angle problem with the color removed. Let $a(A)$ and $a(C)$ be learning rates for independent conditions appropriate to each RRC group where the angle or the color alone was relevant. Trabasso assumed that in transfer a proportion,

$a(A)/[a(A) + a(C)]$, of the subjects would solve during RRC training on the angle while another proportion, $a(C)/[a(A) + a(C)]$, would solve on the color. This assumption is equivalent to setting the focus sample size, s, equal to one in Equation 2.7. In the condition where the angle was emphasized by the color, five subjects showed perfect transfer while 4.72 were predicted to do so; where the color emphasized the flowers, only one subject made no errors in transfer while the theory predicted 1.7 subjects to do so. Assuming that transfer was all-or-none, as was done in Chapter 4, the mean errors for each group was predicted quite accurately. In the emphasis condition, the observed and predicted means were 16.07 and 16.45, respectively; in the counteremphasis condition, these values were 18.11 and 23.60, respectively.

Although Archer and Trabasso provided demonstrations of how the cue salience might be manipulated and learning rate or transfer facilitated, the first systematic investigation of the relationship between discriminability, preference, and speed of sorting attributes in concept identification has been only recently attempted by Imai and Garner (1965). Here discriminability was defined in terms of the physical difference between the attribute values. Imai and Garner varied vertical pairs of dots in (a) distance (the distance between the dots), (b) orientation (the degree of tilt in their alignment from vertical), and (c) position (the distance from the midpoint of the card to the bottom dot). For each attribute, four different levels of discriminability were used. The same subjects served throughout the experiment and two basic conditions were considered: first, each subject sorted cards according to any attribute he wished in a "free classification" condition; and second, subjects were asked to sort according to an attribute chosen by the experimenter in a "constrained classification" condition.

In free classification, two successive subconditions were run. In one, the subjects classified *pairs* of attributes (forty-eight sets involving the three combinations of pairs and sixteen combinations of the discriminability levels of the two attributes); in the other, the subjects classified patterns containing all three attributes (sixty-four sets of eight cards, each set representing one of the possible combinations of the four values from each of the three attributes).

A subject was classified as "preferring" an attribute if he chose it more than 50 percent of the time. On this basis, twelve subjects preferred distance, eight preferred orientation, and four preferred position. The interaction between preference and discriminability was most clearly summarized in a plot of the percentage of choices of the preferred attribute for each discriminable level of the nonpreferred one against the discriminability of the preferred attribute, resulting in a family of four curves. This plot showed that when the preferred attribute was highly discriminable, it was selected nearly all the time, regardless of the discriminability of the nonpreferred attribute. As discriminability of the preferred attribute declined, however, the probability of choosing it also decreased; the largest decrease, to about 50 percent, occurred when the nonpreferred dimension was highly discriminable.

Imai and Garner also assessed the influence of competing attributes on free classification by comparing the attribute-pair data with that obtained when all three attributes were used together. The influence of each attribute on the choice of one over another in free classification appeared to be independent. That is, the probability of selecting one attribute over both of the others, when all three were varied, could be predicted quite accurately by multiplying the probabilities of choosing that attribute over each of the others in the attribute-pair condition. To illustrate, in the attribute-pair condition the probability that a subject selected distance (at discriminable level 2) over position was .87 and over orientation was .81. When the three attributes varied together, the observed probability of choosing distance over both orientation and position was .75, reasonably close to the predicted value of $.87 \times .81 = .70$. Imai and Garner were able to predict accurately all of the three attribute, free-classification data from the attribute-pair data. The accuracy of these predictions suggests that Luce's (1959) constant-ratio rule obtained and that the cue weights (response strengths or v's) of each attribute remained constant across the stimulus conditions. Such a property would be highly desirable in testing the assumptions of the present sampling theory.

In a second experiment, Imai and Garner had six distance-preferring and six orientation-preferring subjects sort cards into two piles according to an attribute determined by the experimenter. In this constrained classification condition, subjects sorted cards into binary classes in 150 successive problems where the stimuli differed in either one, two, or three attributes. The sorting was carried out over five daily one-hour sessions. In all problems the sorting was very rapid and low in error. Of importance here was the finding that *only* discriminability and not preference affected speed of classification. As discriminability increased, so did the speed of sorting, regardless of the subject's preference classification. Furthermore, no facilitation was found when zero competing attributes was compared against the combination of one and two competing attributes, so that no additivity effect was obtained. This result may have occurred because the subjects were extremely well practiced and there were only three attributes; in fact, the range of mean sorting times per set was only from three to seventeen seconds.

151

In summary, Imai and Garner showed that only the discriminability of the relevant attribute in constrained classification (or typical concept identification) is important in sorting speed. In free classification, both discriminability and preference influence the basis of sorting. Besides the demonstration that discriminability affects sorting time (cf. Reed, 1951), the Imai and Garner results are of particular importance to studies that purport to assess the "inherent difficulty" of concepts or preferences for particular attributes. For example, Heidbredder's (1946) empirical ordering of object, number, and form concepts, or Suchman and Trabasso's (1966a) form preference and age results may depend not only on the basic nature of the concepts (degree of abstraction) or experience with the stimuli but also on differences in the ease of discriminability. This problem is not limited to studies in concept learning or stimulus preferences by children; it also relates to an extensive literature in discrimination learning which has sought to determine the relative dominance or preference for such stimuli as color, shape, brightness, and so on by different species of animals. Next we discuss one study on RRC discrimination learning and variation in cue salience.

CUE SALIENCE AND RRC LEARNING

Despite sufficient evidence demonstrating the effect of cue salience upon learning rate, very little evidence exists regarding how relative salience of the two relevant cues affects mode of solution in a RRC problem. Indeed, an experiment by Miles and Jenkins (1965) is the only extensive study we have found that is directly addressed to this issue. Because this relevant experiment is not reported in the published literature (it was a paper read by Jenkins at the 1965 meetings of the Psychonomic Society), we shall describe it in detail.

The basic aim of the Miles and Jenkins experiment was to fix the vividness of one relevant cue and to vary the salience of the other relevant cue in a RRC discrimination, and then to assess the respective degrees of control over differential responding by these two cues. The subjects were pigeons learning a successive ("go-no go") discrimination with discrete trials programmed in a Skinner box. The nine groups ($N = 5$ to 7 each) of immediate relevance in this experiment learned the problems depicted in Table 6.1. The possible trial stimuli were the onset of a continuous tone (T) and the lighting of the response key with one of five intensities; L_1 denotes the brightest key light and L_2, L_3, L_4, and L_5 denote progressively dimmer key lights.

152

TABLE 6.1. TRAINING AND TESTING CONDITIONS IN THE
MILES AND JENKINS EXPERIMENT [a]

Training					
Tone Control		Light Controls		$T + L$ Groups	
+	−	+	−	+	−
TL_1	L_1	L_1	L_2	TL_1	L_2
		L_1	L_3	TL_1	L_3
		L_1	L_4	TL_1	L_4
		L_1	L_5	TL_1	L_5

Test Trials				
	L_1	L_2	L_4	L_5
T				
No T				

(Design from Miles & Jenkins, 1965.)
[a] T denotes presence of a tone; L_1 through L_5 denote progressively
dimmer key lights.

The groups in Table 6.1 divide into one tone control group that
learned a tone-no tone discrimination with a constant key light on
positive and negative trials; four light control groups that had L_1 on
positive trials and L_2, L_3, L_4, or L_5 on negative trials; and four tone-light
RRC groups that had positive trials distinguished from negative trials by
the presence of a tone and a brighter light. For these latter groups, the
tone-no tone cue was of fixed salience while the light-intensity differential
cue varied in its salience, presumably being most salient for the L_1 versus
L_5 difference.

The availability of the control groups permits independent assessment, via their learning rates, of the salience of the tone cue and the four
differential light cues. Thus prediction of learning rates in the additive
tone plus light groups should be feasible. Moreover, the ratio of the light
to the tone salience estimates should provide an index of the relative
degrees of control over responding by the light and tone components in
the $T + L$ groups. This relative degree of control by the two cues was
assessed in the Miles and Jenkins experiment by presenting to each

153

subject during an extinction session the eight test combinations depicted at the bottom of Table 6.1. These tests permit the drawing of a four-point generalization gradient along the light-intensity gradient, one curve obtained with the tone and the other without. The index of tone control was the ratio of tone responses to tone and no tone responses, that is, the sum of the top row divided by the total of entries in the table. This index would be 1.00 if the tone completely controlled responding, and 0.50 if the tone had no control whatsoever over responding.

A few procedural details need be told. A trial consisted in presenting the positive or negative stimulus complex either for eight seconds or until four responses had been emitted, whichever occurred first. Food reinforcement was provided upon completion of four responses within eight seconds on positive trials. The key was darkened between trials, and the next trial occurred after a randomly variable interval (mean of sixty seconds). This procedure necessarily makes the dark key a "negative stimulus," but since pigeons rarely ever peck a darkened key anyway, this aspect of the procedure may be ignored. Initial training involved only the positive stimulus for four days at forty trials a day. Thereafter, for the next twelve daily sessions, each session consisted of forty positive and forty negative trials given in random order. Finally, in the last session ten eight-second nonreinforced tests were given with each of the eight stimuli shown in the bottom of Table 6.1.

Due to the initial all-positive training, the birds began discrimination training pecking both positive and negative stimuli, so discriminative performance was revealed mainly in terms of extinction of responding to the negative stimulus. The mean responses ("errors") to S^- over the twelve discrimination sessions for the nine groups are entered into Table 6.2. These were estimated visually from a graph in the Miles and Jenkins report and are probably accurate to only within ± 10 errors due to the scale of the graph; still, this is a small change relative to the large group differences.

Qualitatively, the mean errors for the nine groups fall in a regular pattern. There is a powerful and orderly effect of the light-intensity differential upon learning rate for both the light-only controls and the $T + L$ groups. The learning rate of the tone-only group falls intermediate between the extremes of the light-only groups. There is a consistent additive effect in the $T + L$ groups: each makes fewer errors than do the respective tone or light control groups trained on the components of the $T + L$ problem.

One may expect a quantitative model to do a reasonable job in accounting for such orderly data. The model to be applied merely says that the rate of differentiation of responding to the positive and negative

154

TABLE 6.2. MEAN RESPONSES TO S^- OVER THE TWELVE DISCRIMINATION SESSIONS FOR THE NINE GROUPS IN THE MILES AND JENKINS EXPERIMENT [a]

Group	+	−	Observed Errors	$c = 1/E$	c	Predicted Errors (E)
Tone	TL_1	L_1	850	.00118		
Light	L_1	L_2	1500	.00067		
"	L_1	L_3	820	.00122		
"	L_1	L_4	450	.00222		
"	L_1	L_5	150	.00667		
$T + L$	TL_1	L_2	530	.00188	.00185	540
"	TL_1	L_3	455	.00220	.00240	417
"	TL_1	L_4	275	.00363	.00340	294
"	TL_1	L_5	80	.01250	.00785	127

(Data from Miles & Jenkins, 1965.)
[a] Other columns give learning-rate estimates as reciprocals of mean errors, and predicted quantities for the additive groups.

stimuli depends on the salience or sampling probability of the relevant cues. If we let q_n denote the probability of the response to the negative stimulus on the nth negative trial, and assume that $q_1 = 1$ due to generalization from the all-positive training, then the relevant equation is

$$q_n = (1 - c_i)^{n-1}$$

The mean number of errors in a prolonged trial series will then be approximately $1/c_i$. Therefore an estimate of c_i is the reciprocal of the mean errors; these estimates are entered into Table 6.2 for the nine experimental groups.

The additive experimental conditions were composed by adding either the tone or light differential to the control component. Therefore, letting c_t and c_i denote the control learning rates for the tone and L_i-light groups, the learning rate for the respective $T + L_i$ additive group is (cf. Equation 2.6)

$$c_{t+i} = \frac{c_t + c_i - c_i c_t}{1 - c_i c_t} \tag{6.1}$$

Since learning rates bear a reciprocal relation to mean errors, we may substitute reciprocal errors for the c's in Equation 6.1 to arrive at the prediction equation

$$E_{t+i} = \frac{E_t E_i - 1}{E_t + E_i - 1} \tag{6.2}$$

155

If the error scores are large, as in the present case, the -1 terms in Equation 6.2 are negligible and can be ignored; this amounts to ignoring the small $c_t c_i$ terms (all less than .00002) in Equation 6.1. This has been done for the predictions shown in Table 6.2. The predicted learning rates for the $T + L_i$ groups were obtained by simply adding the two control c's, one from condition TL_1-L_1 and the appropriate one from the L_1-L_i light condition. It may be seen that the learning-rate predictions are very accurate for the first three groups, but somewhat discrepant for the fastest learners, those in condition TL_1-L_5. The overprediction of errors in the TL_1-L_5 and, to some extent, the TL_1-L_4 condition could have resulted from our ignoring the closeness of the L_4 and L_5 intensities to the dark key that prevailed during the (negative) intertrial interval. Generalization of inhibition from darkness to L_5 might have reduced generalized responding to L_5 at the start of discrimination training, thus reducing errors below that predicted by a theory which ignores this factor.

Turning to the extinction tests designed to assess control of the tone over responding, Table 6.3 lists for each additive group the proportion of all responses made in the presence of the tone. These proportions are difficult to predict exactly because of differential generalization factors (to different L_i values) that enter in for the various groups. However, a very rough index can be composed, based on our previous c estimates, which gives the proper ordering of the various conditions. Let D denote the control index; it is the response rate on tone plus light tests divided by the sum of the response rates to the tone-plus-light tests and the light-only tests. Assuming that response rates depend on $c_t + c_i$ in the $T + L$ tests and on c_i in the L-alone tests, the control index will be approximately

$$D_i = \frac{c_t + c_i}{c_t + 2c_i} \tag{6.3}$$

This rule-of-thumb index is 1.00 when the tone totally dominates (when $c_i = 0$) and is .50 when the tone has no control over responding (when $c_t = 0$).

The c values calculated in Table 6.2 were entered into Equation 6.3 to gauge the relevant indices of control, and these are entered into the last column of Table 6.3. The main point to be gleaned from the data in Table 6.3 is that the control of responding by the tone is inversely related to the salience of the light-intensity cue: if the intensity difference is small, the tone primarily controls responding; if the intensity difference is large, the light controls responding and the tone exerts very little control. Using the c_i estimates from the learning rates of independ-

TABLE 6.3. TONE-CONTROL INDEX CALCU-
LATED AS PROPORTION OF ALL
TEST RESPONSES MADE IN THE
PRESENCE OF THE TONE

Group		Observed D^a	Calculated D
TL_1	L_1	.94	1.00
TL_1	L_2	.89	.74
TL_1	L_3	.65	.66
TL_1	L_4	.61	.57
TL_1	L_5	.64	.53

^{a} Data from Miles & Jenkins, 1965.

ent control groups, Equation 6.3 correctly rank-orders the groups in tone control, except for the small, unexpected reversal of the final two groups. Including in the ranking a sixth group trained on TL_1 versus darkness which gave a D score of .56 (with .50 predicted) on the test trials, the rank-order correlation between predicted and observed tone-control indices is .94. Thus the general quantitative model has done a satisfactory job in relating errors by tone and light control subjects to the errors in acquisition and the extent of tone control over responding in the groups learning with $T + L$ as redundant, relevant cues.

IMPLICATIONS OF CHANGES IN CUE SALIENCE

In the following two experiments, three manipulations of cue salience were attempted in an effort to influence learning rate and what was learned in RRC problems. Should our experimental efforts succeed to the extent that we could affect the weight of one cue but not others, that is, a change in the weight of cue 1, w_1, does not affect the weight of cue 2, w_2, then certain implications of the sampling theory could be rigorously tested. This requirement of independence of the weights is critical, however, and as events turned out our experimental efforts were not exemplary on this point and we failed to keep weights constant. When we altered the salience of one cue through emphasis or when we increased the complexity of the stimuli by adding other, irrelevant cues, we inadvertently added physical amounts of relevant cues or reduced the relative weight of these cues by introducing other, unexpected irrelevant cues. Despite this failure, our experiments provide qualitative tests of the sampling theory and point to the kind of future research that might be conducted on salience and attention in learning. With these initial qual-

157

ifications clearly in mind, we shall now describe the general character of the experiments and what implications they have for our model.

In each experiment, two salience manipulations were attempted. One variable in both experiments was the number of irrelevant cues that were added to the problem. Here, different groups of subjects learned problems with the same RRC's but each had a different number of irrelevant cues. The other variable was the salience of a relevant cue that was altered by changes in discriminability in one experiment and by emphasis in the other. When the discriminability of a relevant cue in the RRC problem was varied, we changed the difference between values of a size dimension; in another experiment we manipulated emphasis by underlining in red ink a relevant letter in a consonant cluster.

If the weight of a cue is unaffected by the addition of other, irrelevant cues and if its weight is increased by changes in discriminability or emphasis, then the relevant prediction equations of the model are Equations 2.1, 2.7, 2.8, and 2.9 of Chapter 2. Equation 2.1 relates learning rate of the problem to the weights of the relevant and irrelevant cues, that is, the rate of learning is directly proportional to the number and weight of the relevant cues in the problem. Regarding learning rate, the expectation is that learning will be slower with more irrelevant cues or with a reduction in the weight or salience of the relevant cues. Equations 2.7 to 2.9 relate solution-type probabilities in the RRC problems to learning rate. Consequently, changes in the weights of the cues which affect learning rate also affect the probability that a subject solves the RRC problem on the basis of cue 1 alone, cue 2 alone, or both cues 1 and 2. Regarding this solution-type distribution, the expectation is that an increase in the number of irrelevant cues will reduce the sampling probability of each relevant cue and therefore will increase the probability that the subject learns only one cue in his solution hypothesis. Let p_1 and p_2 denote the proportions of solutions on either cue 1 alone or cue 2 alone and suppose that the weight of cue 1 is larger than that for cue 2 so that p_1 is larger than p_2. If the weights of these two cues, w_1 and w_2, are unaffected by the addition of irrelevant cues, then the ratio of p_1 to p_2 decreases with increases in the number of irrelevant cues (cf. Equation 2.11). If one cue is more salient than another, so that p_1 is greater than p_2, and if the salience of cue 2, w_2, increases through emphasis without affecting w_1, then the expectation is that both p_2 and $p_{1,2}$, the proportions of subjects solving on either cue 2 alone or on both cues, increase.

Restating these implications, when one makes a discrimination or concept-identification problem more complex by adding other, irrelevant attributes, these irrelevant cues serve as distractors and compete for the

158

subject's attention during the course of learning. Since the subject can only attend to a limited number of cues at any given time (as is reflected in our assumption of a fixed-focus sample size), the likelihood that he attends to both relevant cues at the same time in a RRC problem is reduced. Consequently, he is less likely to learn both cues when the problem is made more complex. This is a commonsense expectation, for with greater distraction, less learning occurs. Similarly, the more a cue "stands out," the more likely it is to be dominant in attention and consequently in what is learned.

EXPERIMENT I

Experiment I used geometric figures as stimuli. For all subjects, the relevant and redundant cues were the size of a central figure and its color. For example, in one problem all the red figures were large and were classified in category 1, whereas all the blue figures were small and were classified in category 2. For a given color and size combination, problems were constructed by adding either one, three, or five irrelevant attributes such as the number and position of the figures. To manipulate the discriminability of one of the relevant dimensions, one group was trained on a problem with three irrelevant dimensions and the size difference between the large and small figures was reduced. Another group was trained with the same three irrelevant dimensions but the size difference was increased. The assumption was that the salience of the size cues would be either reduced or increased by changes in the discriminability of the size dimension. Thus the experimental design of Experiment I was an incomplete factorial with five groups: three groups learned a problem with a moderately salient size dimension and with either one, three, or five irrelevant dimensions; two other groups learned problems with three irrelevant dimensions but the size dimension had either a low or a high salience. Let the letters L, M, and H denote the low, moderate, or high salience of the size dimension and 1, 3, or 5 denote the number of irrelevant dimensions of the problems. The five groups are indexed by the initials $M1$, $M3$, $M5$, $L3$ and $H3$.

Each subject was first trained on the size-color RRC problem to a strong criterion of learning and then was tested separately for what was learned on the size and color attributes. If adding irrelevant cues were effective in reducing the relative salience of size and color, then two results are anticipated. The rates of learning for groups $M1$, $M3$, and $M5$ and the number of subjects learning both the color and size attributes during training in these three conditions should progressively decrease. Thus we expect slower learning and more selective attention with the addition of irrelevant stimuli to the

159

task. If the manipulation of size discriminability were effective, two expectations also follow. If, when the size discriminability is reduced, its salience is decreased, we expect that the learning rate would increase from group $L3$ to $H3$ and that the number of subjects who learned the RRC problem on the basis of size alone or both size and color would increase between the same two groups. The latter expectation depends upon the size being less salient than the color in group $L3$.

Method

Subjects: The subjects were 207 undergraduate students at the University of California, Los Angeles. Each subject was trained and tested in individual sessions. Seven subjects failed to reach the learning criterion and were not tested for what they had learned. These nonsolvers were distributed as follows: one in group $M1$, two in $M3$, three in $M5$, one in $L3$, and none in $H3$. A sufficient number of subjects were run until a total of forty solvers in each group was obtained.

Stimulus Materials and Problems: The stimuli were patterns of outline geometric figures drawn in crayon pencil from templates on white 3×5-inch file cards. In all problems, three dimensions were used: the shape (circle or square), the color (red or blue), and the size (large or small) of the figures. Color and size were RRC's in all problems; the shape attribute was always irrelevant. For the $L3$ condition, where size was of low discriminability, the squares were either 1 inch or $\frac{3}{4}$ inch in width while the circles were either $1\frac{1}{8}$ inches or $\frac{7}{8}$ inch in width. For the medium discriminability conditions ($M1$, $M3$, and $M5$), the squares were either 1 inch or $\frac{1}{2}$ inch and the circles were either $1\frac{1}{4}$ inches or $\frac{5}{8}$ inch in width. For the $H3$, high discriminability condition, the squares were either 1 inch or $\frac{3}{8}$ inch in width and the circles were either $1\frac{1}{8}$ inches or $\frac{1}{2}$ inch in width.

Group $M1$ learned a problem with the shape irrelevant and the color and moderate size relevant and redundant. For group $M3$, two further irrelevant dimensions added: the number of figures on the card (one or two) and the orientation of an interior line bisecting each figure (vertical or horizontal). All figures and interior lines on a card were drawn in the same color (red or blue). For group $M5$, two more irrelevant dimensions were added: the position of the figures on the card (upper right or lower left) and the presence or absence of a rectangular border around the edge of the display card. When present, the border was the same color as the outline of the central figures (red or blue). Groups $L3$ and $H3$ had the same problem as group $M3$ except that the size differential was either smaller or larger. The number of different stimulus patterns was four for group $M1$, sixteen for groups $M3$, $H3$, and $L3$, and sixty-four for group $M5$. The responses were the nonsense syllables,

160

"mib" and "dax." Combinations of the values for size and color and the response assignments were completely counterbalanced within each experimental condition.

Procedure: The training procedure and instructions were identical to those used in Chapter 3. The learning criterion was thirty-two consecutive correct responses. If a subject committed an error after sixty-three trials of training, the experiment was terminated, and he was dismissed and classified as a nonsolver. If the subject met the learning criterion, he was immediately given a detailed questionnaire to fill out regarding his learning of the color and size dimensions. The questionnaire contained specific questions regarding (a) the rule used to classify the cards, (b) other possible bases for classification in case the subject indicated only a single-cue focus, and (c) the possibility of guessing in case the subject offered a two-cue solution. No card-sorting tests were given.

RESULTS

Number of Irrelevant Cues

Including the data from nonsolvers, the mean number of acquisition errors for groups $M1$, $M3$, and $M5$ were 2.03, 4.10, and 7.05, respectively. Analysis of variance on error scores yielded a significant F ratio ($p < .01$) for the differences among the groups. In pair comparisons, the mean difference between groups $M1$ and $M3$ was of borderline significance ($p < .10$) while that between groups $M3$ and $M5$ was significant ($p < .01$). These results corroborate the common finding that learning is slower with more irrelevant dimensions.

The forty solvers in each group were classified according to their stated solution rule. Although the questioning did not constrain the range of possible answers, the only solution rules stated were color alone, size alone, or both. The frequencies of the three types are shown in Table 6.4.

The frequency of two-cue solutions decreases with the number of irrelevant dimensions, as was expected. Although the decline in two-cue solutions is regular, it is not very large in absolute terms (i.e., from 42.5 percent down to 25 percent). A chi-square test on Table 6.4 did not reject the null hypothesis ($\chi^2 = 3.77$, $df = 4$). In this instance the manipulations had a consistent but weak effect on solution type.

Another feature of the solution-type data is that the ratio of the frequencies of color-alone to size-alone solvers *increases* with the number of irrelevant cues whereas we had expected it to decrease. This discrepant result led us to reexamine our methods for introducing new irrelevant cues. In retrospect, a plausible confound is that our method

161

TABLE 6.4. THE NUMBER OF SUBJECTS SOLVING ON SIZE, COLOR, OR BOTH AS A FUNCTION OF THE NUMBER OF IRRELEVANT DIMENSIONS: EXPERIMENT I

	Irrelevant Dimensions		
Solution Type	1	3	5
Size	9	9	8
Color	14	19	22
Both	17	12	10
Totals	40	40	40

enhanced the weight of the relevant color as more irrelevant dimensions were added. When a second figure, an interior line or a border, was added, these were colored red or blue in congruence with the central figure. It is plausible that the probability that the subject sampled the color rather than figure size increased as the number of colored features of the display increased. By this argument, the ratio of the weights of the color to the size cue in this experiment would increase with the number of colored irrelevant features.

Discriminability of the Size Cue

The forty subjects each in conditions $L3$ and $H3$ learned the RRC problem with three irrelevant cues, color relevant, and the discriminability of size of either low or high salience. In acquisition, this variation produced an expected but numerically small and insignificant effect on the number of errors. Mean errors to criterion were 4.23 for group $H3$ and 5.10 for group $L3$ ($t(78) = .70, p < .05$).

Although the effect of change in size discriminability on learning rate was not appreciable, the emphasis of size did affect the frequencies of solution types. The obtained frequencies are given in Table 6.5. When the size cue was low salience, 36/40 or 90 percent of the subjects learned only the color and nothing about size. When the size was made more discriminable so that high salience was obtained, 28/40 or 70 percent of the subjects learned the size, with nineteen of these twenty-eight also learning the color. The difference in solution types for conditions $L3$ and $H3$ is highly significant ($\chi^2(2) = 17.55, p < .01$).

In these data, we encounter a disconfirming relation for the sampling theory which relates solution type to learning rate: here, changes in

162

TABLE 6.5. SOLUTION-TYPE FREQUENCIES FOR GEOMETRIC FIGURES WITH VARIATIONS IN SIZE DISCRIMINABILITY: EXPERIMENT I

	Number of Subjects Solving on:		
Group	Size	Color	Both
L3	3	36	1
H3	9	12	19

size salience strongly influenced solution type but had only a small and insignificant effect on learning rate. However, in qualitative terms, Experiment I supports the general expectations of the model. When we increase the number of irrelevant cues, the learning rate and the number of subjects who learn both cues decrease. When we increase the discriminability of a weaker redundant cue, the learning rate and the number of subjects solving on the weaker cue or both cues increase.

EXPERIMENT II

The next experiment was another investigation of the effects of salience and number of irrelevant cues upon solution types. This was because of deficiencies in the first experiment: that is, an insignificant effect on solution type, and a confounded increase in the color-to-size ratio of weights with increasing irrelevant cues. To correct the latter defect, the stimulus patterns for Experiment II were composed of clusters of letters. Each letter may be considered analogous to a dimension, and the two values of that dimension were whether the letter appeared in upper or lower case (e.g., *F* versus *f*). For each problem two letters were RRC's. Three groups of subjects learned with zero, one, or two irrelevant letters added to the pattern. We shall refer to these as groups 0, 1, and 2. The expectation was that the learning rate and the proportion of two-cue solvers would decline over these three groups.

Three additional groups were run to assess the effect of cue salience. The prediction was the following: if the sum of weights of the two relevant cues is held constant, then the maximum number of two-cue solvers occurs when the two relevant cues are equal in their weights. We sought for a method whereby the salience of one or another or both relevant cues could be manipulated so that the sum of their weights would remain constant. For these purposes we tried emphasizing one or the other relevant letter. The emphasizer was a red-colored underline placed beneath a letter. Ideally an emphasizer should increase the probability that the subject attends to the cue, but the emphasizer itself should not be a differential cue (cf. Trabasso, 1963).

Suppose that the emphasizer has an additive effect in increasing the weight of the cue emphasized. If so, then the sum of weights of the two relevant cues will be the same whether cue 1 or cue 2 is always emphasized. These two conditions yield "unbalanced weights" conditions. For an "equal weights" condition, either cue 1 or cue 2, but not both, was emphasized on each trial, on a random half of the trials. Thus, on half the trials the emphasizer was applied to cue 1, and on half the trials it was applied to cue 2. But in either event, the sum of the two weights was expected to remain constant. If the two relevant letters have equal weights, then the same argument can be made assuming that the emphasizer multiplies the weight of the emphasized cue by a factor greater than unity. That is, random emphasis of cue 1 or 2 should give the same sum of weights as does consistent emphasis of cue 1 alone or cue 2 alone. The test for whether constant sum of the relevant weights has been achieved is whether these three conditions yield equal learning rates. But even if the learning rates turn out to be unequal, so that for extraneous reasons a constant sum is not achieved, it still follows that more two-cue solvers should appear in the equal-salient condition. In the following we will refer to these three groups by the relevant letters emphasized, that is, *J, N,* or both *J* and *N*.

Method

Subjects: The subjects were 168 students from introductory psychology classes at University of California, Los Angeles. They were assigned irregularly to the six experimental conditions and run individually. In each group there were twenty-eight subjects who reached criterion and were tested for what they learned.

Procedure: The training procedure was identical to that of the experiment of Chapter 3 except that the response categories were "Yes," signifying that a card belonged to the correct rule for classification, and "No," signifying that it did not belong. The subject was told that his job was to learn a classification rule and to identify each card as belonging to the rule (respond "Yes") or not (respond "No"). He was told only that the stimulus patterns consisted of upper- and lower-case letters.

The learning criterion was thirty-two consecutive correct responses. After reaching criterion the subjects were tested for what they had learned. The test used a combined sorting and question-answering procedure. Before the test, the subject was instructed as follows:

164

"All right. You have indicated to me that you have solved the problem. Now I am going to show you a deck of cards similar to those you were just shown. Your task is to classify each card according to the rule you have just learned and not anything else."

As each test card was classified, the experimenter asked: "Why did you classify this one as a Yes (or No)?" and the subject's replies were recorded.

Stimulus Materials: The training stimuli were clusters of four typed symbols arrayed in a cross on white 3 × 5-inch file cards. Four dimensions of upper- and lower-case letters were used: (J or j), (Q or q), (N or n), and (F or f). When one of these dimensions was removed, its position in the cross was filled by the number symbol, #.

For all problems, the J and N dimensions were redundant and relevant, appearing only in the combinations Jn or jN. The clockwise order of the letters in the cross was fixed as J, Q, N, F, but they were rotated around the cross from trial to trial. Thus the position of the letters varied randomly and was irrelevant.

In condition 0, with no irrelevant letters, the symbol # replaced Q and F. There were eight cards in total, consisting of the two relevant letter patterns (Jn or jN) appearing in each of the four positions of the cross. In condition 1, the letter Q was added and was irrelevant. There were four different letter patterns, each appearing in four positions, thus totaling sixteen cards for this condition. In condition 2, the letters Q and F were independent, irrelevant cues. There were eight possible letter patterns, each in four positions, totaling thirty-two cards.

Conditions J, N, and JN used the thirty-two cards from condition 2 except one letter per card was underlined in red. For conditions J and N, this underlined letter was always J (or j) and N (or n), respectively. For condition JN, the thirty-two cards were divided into four sets of eight, with j, J, n, and N underlined in each set. When the cards were shuffled, the underline appeared equally often under the J or N dimension, half the time with the upper-case and half with the lower-case value.

The test stimuli consisted of eight cards each with four letters in a cross. Four cards contained only a single relevant letter (J, j, n, or N) with the remaining positions filled with the novel letters (H or h), (T or t) and (B or b). Two cards contained both relevant letters, Jn on one, jN on the other. The last two cards contained neither relevant dimension with Q on one and f on the other. All test cards contained two upper- and two lower-case letters.

During training, the specific classification rule was counterbalanced, half the subjects learning "Yes" to Jn and "No" to jN, and half learning the opposite pairings.

165

RESULTS

Number of Irrelevant Cues

As expected, learning rate was decreased by adding irrelevant cues. The mean errors to criterion for groups 0, 1, and 2 were 3.93, 6.36, and 11.46, respectively. These values differed significantly ($F(2.81) = 7.47$, $p < .01$). The corresponding estimates of learning rates were .254, .157, and .086. For samples of subjects as large as those in the present experiment, the maximum-likelihood estimates are normally distributed with variance $c^2(1 - c)/N$, and the standard deviations of the estimates are .0415, .0174, and .0155 for conditions 0, 1, and 2, respectively. Pairs of estimates were compared by normal distribution tests and all pairwise differences were significant ($p < .02$ or better).

The subjects were divided into the three solution types: those who learned *J* alone, *N* alone, or both *J* and *N*. The effect of irrelevant cues upon solution type is depicted in Table 6.6. There was a substantial

TABLE 6.6. FREQUENCY OF SOLUTION TYPES RELATED TO THE NUMBER OF IRRELEVANT CUES: EXPERIMENT II

Solution	0	1	2
J	0	10	12
N	1	9	14
Both	27	9	2
Totals	28	28	28

decline in two-cue solvers as more irrelevant cues were added. The differences among conditions were reliable ($\chi^2(4) = 48.3$, $p < .01$).

The mean errors to criterion were 6.18, 8.86, and 3.35 for groups *J, JN,* and *N,* respectively. These groups collectively learned faster than the unemphasized letter control group 2 which averaged 11.46 errors. Among themselves, however, the emphasized groups differed significantly ($F(2, 82) = 7.11$, $p < .01$) and all pairwise comparisons were significant ($p < .05$). Thus the letter weights were not equal to begin with and the manipulation of stimulus emphasis did not produce equal learning in the alternate emphasis condition. The slower learning by group *JN* might be explained by viewing the changing letter positions of the red emphasizer as an additional, irrelevant cue. The difference between groups *J* and *N* suggests that *N* was more salient than *J*. These

166

differences in learning rate make it virtually impossible to obtain quantitative fits of these data from a single set of parameters.

The frequencies of solution types for the three emphasizer groups are shown in Table 6.7. There was an appreciable effect of the emphasizer on which cues were learned. When only one letter was emphasized, 80 percent of the subjects learned only that letter, 5.4 percent learned

TABLE 6.7. FREQUENCY OF SOLUTION TYPES RELATED TO REDUNDANT LETTER EMPHASIZED: EXPERIMENT II

Solution Type	Emphasized Letter		
	J	N	JN
J	22	0	4
N	3	23	6
Both	3	5	18
Totals	28	28	28

only the unemphasized letter, and 14.6 percent learned both. Stated differently, there was about a 95 percent chance that a subject would learn the emphasized letter in the J and N conditions. In condition JN, where each relevant letter was emphasized on half the trials, there was a large increase in the frequency of two-cue solutions. In this condition, the single-cue solvers were approximately evenly divided, although the letter N was learned more often than J in the J and N conditions, a result consistent with the finding that group N learned faster than group J. In any event, in RRC problems with one cue more salient than another, subjects solve primarily on the salient cue; when the two cues are equally salient, an increase in two-cue solutions occurs.

Theoretical Calculations

To predict the learning rate and frequency of the solution types in Experiments I and II, one needs, for each condition, estimates of the sampling probabilities, $a(1)$ for cue 1 and $a(2)$ for cue 2, and the sample-size parameter, s. Ideally, for each condition, one should have two control groups, as were used in experiments of Chapters 3, 4, and 5. One group learns a problem with cue 1 relevant and cue 2 irrelevant; the other learns with cue 2 relevant and cue 1 irrelevant. These two conditions would provide us with *independent* estimates of the sampling probabilities for each cue and permit prediction of the learning rate for the group that learns the RRC problem. Since we had eleven conditions in Experiments I and II, this would have necessitated the expensive procedure of running an additional twenty-two conditions for prediction purposes. Hence no strong numerical predictions are possible.

It is possible, however, to "fit" the solution types for each condition or a group of conditions as a consistency check of the sampling theory. For each group fit, the learning rate, $a(1.2)$, and the proportions of subject who solve only on cue 1, $p(1)$, and only on cue 2, $p(2)$, can be used to estimate $a(1)$, $a(2)$, and s for that condition. The three equations in three unknowns are:

$$a(1.2) = a(1) + a(2)$$

$$p(1) = \frac{a(1)}{a(1) + a(2)} (1 - a(2))^{s-1}$$

and

$$p(2) = \frac{a(2)}{a(1) + a(2)} (1 - a(1))^{s-1}$$

One may proceed by equating these three equations to the observed values for each condition, and then search for the triplet of parameter values that gives the best fit of the data for each group. This method would fail if the data were such as to require either negative estimates of the sampling probabilities or nonsensical values for one or more of the parameters.

We carried out this procedure for the data in Tables 6.4–6.7, using the observed learning rate to fix $a(1) + a(2)$ and searching for values of $a(1)$ and integer values of s to find the pair that minimized the chi-square fit to the solution-type frequencies. These chi-square values have no degrees of freedom and they show simply that the data can be fit by the model.

In all eleven conditions, we obtained nonsignificant, minimum chi-square values with positive estimates of $a(1)$, $a(2)$, and s, indicating that we could indeed fit these data. The main reason for obtaining this goodness-of-fit is that the data were qualitatively in agreement with the expectations of the sampling theory. Examining the parameter values, however, the sample-size parameter did not remain invariant across conditions. In Experiment I, it *increased* with the number of irrelevant cues; but in Experiment II, it *decreased* with the number of irrelevant cues, so that this outcome has no reliability. Likewise, when discriminability varied, the s estimates increased with changes in salience in Experiment I; in Experiment II, the same estimate ($\hat{s} = 2$) fit groups J and N but a large one ($\hat{s} = 19$) was needed to fit group JN.

When we tried to keep the parameters invariant across conditions, reasonable fits were obtained for all conditions in Experiment I but were significantly in error for Experiment II. The basic difficulty is that parameters which theoretically should be invariant over conditions were not. As we indicated, the weights of the cues in the experiments did not remain constant with changes in the stimuli. In the geometric conditions, when we added irrelevant cues or when we changed the size of the figures, we also added more color so that $a(C)$ would not be constant across conditions. If we hold $a(C)$ constant, then the variation shows up in the parameter, s. With the letter stimuli, an examination of the learning rates indicates that when irrelevant cues were added, the amount of change in the learning rate was much greater than that expected if the weights of the letters were equal; and in the emphasis conditions, some letters were learned more readily than others so that, again, their weights were unequal.

It is possible that each added irrelevant letter introduces other irrelevant cues such as positional ones in conjunction with the new irrelevant letter ("q in the topmost position") or conjunctive hypotheses involving several letters in several positions ("q and J in lower half of the display"). The emphasizer, which shifted locations, may itself have acted as an irrelevant cue. For example, the shifting underline may have increased the probability that subjects used hypotheses involving the underline in conjunction with a location rather than a letter ("underline in the East or West is in category Yes"). The greater number of subjects solving on two cues in this problem could have occurred for several reasons: some subjects may have learned the general hypothesis that "underlined letters are relevant" and, following this, learned the specific paired associates, that J or n go with one classificatory response while j or N go with the other. Second, a subject might have learned initially on the basis of only one letter but, during his criterion trials, added to his sample focus the other emphasized letter.

Although these conjectures are ad hoc and speculative, they have testable consequences; they also indicate the experimental pitfalls that one has to avoid in order to be sure that the boundary conditions of the theory are not exceeded so that a reasonable quantitative test can be made. For example, if the shifting emphasizer acts as an irrelevant cue, shifting the emphasis between two irrelevant cues should retard learning more than would the constant emphasis of one irrelevant cue. The possibility of the subject enlarging his solution focus during criterion could be tested by various overtraining designs in which the location of the emphasizer changes from the training to the overtraining series. For example, initial training could be done with the J problem and overtraining then could be carried out with either the N or JN stimuli. An appreciable learning of the N cue would indicate that emphasized cues

169

have a high probability of being incorporated into a previously restricted sample focus. This would be compared to the null effect obtained in Chapter 3 where a previously irrelevant cue was made relevant and redundant during overtraining.

In addition, we should mention the possible role of memory in these findings and its influence on the parameter s. When there were several irrelevant dimensions (here, two or more) the theory fit well across conditions; but it failed when the number of dimensions was small. With a small number of patterns (e.g., condition 0 of Experiment II had only two letter combinations), the subject may have sufficient opportunity to memorize all combinations so that changes in position of the letters is of no major consequence in affecting the number of two-cue solutions. However, with a larger number of stimulus patterns, specific memorizing would be more difficult because each pattern contains more elements and the large number of similar patterns provides several opportunities for interference to produce forgetting of specific past information. When there is a massive overload of incoming information, the subject might be expected to resort to the "focus sampling" with which the model deals. If this conjecture proves to be correct, then applicability of our model is restricted. The process model is not presently formulated to allow for attachment of a "specific memory" mechanism.

The important thing that we learned from our experimental *faux pas* in this chapter was that we should have taken care to ensure that our stimulus weights would be constant despite changes in the patterns. As indicated in our review of the Imai and Garner (1965) results, such patterns are possible to construct. What we seek, then, are patterns in which the addition or removal or change in emphasis of one attribute does not change the appearance or amount of another attribute. For example, the addition or removal of our dot cues in Chapter 3 probably would not affect the weight of the shape cues and vice versa. Thus, in order to give the theory the kind of test that would permit quantitative predictions, we would seek stimulus materials that produced disjoint sets of cues. Current work in our laboratory on this problem is being conducted by Howard Rollins as a dissertation project.

In the next section, we discuss how one might independently assess cue weights in order to test their effects on learning and concept identification. We do this by further elaboration on the notion of an attending hierarchy introduced in Chapter 1.

The Hierarchy of Cue Weights

Of fundamental importance to the sampling theory is the postulation of a hierarchy of analyzer or attention responses. At the outset of a problem these responses are assumed to be arranged in an increasing order according to their strength or weight, w_i. The discriminability of cues and perceptual and experiential factors all influence these weights. These hypothetical cue weights are the determinants of learning rate and solution type since they determine the likelihood that the relevant cues are sampled. The w values were noted to play much the same role in the sampling theory as do the response strengths (v values) in Luce's (1959) choice theory.

The basic notion of a hierarchy of encoding responses is hardly novel (e.g., Baron, 1965), since any theory that addresses itself to attentional phenomena must have some representation of an ordering of the cues competing for attention. The specific verbal labels for what orders the cues vary from one theorist to the next: channel bias (Broadbent, 1958), amplifiers or weights on feature counters (Uhr & Vossler, 1963), probability of particular observing responses (Zeaman & House, 1963), or probability that particular stimulus analyzers are switched in (Sutherland, 1964); but all these approaches commonly begin with postulating a hierarchy or ordering of cues according to their attention-getting values, no matter how these theories may differ in other respects.

Since this attentional hierarchy plays a central role in the present account of discrimination learning, a useful line of investigation would be to devise methods that provide some independent assessment of this hierarchy, that is, independent of the learning phenomena to be explained by reference to the hierarchy. Although little work has been done along these lines, several procedures suggest themselves as assessment techniques.

A first technique hinges upon the fact that human adults already have verbal labels for the attributes typically used in our experiments (color, shape, size, etc.). Thus, if a subject inspected a series of stimulus patterns and then was asked to describe how they differed among themselves, he would describe most of the attributes and emit the descriptions in some particular order. If we coordinate cue weight to the availability of the verbal label for that cue, the weight of cue i should then be reflected by the proportion of subjects who report cue i and the ordinal position of the label's occurrence in the subject's listing. This procedure is suggested by analogy to the way a response hierarchy is constructed from free-association tests to a stimulus word. The "stimulus" in this case is the entire series of patterns shown before the subject gives his descriptions of how the patterns varied. By testing large groups of homogeneous subjects on the same series, a set of empirical norms could be obtained. As in word-association norms, the available cues of the series would be ordered by a composite index referring to their relative frequency and average order of occurrence in the subjects' listings. If something like Marbe's law holds, then in free recall the labels given most frequently should also tend to occur earlier in the recall, and these should be the more salient dimensions of the stimulus series for this population of subjects. The assessment of the hierarchy thus obtained could be cross-validated by using it to predict the order of learning difficulty for problems involving the series of patterns and varying which cue is relevant.

An alternative assessment would involve Imai and Garner's (1965) method of "free classification" in which the subject would be asked to classify consistently the patterns into two piles according to any dimension he wished, and there would be no feedback to direct his classification. Presumably the dimension chosen for classification in this unconstrained situation would represent the most salient dimension for the subject. One pass through the deck of cards, however, would provide limited information about the subject's hierarchy.

The foregoing method can be extended in two different ways. One is by analogy to the paired-comparison method for scaling N objects (dimensions here). A short series of two-cue patterns could be presented, in each of which the subject chooses between the two available cues for classification (the other $N - 2$ cues are held constant). By presenting all $N(N - 1)/2$ paired comparisons, one could accumulate information about which cues are preferred consistently, and thus assess their ordering in the hierarchy. The alternative way to estimate this ordering would be by successive elimination of the chosen attribute (cf. Luce, 1959). Starting with all N attributes in the deck of cards, a first unconstrained sort would give the presumptive first-ranked dimension of the N available. This dimension is then removed, and the subject is requested to make another sort of the $N - 1$ dimension deck, yielding the second-ranked dimension. By following this elimination procedure through $N - 1$ sorts (the last involves the two dimensions not previously chosen), all N dimensions would have been ranked according to the cue weights associated with each dimension.

A single cycle through this procedure yields a ranking by one subject, but provides no assessment of distances between successive weights in the hierarchy nor of the weights themselves. In other words, the one-shot ranking provides ordinal but not interval or ratio measurement of the cue weights. However, the complete ranking can be repeated by the same subject (or averaged over several subjects tested once) and, from the ranking of the obtained probabilities, estimates of the cue

172

weights can be derived using Luce's choice theory (cf. Atkinson, Bower, & Crothers, 1965; Luce, 1959).

A third procedure, similar to the method of triads, was employed by Suchman and Trabasso (1966a) for assessing cue preferences of young children. A child was shown cards containing three stimulus objects, each differing from the others in two attributes but identical to one other pattern in one attribute. For example, the three patterns might be: a = large red circle, b = small blue circle, and c = small red triangle. Typical of the method of triads, the subject was asked to pick out the two patterns that are "most alike" (or most similar, or go together, etc.). Logically, the test involves a conflict between three possible bases for judged likeness, size, color, and shape, and it was presumed that the subject's choice reflected for him the more salient attribute of the three. Thus, choice of a, b implies shape dominance, of a, c color dominance, and of b, c size dominance. A series of triad cards of this kind (with either restricted or unrestricted values being compared) could be given to the subject to determine the consistency of his choices. Each of the possible triads of N dimensions can be tested with this procedure. Suchman and Trabasso (1966a) assessed only size, color, and form; they found individual children to be quite consistent in their choices, with a predominant color preference for very young children changing over to a shape preference for older children. The size cue was chosen infrequently at all ages tested.

Regardless of how the hierarchy is assessed, the obtained ranking could be used to make at least ordinal predictions about the discrimination learning of a subject. Learning should be slower as the rank of the relevant cue is lower in the hierarchy. Also the estimated hierarchy could be used to rank-order different RRC problems according to the likelihood that the subject would learn both cues. In general, the lower the average rank of the two RRC's, the less probable it is that the subject will learn both cues.

A related experiment by Suchman and Trabasso (1966b) validated their cue-preference measures for children. Following the assessment tests (with triads varying in color, form, and size), the child learned a color, or form, or color and form problem involving the same stimuli. In the first two single-cue problems, the form or color was irrelevant, respectively. Those children assessed as having a color preference learned the color problem rapidly but the form problem slowly; those assessed as having a form preference showed the reverse order of learning rates. Moreover, on the color and form RRC problem, the assessed preference predicted the dominant cue in the child's solution focus, that

173

is, children preferring color tended to solve on color but not form. However, a few of the subjects in each preference subgroup learned both the color and form cues. In this instance, then, the "nonlearning" assessment of cue salience was validated by the discrimination learning performance.

The assessment methods suggested above are not easily adapted to animal subjects, since instructions and nonreinforced testing are essential to those procedures. Independent assessment procedures for animals would be difficult to devise and validate since so much of the role of instructions in human experimentation corresponds to explicit discrimination training for animals. The most direct assessment, of course, involves transfer tests after initial RRC learning: cues of low salience would not be very well learned, so deleting, neutralizing, or even opposing them would not substantially affect performance to the remaining cues. That is, the "stimulus equivalence" class includes variations in poorly learned cues of low salience in the compound. Contrariwise, alterations in a highly salient and well-learned cue of the RRC compound would lead to a large generalization decrement.

But these transfer procedures involve discrimination learning. Are there other assessment procedures that do not require a history of differential reinforcement to the cues? One possibility is use of an "habituation" preparation. Some index of an orienting reflex is recorded which is elicited by an abrupt change in an habituated compound. Specifically, a stimulus compound would be presented repeatedly in close temporal succession until the animal habituated to it. After this occurred, the repetition of the compound continues except that now it would be occasionally presented in altered form, where one or another element is either removed or changed in value. For example, electrode recordings from the visual cortex of monkeys might be taken during repetitive flashes of a large red square. Then, two or three consecutive flashes of a small red square might be interspersed among the flashes of the large red square. Alternatively, the color or shape could be changed more or less along a gradient. The expectation is that the change in a monotonous series would "release" habituation—evoke an orienting reflex (OR)—and that the magnitude of this OR would increase with the salience or weight of the altered element in the compound. The magnitude of the OR would also be expected to vary with the amount or discriminability of change in a single component, yielding a typical gradient. If results are as expected, this procedure would provide a crude assessment of the salience of a given component (dimension) in a compound stimulus. And this could be cross-validated by prediction of the dominance relations in RRC discrimination training and transfer.

174

It could be claimed that the OR assessment above is not a "non-learning" procedure, since habituation may be viewed as the conditioning of inhibition (of arousal) to the repeated stimulus pattern (Stein, 1966). Accordingly, the increase in OR released by the altered stimulus pattern would be viewed as "disinhibition" of the conditioned inhibition. Thus the procedure resembles (in reverse) that of positive conditioning of a CR to a compound CS, with generalization tests to altered components in the compound. If this view is correct, then it makes very difficult any search for a "nonlearning" procedure to independently assess salience of cues in animal experiments.

We indicated earlier that the hierarchy of cue weights could be manipulated in several ways, and that one method was to vary the discriminability of the two values of a dimension that appear over successive patterns in the series. From this it follows that demonstration of a simple "preference" for attribute A over attribute B gives equivocal evidence, since we do not know whether to interpret this as showing some kind of "innate preference" or as showing that the discriminability of the particular A values was higher than the B values in this instance. Thus, if one is concerned with stable preferences for particular dimensions, then it is advisable to use for comparison pairs of values that have first been scaled for equal discriminability (cf. Imai & Garner, 1965).

An experiment by Hara and Warren (1961) is an exemplary model of how to proceed to establish such conclusions about cue preference. Using cats in a modified Grice box, Hara and Warren first had their cats do discriminability scaling of three separate and independent dimensions of two test rectangles: the two brightnesses, the two sizes, and the two forms (ratio of horizontal to vertical length). By this means they found two brightnesses, two sizes, and two rectangles that were separately discriminated, say, with 80 percent accuracy. Among the several tests given after this assessment were some "opposition" or conflict tests in which two equally discriminable attributes were pitted against one another. The choices on these opposition tests varied from 50 percent to about 75 percent to one attribute, with six or twelve tests giving choice percentages that significantly deviated from 50 percent. The brightness cue was preferred most often to either the size or form cue, whereas size and form were chosen about equally often by the cats. This was a genuine preference in the sense that the opposed cues were equated for discriminability before the opposition test.

Reducing the difference between the two values of an attribute could, in principle, reduce performance in two exclusive ways: first, it could lower the probability that the subject will notice and sample this cue; and second, it could lower the probability of a correct response

175

given that the subject encodes the patterns according to this attribute. We may use Thurstone's (1927) concept of the "discriminal dispersion" to clarify this latter point. The basic notion is that over successive trials with the same stimulus value being put into the system, the output from a particular analyzer fluctuates quantitatively about a mean value with some variance. This probability distribution of outputs from a given analyzer for a given input value corresponds to Thurstone's discriminal dispersion. If the two physical values are close together, then the distributions of encoded outputs for the two are also close together, overlapping to a considerable extent. Consequently, in the zone of overlap, equivocation and incorrect responding may occur.

Although these two effects of value differences are correlated, sampling probabilities should increase with value differences beyond those that would provide 100 percent discrimination with this cue. The size variation used in Experiment I in Chapter 6 is a case in point. Subjects could discriminate perfectly between the two values in the "low salience" (group $L3$) condition when asked to do so. Yet when not preinstructed to look for size differences, they learned the size cue less frequently the smaller was the physical separation between its two values. If discriminability were defined in terms of the percentage correct responses when encoding a given cue, then the three size differences in that experiment were 100 percent discriminable, yet they had increasing effects on method of solution. And this, of course, we would interpret in terms of their increasing sampling probabilities. The artificial ceiling on the percentage correct measure could be avoided by using summated JND's as the discriminability measure. Then, cue-sampling probability would improve continuously with the JND's separating the two values of that dimension.

SUMMARY

The experiments in this chapter tested predictions regarding solution types as the salience of the two redundant and relevant cues varied. The expectation was that an increase in the number of irrelevant cues would lower the saliences of the relevant cues and thus reduce both the learning rate and the frequency of two-cue solutions. These outcomes were obtained in both experiments, and the effects were stronger with the letter than with the geometric stimuli. In the first experiment, it was expected that an increase in the salience or discriminability of one relevant dimension (size) would increase both the learning rate and frequency of subjects who learn this dimension. The effect on learning rate was small and insignificant, but the effect on solution type was

176

substantial and in the expected direction. In the second experiment, the salience of a letter was increased by an emphasizer (a red underline); some subjects had only one letter emphasized whereas others experienced an alternating emphasis on each relevant letter. The expectations were that these groups would learn faster than the unemphasized control group, that the subjects with single-letter emphasis would mainly learn only this cue, and that the alternating emphasis would increase the likelihood of two-cue solutions. This pattern of results was obtained. All emphasized groups learned faster than the unemphasized controls. In the single-cue emphasis condition, 95 percent of the subjects learned the emphasized cue while 20 percent learned the unemphasized cue (counting two-cue solvers in both percentages). The shifting emphasizer increased the relative frequency of two-cue solutions from the control level of 7 percent to 65 percent. In qualitative terms, these results confirm the general type of theory proposed.

7

SELECTIVE ATTENTION
AND OVERTRAINING

In Chapter 2 we assumed that the subject operated alternately in two modes during training: a search mode and a test mode. The search mode was activated after commission of an error. On such occasions the subject presumably searches among the cues that are available and selects a sample. Hypotheses are formed by assigning the reinforced responses consistently to the two values of each sampled dimension; these hypotheses constitute the focus sample to be tested on the next trial. If the response to the next stimulus pattern is correct, those hypotheses consistent with the feedback information are supposedly retained, whereas those inconsistent with it are eliminated from the focus at that moment. If the response to the next pattern is incorrect, then the sample focus is given up and a new search occurs. This alternation of search, sample, and test goes on until the subject solves the problem.

These assumptions imply that the subject's attention to cues is even more selective after than before mastery of a problem. That is, the subject should learn only those relevant cues that are selected for his focus sample on the last error trial; other relevant cues not in the sample at that time should not be learned. Furthermore, when the criterion run is sufficiently long, any irrelevant cues contained in the focus will be eliminated, so only the relevant cues selected in the focus sample at the last error trial will be retained. The implication tested in this chapter is that a subject who has learned only one of two RRC's in training should not learn the second relevant dimension during extended overtraining.

Some of the results reported in Chapter 3 bear on this assumption and appear to support it. In the experiment reported there, an irrelevant dimension was made relevant and redundant after the subject had first mastered the problem on a single relevant dimension. Of eighty-six subjects tested in this condition, none indicated having learned anything

178

about the added relevant dimension. These subjects uniformly verbalized only the first dimension as their solution hypothesis and sorted at chance on the test cards involving the second, added dimension. Although these results support our theory, an alternate interpretation of them is possible. One might argue that these subjects sampled and rejected during training the initially irrelevant cue and thus did not consider it again during overtraining. Some support for this rejection interpretation may be found in recent studies by Erickson (1967), Levine (1966), Trabasso and Bower (1966), and Trabasso and Staudenmayer (1967). Consistent with this interpretation would be the further view that during overtraining subjects continue to sample and learn responses to cues which they had not previously rejected.

OVERTRAINING AND RRC LEARNING

In one experiment bearing directly on the overtraining issue, Sutherland and Holgate (1966) trained rats on a RRC problem involving brightness and orientation cues. One group of rats was trained until they met a mild criterion of learning and a second group was overtrained. When the training was to a mild criterion, the correlation between errors on brightness and orientation tests was negative ($-.56$), indicating that the animals learned more about one cue than the other. However, with 200 overtraining trials, the correlation was virtually zero, because the rats had learned both cues fairly well. Thus, rats appear to resample or learn other relevant cues during overtraining in contradiction of our sampling assumptions.

OVERTRAINING AND PARTIAL VALIDITY

Hughes and North (1959) investigated the effect of *partially* reinforcing a cue during overtraining by assessing what was learned in a transfer design. Rats were first trained on a horizontal versus a vertical discrimination with black and white cues irrelevant (50 percent correct). During overtraining the white cue was made partially relevant by pairing it with the positive discriminanda either 75 percent or 25 percent of the seventy-two overlearning trials. In transfer the white cue became positive, black became negative, and the orientation dimension was removed. Subjects that had had white paired with the positive discriminanda 75 percent of the time learned faster than those that had had white paired 25 percent with the positive discriminanda. Mean errors were 4.5 and 8.5, respectively, for the 75 and 25 percent conditions. On the first transfer trial, no significant preference for the 75 percent cue

179

was demonstrated. These results, however, indicate that some learning occurred for the partially relevant cue during overtraining even though the subjects first mastered the discrimination on a 100 percent relevant cue in training. These data constitute a second negative finding with respect to our sampling assumptions, at least as applied to experiments with rats.

The experiment by Hughes and North demonstrated that a cue made partially relevant during overtraining is learned in some degree by rats. Somewhat less critical data for our theory comes from experiments involving partially relevant cues introduced at the outset of training on a discrimination. The results here are conflicting. Working with rats, Babb (1956) and Bitterman and Coate (1950) found some positive transfer to a cue that was partially relevant in an initial discrimination. However, an extensive experiment on human concept identification by Bourne and Haygood (1960) found little, if any, learning on a partially relevant cue even with much overtraining.

In the Bourne and Haygood experiment one cue was partially relevant, being paired with the correct response on either 90, 80, 70, or 60 percent of the trials for different groups of subjects. Two further groups were run; for one, the cue was redundant with the relevant cue (100 percent); for the other, the cue was completely irrelevant (50 percent). These basic six conditions were replicated with one, three, or five irrelevant (50 percent) cues added, thus making eighteen groups in all. All subjects were overtrained, receiving at least eighty trials after their last error, before being shifted to a problem in which the previously relevant cue was made irrelevant and the previous partially relevant cue was made completely relevant. Table 7.1 summarizes their findings in terms of mean errors to mastery on the transfer problem.

In transfer, the 100 percent groups which had both cues relevant and redundant showed positive transfer. This result is consistent with our transfer findings in Chapter 4. Regarding those conditions with partially relevant cues in training, Bourne and Haygood claimed that errors in transfer decreased as a function of increases in partial validity. However, closer examination of their data suggests that their conclusion may be unwarranted. There were several inconsistencies in trend and no statistical comparisons of the data were made which excluded the 100 percent groups. Averaging over the number of irrelevant dimensions per problem, we estimated mean transfer errors to be nearly equal for groups with the 50, 60, 70, 80, and 90 percent cue, respectively (see their Fig. 1, p. 373). From these data we would conclude that if one cue is relevant throughout training, a second, partially relevant cue is not learned as evidenced by lack of positive transfer to a problem in which

180

TABLE 7.1. MEAN NUMBER OF ERRORS MADE IN TRANSFER TO A DIMENSION THAT VARIED IN ITS DEGREE OF PARTIAL REINFORCEMENT DURING TRAINING

Percent Partial Reinforcement	Number of Irrelevant Cues			
	1	3	5	Average
50	5.8	10.9	17.4	11.4
60	4.8	13.9	13.4	10.7
70	5.2	12.9	15.5	11.2
80	6.8	9.9	10.5	9.1
90	10.7	10.1	12.9	11.2
100	1.0	5.4	4.1	3.5

(Data from Bourne & Haygood, 1960.)

the partially relevant cue becomes relevant. This is consistent with the sampling assumptions we have made for human concept identification.

BLOCKING AND FADING PROCEDURES IN OVERTRAINING

Our result, that prior training to classify stimuli according to one dimension reduced or "blocked" the acquisition of control of responding by a second cue later made redundant with the first, is not an isolated finding nor is it exclusively confined to human subjects, since reports by Jenkins (1966), Kamin (1966), Lawrence (1949, 1950), and Miles and Jenkins (1965) have shown it clearly with rats and pigeons.

In the experiment by Miles and Jenkins (1965), it will be recalled that pigeons first learned a key-brightness discrimination where they were reinforced for pecking the key when it was illuminated with one brightness (L_1) but not with a different brightness (L_2). After this, a tone was then sounded along with L_1 but not with L_2, and this compound discrimination was trained for twelve hourly sessions. Then generalization tests were carried out along the brightness continuum with the tone absent or present. The test outcomes showed that the presence or absence of the tone had practically no effect upon the pigeon's responding at a given key brightness. That is, the tone acquired no associative strength with respect to the response when it was added following learning of the brightness discrimination. As reviewed in Chapters 1 and 6, if the presence-absence of the tone was available at the outset of learning as a relevant cue redundant along with the bright-

181

ness difference, then the tone acquired substantial control over responding. Miles and Jenkins' results on errors in compound training and the degree of tone control are well accounted for by our model for additivity of cues and for relating learning rate to cue salience and degree of control (dominance) by elements of the compound (see Chapter 6).

Kamin (1966) has done an extensive series of studies of blocking, using rats in the "conditioned emotional response" (CER) paradigm. The CER refers to the fact that animals lever-pressing for positive reinforcement cease responding when a stimulus is superimposed which has been paired with an unavoidable noxious stimulus like electric shock. This stimulus-controlled suppression of positively reinforced behavior is evidently due to the classical conditioning of fear responses to the imposed stimulus. Hence the amount of suppression can be treated as though it were an index of the strength of a classically conditioned response, and over a long series of parametric studies Kamin has demonstrated the heuristic value of this identification.

In this paradigm the basic blocking experiment is as follows: first the rat receives, say, sixteen trials of a noise (N) stimulus paired with shock; then sixteen trials of the compound, noise plus light $(N + L)$, paired with shock; and then no-shock tests with the light alone (L). The basic observation is that this sequence produces virtually no suppression to the light CS, the added redundant cue. The same type of effect obtains if the sequence is L alone, then $N + L$; here, tests with N show no suppression, so it is not a modality-specific effect. Also initial training to $L + N$ from the outset produces some suppression to each element singly, so suppression can be conditioned somewhat to both elements of a compound unless blocking occurs. Kamin has investigated several aspects of this phenomenon, specifically concerning how degree of blocking (of L in $L + N$ following N alone) varies with degree of suppression to N before compound training begins. Several variables (number of shocked trials to N alone, extinction to N alone following shocks to N alone, intensity of the noise CS) which make for less learning or less suppression to N by the end of the prior series also reduce the blocking effect of N upon the redundant element (L) in the compound. Roughly speaking, the more the rat has to learn (to show total suppression) during the compound trials, the more control of the CER is gained by the new redundant element of the compound.

Both Kamin (1966) and Jenkins (1966) relate their results on blocking to results on "overshadowing" (what we have called dominance) whereby the control acquired by a weak discriminative cue is lessened if a salient redundant cue is concurrently present from the outset. They point out that since the salient cue is probably learned

182

sooner than the weaker cue, the earlier learning of the salient cue will block learning of the weaker cue. Dominance in RRC training would thus be a consequence of a blocking of the slower learned cue by the faster learned cue when both are present from the outset of training. This view is consonant with our theoretical model insofar as we wish to transpose details from the human to the animal learning context. The assumption that the subject does not increase his sample focus when he responds correctly gives the same account of overshadowing and blocking. Overshadowing results when the subject "by chance" learns on the basis of a sample containing only one of the relevant cues, and because he henceforth responds correctly this blocks the subsequent acquisition of the alternate cue. In theory, a subject learns both cues only if both are in a particular sample (taken following an error) that eventuates in a solution.

The animal studies reviewed earlier appear to show extreme results on blocking; that is, there was little if any differential conditioning to the blocked cue. However, such extreme results are not the general outcome, and the prediction of complete blocking simply would not be sustained by the general results in animal work. To mention just a few of the alternate results, some learning of a blocked cue by rats has been reported by Bruner, Matter, and Papanek (1955), and by Hughes and North (1959). These studies showed some positive transfer to a problem in which the allegedly blocked cue was relevant. Kamin (1966) reported such positive transfer ("savings") in CER retraining to L alone in his blocking experiments, despite the fact that there was no suppression evidenced in extinction tests with L alone. Moreover, Mackintosh (1965b) and Mahut (1954) have reported that while rats may develop strong position habits during presolution of a visual discrimination, the latencies of their responses to the visual S^+ and S^- stimuli may begin to draw apart. Thus latencies revealed differential response tendencies to values of a dimension that was not currently controlling the choice response.

In lieu of such evidence, a more defensible position (cf. Mackintosh, 1965a) would be that blocking is a graded phenomenon: the more the subject has been biased to attend and respond to cue A, the less he learns per trial about cue B which is relevant and redundant with cue A. This lesser learning need not be "zero," and its amount could be assessed relative to controls not having had compound practice and other controls having had compound practice but without a prior bias toward one of the relevant cues.

If blocking is a graded effect, then what experimental arrangements would result in more or less blocking of the added cue? Four variables

183

have been investigated in this context, and there doubtless are many others to be examined. From the experiment by Bruner, Matter, and Papanek (1955), it is known that blocking increases (transfer decreases) the higher the drive level of the rat during training and the higher the degree of prior training on cue A before the $A + B$ redundant phase begins. Their interpretation, that overtraining and high drive are factors that rigidify and narrow the breadth of the resulting cognitive map, is colorful description but short on explanatory depth. Another factor is the relative salience of cues A and B: the less salient is the prior biased cue A relative to the added redundant cue B, the less blocking that occurs to B (Mackintosh, 1965b). This result was also found to some extent in Chapter 3 for groups S' and D' where subjects more frequently learned the added (novel) salient dot than the weaker shape dimension.

Finally studies have been reported using "fading" procedures which can be introduced in one of two places in the three-phase experiment. The three phases are depicted diagrammatically in Figure 7.1: phase 1 consists of training with a vertical gray rectangle positive and a horizontal gray rectangle negative; in phase 2, brightness is used as a redundant cue for overtraining; in phase 3, testing occurs with brightness relevant and shape neutralized (both are squares here). One procedural variable is the abruptness of the transition from the stimuli of phase 1 to the stimuli of phase 2; here, one gradation of fading in the brightness

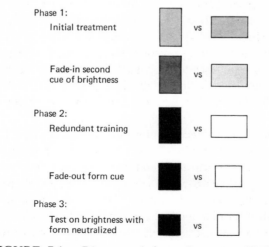

FIGURE 7.1. *Diagram of three phases in a blocking experiment using brightness and shape cues with fading between each phase.*

differential is illustrated. The other variable is the abruptness of the transition from the stimuli of phase 2 to the test stimuli in phase 3.

An experiment by Mackintosh (1965b) employed fading in between phases 1 and 2. He found that his rats learned more about the brightness cue when it was introduced abruptly, in one step, than when it was faded in as illustrated in Figure 7.1. An experiment by Terrace (1963) used fading out between phases 2 and 3. The first discrimination was to red-green colors learned without errors, and the second cue was orientation of a white line projected onto the colored key. Terrace reported that phase 3 performance was perfect (errorless) for pigeons exposed to the fading routine between phases 2 and 3, and was much poorer for those experiencing an abrupt shift from phase 2 to 3.

These results are comprehensible, though hardly derivable from extant formal theories. The beneficial effect of the abrupt transition from phase 1 to 2 is understandable in terms of the higher probability of an orienting reflex and attention to the novel dimension that is introduced abruptly. The opposite effect of fading between phases 2 and 3 is understandable in terms of the gradual reduction in the salience of the first learned cue, permitting more attention to other cues.

These variables have been investigated with animals and with problems wherein the redundant cue in phase 2 was not present and irrelevant in phase 1. These fading methods should be explored with human subjects learning concept-identification problems wherein the later redundant cue is initially irrelevant. Interpreted in its strictest sense, the sampling theory implies that perfect transfer to the redundant cue could not be produced (by fading or otherwise) without some errors occurring between phases 2 and 3. What the theory now foresees is that attention and correct performance to the first-learned cue should continue until its discriminability has been faded sufficiently so that guesses and overt errors begin to occur, at which point the subject would begin searching for another relevant cue. In effect, the theory supposes that the subject exposed to the fading procedure will have as much difficulty learning the second cue as would a control subject who does not have the phase 2 redundant overtraining and fading but is put directly onto the phase 3 problem (one-trial "fading"). This implication is clearly incorrect for Terrace's pigeons and is probably incorrect for human subjects as well.

The foregoing implication about fading agrees with the general implication of the theory that blocking is a complete "all-or-none" phenomenon, that is, *no* learning on the blocked cue. This follows from the way the axioms of the theory use attention to tie together performance and learning. Roughly speaking, the theory supposes that the subject can learn nothing about cues which had no weight in determining

185

his choice on a trial. These axioms characterize trial events as follows: at the onset of a trial the subject is preset to attend to the values of one or more dimensions, and his response is determined by *averaging* over the conditional connections of the dimension values sampled; at the end of the trial, the reinforcement feedback may alter the conditional connections of the values sampled and may also change (by eliminating error-indicating irrelevant cues) their sampling probabilities for the next trial. Two implications of our system are relevant to its prediction of complete blocking: first, when the subject responds correctly, he should never increase his sample focus, although he may reduce it by discarding irrelevant cues; and second, if the subject is responding correctly 100 percent of the time, he therefore must not be sampling irrelevant or unlearned cues—otherwise the averaging rule for performance implies less than perfect performance. Thus an unlearned redundant cue added in overtraining should not be sampled; and if it is, it should produce some errors, which typically are not observed in experiments showing less then complete blocking. In the next chapter, we shall describe a more general theory which separates performance from learning and handles graded blocking phenomena.

NOVELTY AND CUE SELECTION
DURING OVERTRAINING

When novel cues are added during overtraining, the restrictive sampling assumptions of the model are known to fail. In Chapter 3 we found that novel, relevant, and redundant cues were learned by some subjects during overtraining. Recently, Guy, VanFleet, and Bourne (1966) studied concept-identification problems where during overtraining they introduced a novel relevant cue, irrelevant cue, or partially relevant cue. After overtraining the subjects were transferred to problems in which the novel cue alone was relevant and the previously relevant cue became irrelevant. Comparisons of transfer performance were used to infer whether subjects had learned anything about the function of the novel cue.

In their first experiment, Guy, VanFleet, and Bourne did not inform their subjects regarding the possible stimulus dimensions, and a salient background cue was used as the added dimension. Subjects received zero, ten, or twenty post-criterion trials. For each of these overtraining conditions, three groups were run: one group had a novel irrelevant cue; one group had a novel relevant cue; the third group had no novel cue added during overtraining. All three groups were transferred to a common problem with only the novel background cue as the relevant dimension. The results showed no increase in positive transfer as a function of the amount of overtraining with a novel relevant cue. However, if in overtraining the novel cue was irrelevant, transfer to it was increasingly negative with more overtraining. These data suggest that subjects sampled the novel cue during overtraining and rejected it because it was irrelevant. Taken together, however, the results in the Guy, VanFleet, and Bourne experiment appear to be inconsistent: on one hand, they find evidence for sampling and rejection of a novel, irrelevant cue during overtraining; but on the other hand, they do not find sampling and learning of a novel, relevant cue during overtraining. Interpretation of their study is complicated further by the fact that the groups that were simply overtrained (without the novel cue) showed the most positive transfer to the novel cue problem. Apparently, overtraining on the original set of stimuli enhances the surprise or novelty of the cue introduced at the beginning of transfer, thus enhancing attention to it.

In the second experiment, Guy, VanFleet, and Bourne again did not instruct the subjects as to what dimensions would be used and the salient background cue was the novel dimension. Four groups were run. During twenty post-criterion trials, the added cue was either irrelevant (50 percent correct), partially relevant (75 percent correct), relevant (100 percent correct), or absent. On transfer, the four groups averaged 37, 31, 16, and 8 trials to criterion, respectively. The difference between the relevant and absent groups was significant; but differences were not statistically reliable between the irrelevant, partially relevant, and relevant groups. Despite the lack of significant findings, the trend of the data suggests that some cue rejection or resampling occurred during overtraining. In a subsidiary analysis, the authors reported that the backward learning curve for the 312 subjects was stationary at .50 correct over all trials prior to the last error before learning. This finding is consistent with hypothesis-testing models, although the overtraining results are not.

In a similar study, Hergenhahn, Myers, and Capehart (1966) investigated the effect of introducing a novel, relevant, and redundant cue during overtraining in a concept-identification task. A control group learned to a criterion of ten successive correct responses, received ten overtraining trials, and then was transferred to a problem with a novel cue relevant and the previously relevant cue removed. A second group learned the problem with a single cue relevant, then had ten overtraining trials with a novel relevant and redundant cue added, and then was transferred to the problem with the novel cue relevant and the formerly relevant cue removed. The second group showed more positive transfer performance than the control group, indicating learning of the novel relevant cue during overtraining. Note that the results here are just the

187

opposite of those found by Guy, VanFleet, and Bourne, where the transfer problem included the formerly relevant cue as an irrelevant cue, requiring a "nonreversal" shift.

In concept identification, then, novel cues introduced during over-training may be attended to and learned, although the conditions promoting more or less of this, and causing the conflicting results, are presently obscure. Presumably, a novel stimulus may elicit an orienting reflex when it is first introduced, thereby increasing the chances that it will be sampled and learned. An interesting auxiliary relation here is that continued exposure to older cues can enhance the novelty effect, as suggested by the results of Guy, VanFleet, and Bourne (1966). A more definitive experiment on this effect would be to hold the number of overtraining trials constant but to introduce the novel relevant cue at different points. Following overtraining, all subjects are tested for what is learned. The expectation would be that the later the novel cue was introduced, the more it would be learned and the better would be transfer to it. This expectation goes counter to a simple reinforcement theory.

CUE NOVELTY, SELECTION, AND THE NUMBER OF PRIOR
OVERTRAINING TRIALS

In the Guy, VanFleet, and Bourne experiment, three events were confounded which may have contributed to their findings: the number of trials prior to the introduction of the novel cue, the forcing of errors by making the previously relevant cue irrelevant (a nonreversal shift problem), and new learning in transfer. A small pilot study carried out by Robert Rosenbaum at UCLA aimed at removing these confounds and testing the notion that the novelty of a cue depends upon the number of prior overtraining trials on the original problem.

Rosenbaum's experiment was analogous to the second study of Guy, VanFleet, and Bourne except that he used no transfer problem to assess what was learned. Instead, during overtraining, subjects were shifted onto a problem with a novel cue while the original relevant cue was retained. Hence overtraining performance was errorless and the question of interest is whether or not the subjects would learn the relevance of the novel cue when it became a RRC along with the original relevant cue. After overtraining the subjects received nonreinforced tests on each of the component cues in order to assess what was learned. The problems of nonreversal shift effects, errors, and so on are thus removed and one may vary directly the number of trials prior to the introduction of the novel cue in overtraining.

188

The stimuli were geometric patterns identical to those used in Chapter 3 except that they were drawn in India ink rather than color pencil, and the responses were Alpha and Beta. It will be recalled that the attributes were the shape, location of a dot, number of interior lines, and position of an open side; the shape was the relevant cue in original learning and the other three attributes were irrelevant. Color was not present as a dimension in the original problem but was introduced as the novel cue by using red or blue instead of white index cards as backgrounds for the central figure.

All subjects learned the shape problem to a criterion of ten successive correct responses and then underwent one of four overtraining conditions. Following this, they received single-cue tests for their learning of the shape and the novel color cues. There were forty subjects; ten subjects each were randomly assigned to one of the four conditions.

In a "control" condition for novelty, group R had the color of the stimulus card introduced as a novel RRC with shape immediately after reaching the learning criterion. In this condition, twenty overtraining trials on the RRC problem were given, followed by individual tests on the color and shape attributes along with a questionnaire. To test for novelty, defined as the number of prior overtraining trials, group N was first given forty-eight additional overtraining trials on the shape problem after reaching criterion. The color was then introduced as a novel RRC for twenty trials which, in turn, were followed by testing. If novelty of the color were enhanced by the number of prior overtraining trials, then one would expect more subjects in group N than in group R to learn the color.

Rosenbaum also tested for the learning of a partially valid novel cue during overtraining. In group I, subjects were introduced to the color immediately after reaching criterion but it was irrelevant (50 percent pairing with the classificatory responses) for forty-eight trials. The color became a RRC for an additional twenty trials and testing followed. In a partial validity condition, group P had the novel color attribute introduced immediately after criterion. Each value was paired 75 percent of the trials with one classificatory response (e.g., red was associated with Alpha for eighteen trials, with Beta for six trials, and blue was associated with Beta for eighteen trials, with Alpha for six trials). Then, as in condition I, the color became a RRC for twenty trials and testing followed. If the subjects learned the partial validity of the novel color cue during overtraining, one would expect more learning of the color in group P than in group I.

In acquisition, the four groups showed nearly identical performance. On the questionnaire, 31/40 subjects indicated having learned

189

only the shape; thus nine subjects had resampled and learned the novel color cue during overtraining. In the sorting tests, the thirty-one subjects who learned only the shape sorted 100 percent correctly on this cue but only 53 percent correctly on the color; the nine subjects who verbalized both the color and the shape sorted 100 percent correctly on the shape tests and 86 percent correctly on the color tests. Two subjects contributed the errors on the color tests and they indicated having regarded the neutralized shapes (squares) on the color tests as similar to triangles; this kind of error was infrequent in other experiments.

For novelty and RRC learning, we compare the number of subjects who learned both the color and shape in groups R and N. In group R, which had the novel color introduced as a RRC immediately after reaching criterion, two out of ten subjects learned the color cue; in group N, which received considerable overtraining before the color was introduced, six out of ten subjects learned the color. This difference approached significance by a Fisher exact probability test ($p = .08$). Resampling of novel redundant cues during overtraining was apparently facilitated by more overtraining on the original problem prior to introduction of the novel cue. These data support the idea that novelty may be directly manipulated in this manner.

There was, however, no effect of making a cue partially valid during overtraining. For group P, which had 75 percent valid color cues introduced after criterion, no subjects learned the color. For group I, where the novel cue was irrelevant, one subject learned the color during the last block of twenty RRC trials. This finding is inconsistent with those of Hughes and North (1959) and Guy, VanFleet, and Bourne (1966), and supports the sampling theory regarding the learning of partially valid cues.

This experiment on cue novelty, although a pilot study, indicates that subjects resample novel cues during overtraining and that continued overtraining enhances the novelty of a cue. Presumably, a larger orienting reflex is elicited after longer exposure to the familiar cues of the original problem.

OTHER OVERTRAINING EFFECTS

Considerable discussion has centered recently on the finding that overtraining facilitates the learning of a discrimination reversal by rats. For example, rats are trained to approach the black arm of a T maze for food reward. After reaching a learning criterion, the animals are then divided into two groups. One group is immediately shifted onto the reversal problem, to approach white and avoid black; the other group is given an additional, large number of overtraining trials on the original discrimination before being shifted onto the reversal problem. If the group receiving overtraining learns the reversal faster than the group that learned to a criterion, then one obtains what has come to be termed the overtraining reversal effect (ORE).

The many and seemingly contradictory investigations on the ORE have been given extensive treatment in reviews by Mackintosh (1965a), Paul (1965), and Sperling (1965a, b), so that little more can be added to their discussion here. In general, two factors seem to relate to the finding of the ORE. One factor is the amount of reward: if the rats receive large rewards, they reverse faster than when they receive small ones, regardless of the kind of discriminanda (cf. Theios & Blosser, 1965). The second factor is the kind of discriminanda. In general, if the stimuli are visual, then the ORE is obtained; if the discrimination is positional, it is less likely to occur. Gardner (1966) has warned of the dangers in using the "box score" method to draw such conclusions, however, pointing out that there is a relationship between date of publication and negative results on finding of the ORE. It seems that the majority of findings prior to 1961 are positive whereas those since 1961 tend to be negative. Such a correlation could be a result of refined experimentation and the unreliability of the phenomena in question, although recent well-controlled experiments by Mackintosh and Theios and Blosser would seem to rule out this conjecture.

So far as attentional theory is concerned, Lovejoy (1965) and Mackintosh (1965b) have interpreted the ORE as supporting some version of a two-process, attentional theory of discrimination learning. In theory, the rate of reversal learning depends on (a) the strength of the relevant analyzer at the start of the reversal series and (b) the specific quantitative effects of rewards and nonrewards in altering both the responses associated to the values of the relevant attribute and the strength of the relevant analyzer. Roughly speaking, if the relevant analyzer is strong and if changes in the output-response connections occur faster than changes in the analyzer strengths, then reversal learning will be fast, because the relevant analyzer will almost always be switched in. If initial learning of the relevant analyzer is slow, then overtraining may speed up reversal learning because it enables the analyzer strength to grow to a high value, from which it can endure despite the early nonreinforcements during reversal. Lovejoy has argued that the differences in ORE provided by visual versus spatial discriminations in rats are due to the visual and spatial analyzers being of initially low or initially high strengths, respectively; if so, then the overtraining increment to the relevant analyzer (and hence the ORE) would appear in the

191

former but not in the latter case. Of further relevance to the attentional theory is its prediction that overtraining will retard a nonreversal shift whereas it will facilitate a reversal shift; evidence supporting this prediction has been reviewed by Mackintosh (1965b).

The present sampling theory does not handle these ORE results. In fact, the larger problem of the effects of overlearning per se (cf. Mandler, 1962) are simply outside the scope of the present essay. We mention these problems to indicate our awareness of them and to indicate that we recognize the limitations of the specific model we are using in our investigations.

OVERTRAINING AND PAIRED-ASSOCIATE RRC LEARNING

We now consider some human data in paired-associate experiments involving the RRC overtraining design. The two experiments available at this writing provide conflicting results. One experiment, by Houston (1967), found no evidence for an increase in learning of the weaker cue during overlearning; the other, by James and Greeno (1967), found a slight increase in cue learning with overlearning.

The first experiment by Houston (1967) involved seven stimulus compounds consisting of trigrams surrounded by colored borders. This PA list was learned for one, three, twelve, or twenty trials by different groups. Within each degree of learning, three independent groups were given five transfer learning trials with a problem involving both the color and the trigram, or the color alone, or the trigram alone. Table 7.2 summarizes Houston's transfer data. In the table it can be seen that correct responding on transfer was about the same for the color and the color-trigram groups. This, in conjunction with the poor transfer to trigrams, indicates that the color was the dominant cue in the com-

TABLE 7.2. MEAN NUMBER OF CORRECT RESPONSES IN TRANSFER

Transfer Stimuli	Degree of Training in Trials			
	1	3	12	20
Color and trigram	25.2	27.7	32.7	34.7
Color	25.1	25.2	34.1	34.4
Trigram	11.3	15.8	16.9	17.6

(Data from Houston, 1967.)

192

pounds. With twelve trials of initial training, learning was nearly asymptotic on the compounds and the colors, so the comparison of immediate interest is between the twelve- and twenty-trial groups in their transfer to the weaker, trigram cue. It can be seen that no substantial increase in transfer occurred for the trigram components (16.9 versus 17.6). From this, it appears that five overtraining trials did not increase subjects' learning of the weaker, redundant cue in PAL. And this result is consistent with our sampling assumptions. In a second experiment, Houston instructed subjects before learning that they would be tested for transfer to the trigrams. This instruction produced somewhat more transfer to the trigrams but again there was no difference in correct responding on either the first trial or overall transfer for the groups receiving twelve and twenty training trials.

In the James and Greeno (1967) study, subjects learned a list of eight paired-associates with a word plus a nonsense syllable as RRC's for a digit response. After subjects were trained to a criterion of either four out of eight correct responses, a single perfect trial, or one perfect trial plus ten overtraining trials, they received a transfer test with the eight words alone and the eight nonsense syllables alone as stimuli. More transfer occurred to the words than to the nonsense syllables in all groups. Subjects trained to one perfect trial showed the same low transfer to the syllables as did subjects trained to only four out of eight correct responses. However, subjects who were overtrained showed a greater proportion of correct responses to the weaker syllable cue on transfer. These results were replicated in a second experiment. In a third experiment, subjects were first trained to a criterion of one perfect trial and then received further training on the mastered items as well as on some newly introduced items. These subjects showed no more transfer to the nonsense components of the first learned items than did subjects receiving only training to criterion before the transfer test. The interpretation given was that subjects initially select the more salient stimulus aspects until the list is mastered, but following mastery attention is "freed" to notice less obvious features of the stimulus compounds.

This completes our review of the conflicting literature on overtraining and incidental learning of cues as these bear upon our sampling assumptions.

SOME NEW EXPERIMENTS
ON RRC OVERLEARNING

None of the studies of concept identification has tested our sampling assumptions under ideal conditions in which novelty effects are avoided. We carried out two experiments on this topic. In both experiments, subjects first learned a problem involving two RRC's to a criterion of ten successive correct responses; half of these subjects immediately received single-cue tests for what they learned, and the other half received fifty overtraining trials before testing. If resampling of cues does not occur when a subject responds correctly, then the proportion of subjects who learn both cues should be the same in the two groups. If resampling occurs, then the proportion of two-cue learners should be greater in the overtrained group.

Experiment I used letter clusters as stimuli, and Experiment II used geometric patterns. In the latter experiment, we attempted to manipulate attention to the relevant cues by placing them physically close or far apart in the stimulus display.

EXPERIMENT I
Method

Procedure: The experiment consisted of three phases. Subjects first were trained individually to a criterion of ten successive correct responses on a concept-identification problem involving relevant and redundant letters. Half of the subjects then were immediately tested for their learning on individual letters and compounds by sorting test cards into categories; the other half were given fifty overtraining trials before testing. After sorting, the subjects were questioned about their solution hypotheses.

The subject was instructed that his task was to learn to classify a set of cards containing letters according to a rule known to the experimenter. If he thought a card fit the rule, he was to respond "Yes," if not, "No." Cards were presented one at a time on a holder. The subject classified the cards at his own pace. He was shown the card and its correct classification for four seconds after responding. Then a new card was presented for him to classify after removal of the preceding card and its classification. A different order of stimulus presentations was given to each subject by shuffling the deck of cards before training and each time the stimulus deck was reused.

After the subject reached criterion or finished overtraining, the experimenter instructed him to sort test cards into Yes, No, and Question Mark (?) categories according to the rule he just learned. After sorting through the deck, subjects who used the (?) category were asked to resort cards from that category into Yes and No. Then, questions regarding the rule and basis for sorting followed. In asking the latter questions, the experimenter went through each letter in a random order. Then the experimenter asked if the subject had guessed on any cards when sorting.

194

Training and Test Stimuli: The stimulus patterns were four capital letters typed in a diamond arrangement on white 3×5-inch file cards. The four "dimensions" were the four letter pairs (F, B), (Z, H), (W, J), and (K, N). One letter from each of these four pairs was drawn to compose a stimulus pattern. The relevant letter pairs were (F, B) and (Z, H) and these were redundant, that is, only FZ or BH would occur. Thus patterns containing FZ belonged to the "Yes" class and those containing BH belonged to the "No" class. In one problem the relevant and redundant letters appeared at random in all four positions around the diamond pattern; in the other problem the two relevant letters always occupied opposite locations in the diamond, although their exact locations were varied over trials. There were two redundant pairs, four irrelevant letter combinations, and eight permutations of positional arrangements of the relevant and irrelevant letters, making a total of sixty-four different patterns in all.

The test deck consisted of seventy-two different patterns. All irrelevant letters were used in the tests. Four subsets of eight patterns each tested the single relevant letters; in the B and F tests, the neutral letter X replaced the Z or H letter; in the Z and H tests, the neutral letter D replaced the B or F letter. Four subsets of eight patterns each tested the combinations of the relevant letter pairs: sixteen cards tested the original relevant pairs used in training (FZ or BH) and sixteen cards opposed the relevant training letters (FH or BZ). Finally, eight cards contained only the irrelevant letters and the D, X substitutes.

Experimental Design and Groups: The experiment involved a 2×2 design with the following factors: (1) position of the two relevant letters, either opposite or random, and (2) the degree of training, either to a criterion of ten successive correct responses or to the same criterion plus fifty overtraining trials. There were four experimental groups. The groups are designated LO, LO-50, LR, LR-50, where 50 refers to overtraining and LO and LR denote opposite or random letters, respectively.

Subjects: The subjects were sixty-four undergraduates from introductory psychology classes at the University of California, Los Angeles. Subjects were randomly assigned to four groups of sixteen with the restriction that the proportion of males and females be equal across experimental conditions.

RESULTS

The four groups did not differ significantly from one another in speed of learning as shown either by mean number of errors or by trials

195

to criterion. In overtraining, subjects in group *LO*-50 made a total of four errors; those in group *LR*-50 made seven errors.

Recall that each subject was asked to first sort the test cards without feedback into three categories: Yes, No, and (?). If the subject used the (?) category, he was then asked to resort those cards into Yes and No categories. Finally, he was asked to state the hypothesis that he used to classify the cards during training.

In terms of stated hypotheses, subjects used one of two forms: *complementation* or *dimensionalized* hypotheses. For subjects who learned one component, the two kinds of hypotheses were either of the form "*A* is a Yes and not-*A* is a No" or of the form "*A* is a Yes and *C* is a No." For those who learned two components, the hypotheses were either of the form "*A, B* is a Yes and not-*A, B* is a No" or of the form "*A, B* is a Yes and *C, D* is a No." The number of subjects offering each type of hypothesis in each of the four letter conditions is reported in Table 7.3.

In Table 7.3, 38/64 or 59 percent of the subjects gave complementation hypotheses but the frequency of this type of hypothesis bears no relation to the training condition. We regard these complementation hypotheses as resulting from the use of nondimensionalized letter pairs as stimuli. In contrast, when geometric patterns with known dimensions are used, as in the next experiment, such hypotheses are very infrequent; that is, subjects will state "red is in category 1 and green is in category 2" and not "red is in category 1, everything else is in category 2."

The random and opposite arrangements of relevant letters had no effect on the number of subjects stating two-letter solutions. Therefore

TABLE 7.3. NUMBER OF SUBJECTS STATING VARIOUS SOLUTION HYPOTHESES

Group	Type of Hypothesis			
	One Letter		Two Letters	
	A; Not-*A*	*A, C*	*A, B;* Not-*A, B*	*A, B;* *C, D*
LO	4	4	6	2
LO-50	5	1	5	5
LR	3	4	6	3
LR-50	4	5	5	2
Totals	16	14	22	12

the results of groups *LO* and *LR* (criterion groups) and of groups *LO*-50 and *LR*-50 (overtraining groups) were combined to evaluate the overtraining effect on cue selection. By this combination, the frequency of one-cue solvers (15) and of two-cue solvers (17) is identical for the overtrained and criterion groups. Thus this first experiment supports our sampling assumption that subjects do not learn new cues on correct response trials but learn only those relevant cues that were in the focus sample on the last error trial.

The sorting data with this experimental arrangement were somewhat complicated and a subject's sorting behavior can best be understood in conjunction with his verbalized hypothesis. A check for a consistency of the sorting with the stated hypothesis revealed that subjects were consistent, but that some used different sorting strategies for the same kind of hypothesis. Therefore, instead of presenting the sorting data alone, we shall report this consistency analysis. Table 7.4 summarizes the analyses and gives the solution hypotheses along with the sorting strategies and observed outcomes. No differences were found among the four groups so their data were combined in Table 7.4.

In Table 7.4 it can be seen that the single-cue solution hypotheses (*A*, Yes, not-*A*, No; or *A*, Yes, *C*, No) led to unique sorting strategies by the subjects. For the *A*, not-*A* type, all sixteen subjects sorted the *A* component cards into the Yes category and the remaining components (including the reinforced *B*, Yes component) into No. For subject stating the *A*, *C* hypothesis, the *A* component was sorted correctly into Yes and the *C* component correctly into No, but the unlearned relevant *B* and *D* letters were sorted randomly and were correct only 51 percent of the time.

For the two-letter hypotheses (*AB*, not-*AB*; or *AB*, *CD*), the sorting strategies differed within and between types. For the *AB*, not-*AB* type, ten of the subjects responded as if they had learned all four relevant letters; they sorted the *A* and *B* components into Yes, and *C* and *D* into No. The other eleven subjects of this *AB*, not-*AB* type treated all components as No. In a sense, these subjects "patterned" their solutions by responding correctly to compounds but not to components. One subject of this type sorted components randomly. Finally, ten subjects stating the *AB*, *CD* hypothesis tended to sort correctly on components, while two subjects of this type sorted the components at random.

As suggested earlier, the varied sorting behaviors in this experiment were likely a result of two factors—the use of nondimensionalized (arbitrary) letter pairs as stimuli, and the "Yes-No" format in which the concept learning was cast. That format tends to induce a set for asymme-

197

TABLE 7.4. SOLUTION HYPOTHESES AND SORTING STRATEGIES FOR LETTER PROBLEMS

Verbalized Solution Type	Number of Subjects	Component Sorting Strategy
One letter:		
A, Yes; not-*A*, No	16	*A* in Yes; not-*A* in No
A, Yes; *C*, No	14	*A* in Yes; *C* in No; *B*, *D* random
Two letters:		
AB, Yes; not-*AB*, No	10	*AB* in Yes; *CD* in No
	11	All components are No
	1	Sort components randomly
AB, Yes; *CD*, No	10	*AB* in Yes; *CD* in No
	2	Sort components randomly

try in the subject's partitioning of the stimulus population. It may be recalled that such diverse sorting behaviors were not obtained in the "letters" experiment in Chapter 6 where a "dimension" was coordinated with a single letter that appeared in upper or lower case. Presumably, the two values (*F* and *f*) are treated as related elements and the unit is selected as though it were a single dimension, much like the attributes of geometric figures.

EXPERIMENT II
Method

Procedure: The procedure of Experiment II was the same as that for Experiment I, except that the stimuli were geometric figures, the responses consisted of pressing buttons, labeled One and Two, and no "question mark" category was used in the test series. Feedback lamps, one above each button, informed the subject of the correct button during training; in testing, feedback was omitted and the subject pressed a button to each test card. The instructions were virtually identical to those used in Chapter 3 with additional comments on using the buttons and the role of the feedback lamps.

Training and Text Stimuli: The training stimuli were geometric figures drawn in colored pencil on white 3 × 5-inch file cards. On each card

TABLE 7.4. (CONTINUED)

Number of Cards	Proportion Consistent	Proportion Correct on Compounds
128	.97 (.06) [a]	.99
384	.96 (.06)	
112	.94 (.04)	.94
112	.94 (.04)	
224	.51 (correct) (.08)	
160	.85 (.07)	.94
160	.73 (.06)	
352	.98 (.01)	.94
16	.50 (correct)	1.00
160	.79 (.03)	.95
160	.79 (.04)	
32	.53 (correct)	1.00

[a]Number in parentheses is average deviation of the individual proportions from the mean proportion.

there were three black outline figures. Two figures were constant: an arrow and a circle; one figure varied in shape and was either a square or a triangle, thus providing one of the dimensions. Two dimensions were irrelevant: the direction of the arrow (pointed up or down) and the size of the circle (large—one inch in diameter; or small—one-half inch in diameter). The shape, arrow direction, and size dimensions varied independently and their positions were completely counterbalanced in the deck, totaling $2^3 \times 3! = 48$ different training patterns.

The relevant and redundant cues were the shape dimension and the color (red or green) completely filling one of the figures. In one condition, the relevant dimensions were physically contiguous: the triangles were colored red and the squares were colored green. In another condition, the cues were separated: whenever a card contained a square (triangle), the circle was colored green (red).

In testing, there were a total of forty cards. Sixteen cards tested for color by removing the triangles or squares. Sixteen cards tested for shape by removing the colors. Eight cards contained only the arrows and circles, omitting the colors and shapes, and were included to reduce the possibility of selecting and using the color or shape by chance during the test series.

199

Experimental Design and Groups: There were four groups in the experiment which constituted a 2×2 factorial design. The factors were the degree of training (ten consecutively correct responses or ten consecutively correct responses plus fifty overtraining trials) and the spatial proximity of the two relevant dimensions (either together or separate). The four groups will be designated as T, T-50, S, S-50, where 50 denotes the overtrained groups and T or S refers to the relevant cues being together or separate, respectively.

Subjects: The subjects were ninety-six undergraduates from introductory psychology classes at the University of California, Los Angeles. The subjects were randomly assigned to four equal groups of twenty-four with the restriction that the proportion of males in each group be the same.

RESULTS

The four groups did not differ significantly from one another with respect to errors or trials to criterion in training. In overtraining, seven subjects in group S-50 and two subjects in group T-50 made one error each.

On the basis of their verbal reports, the subjects were classified as to solution type: color, shape, or both color and shape. Table 7.5 summarizes these classifications for the four groups.

In Table 7.5 it can be seen that overtraining led to an increase in the number of subjects who learned both cues. Given training to criterion, the probability of a two-cue solution was .17; given overtraining, it was .46. The difference was statistically reliable ($\chi^2 = 9.50$, $p < .01$). These data indicate that, with geometric figures, further sampling of cues occurred during overtraining while the subjects were making correct responses. These data directly contradict our sampling assumptions.

TABLE 7.5. NUMBER OF SUBJECTS WHO SOLVED ON COLOR, SHAPE, OR BOTH: EXPERIMENT II

Group	Solution Type		
	Color	Shape	Both
Criterion:			
T	20	0	4
S	16	4	4
Overtraining:			
T-50	10	1	13
S-50	14	1	9

In Table 7.5 there is about a threefold increase in two-cue solutions with fifty trials of overtraining. The ratio of total trials in overtraining to trials in training was about 12 to 1 for group *S*-50 and 8 to 1 for group *T*-50. The quantitative relations among the numbers do not provide much support for the conjecture of James and Greeno (1967), that subjects *relax* their attention and learn more cues after mastering the problem. That is, an eight- or twelve-fold increase in trials (beyond mastery) produced a 3.25- or 2.25-fold increase in the frequency of two-cue learners for groups *T*-50 and *S*-50, respectively. The ratio of overlearning-to-learning trials for the two groups is reversed from the amount of increase in two-cue solvers. And in either case, a very large amount of overtraining still left over half the subjects ignorant about the weaker relevant cue.

TABLE 7.6. CORRECT CLASSIFICATIONS ON COMPONENT TESTS AS A FUNCTION OF STATED SOLUTION TYPES

Stated Solution	N	Proportion Correct	
		Color Tests	Shape Tests
Color	960	.91	.54
Shape	96	.51	.88
Both	256	.99	.96

Although we had expected that more two-cue solutions would result from physical proximity of the colors and shapes (condition *T*), the data in Table 7.5 show only a slight increase in the number of two-cue solutions (from 13 to 17) when the stimuli appeared together rather than separated. The probability that subjects learned both cues was .35 when they appeared together and .27 when they were apart, an insignificant difference ($\chi^2 = .78$, $p > .05$).

The sorting test results were compared with the verbal hypotheses. Generally subjects sorted consistently with their verbal hypotheses. Table 7.6 gives the proportion of correct classifications as a function of the stated solution type.

As can be seen in Table 7.6 for subjects who stated having solved on a given dimension, classifications on that dimension were quite accurate; for dimensions not stated as a solution, the classifications were near chance correct. The less than perfect sorting on stated dimensions was attributable to a few subjects in each condition who sorted all components at chance. These subjects, when questioned, indicated that they were trying to be consistent throughout the test series and the only cue they could use to do this was the (irrelevant) arrows. It will be noted that the shapes and colors were absent from the color and shape tests, respectively, but that the arrows were in all tests. There were no cases in which a subject sorted correctly on a cue but did not verbalize it as a solution. For the color solvers, nine subjects sorted both components at chance; for the shape solvers, one subject sorted both components at chance; and for the both solvers, one subject sorted both components at chance. This discrepancy between verbal hypotheses and sorting data was not found as markedly in our previous studies with geometric figures.

SUMMARY

This chapter concerned the effect of overtraining beyond mastery upon the probability that a subject learns both relevant cues in a RRC problem. The sampling theory presented in Chapter 2 implies that further learning would not occur during post-criterion trials. Some experimental literature related to this question was reviewed, including both animal and human work. In both cases, the literature was conflicting regarding any general proposition: under some presently ill-defined circumstances, subjects (animals or humans) apparently learn little, if anything, about an alternate relevant cue during post-criterion trials, whereas under other circumstances some incidental learning occurs with the relevant cue. Either novelty of the new cue or gradual fading out of the old cue apparently increases the chances of the new cue being learned during overtraining. A pilot study was reported which used human subjects and concept identification. This study showed that novelty depends upon the number of prior overtraining trials and that subjects do not learn partially valid cues.

In two larger experiments human subjects were overtrained on a concept-identification task where both relevant cues had been present from the outset of training. One experiment used arbitrary pairs of letters as pseudo-dimensions of letter patterns. Some subjects were trained to criterion and others were overtrained for fifty trials post-criterion on a RRC problem. In that experiment, overtraining had no effect on the proportion of two-cue solvers: 53 percent of the subjects in each condition stated solution hypotheses involving both cues. In the second experiment, patterns of geometric figures were used as stimuli for a RRC problem. Again one group was trained to criterion and the other received fifty post-criterion trials before single-cue testing. In this experiment, post-criterion training significantly increased the proportion of two-cue learners from 17 to 46 percent.

Although these studies contribute to the literature information on a new combination of conditions and overlearning, they provide little help in resolving the conflicting evidence on the issue of overtraining and incidental cue learning. A number of task-situational variables controlling the effect remain to be identified. An obvious controlling variable in the concept-identification studies is the dimensionalization of the relevant stimulus variable, as our results show. The negative evidence in the literature indicates that our sampling assumptions are not generally valid regarding overlearning—that is, subjects *can* learn something about incidental cues during overtraining in which their performance is being controlled primarily by the first cue learned. A somewhat more general theory is needed which implies that amount of incidental cue learning is a graded phenomenon, with less of it (not necessarily zero) occurring when another relevant cue is predominantly controlling the subject's behavior. A more general theory of this type is tentatively advanced in the last section of the next chapter.

8

OVERVIEW AND DISCUSSION

This final chapter presents a brief overview of our findings and their interpretation. Some topics and issues that were either omitted or not discussed appropriately in the preceding chapters will be considered.

In overview, we have sought to establish a firm relation between the attention value of a cue, the rate of learning a discrimination problem in which it is relevant, and the likelihood that the cue is learned in a RRC problem. The mathematical model in Chapter 2 is only one of several possible implementations of these general ideas. The advantages of that specific model, relative to others briefly considered, are its tractability and the fact that its predictions are a function of a few parameters for which estimates are easily obtained. The strategy was to use this model to guide us through studies of RRC learning, and to determine the extent to which these experiments could be interpreted in the specific terms of this model.

The first major experiment (in Chapter 3) showed that adult human subjects solved a RRC problem in one of three exclusive ways: on cue *A*, or cue *B*, or on both cues. These appeared to be all-or-nothing solutions in that the subject responded perfectly to a learned cue, but responded at chance to an unlearned cue, and, in the latter case, had no idea that the unlearned cue was relevant. The method of testing on each cue singly with each subject was noted to have many advantages over traditional methods of averaging over subjects transferred to problems involving one or the other retained relevant cue. This would appear to be a significant methodological point for future studies of what is learned in RRC problems.

The initial experiment established that the model could predict both the learning rate and the probability distribution of solution types in a RRC problem from knowledge of the learning rates for control subjects who learned problems involving the single relevant cues. The cue that was learned faster also dominated in the solution type. This experiment also demonstrated a "blocking" effect, whereby a first-learned cue "blocks" the learning of a redundant relevant cue added during over-training. When the added, redundant cue had been irrelevant during initial training, no subject learned its relevance. When the added, redundant cue was novel, a small percentage of the subjects learned its relevance. This blocking effect also occurred when subjects were required to label overtly the stimulus attributes during the post-criterion, redundant phase; this result forces a conceptual distinction between noticing and using a cue in a sample focus for classification. The assumption that subjects do not resample when they are correct is adequate to explain this blocking effect; the effect is similar to that reported by Thorndike (1928) on "belongingness" which appears also to be due to low sampling (and rehearsal) probabilities for certain "incidental" cues later tested for association.

The experiment in Chapter 4 extended these findings to the prediction of transfer to single-cue problems following learning of a RRC problem. If following $A + B$ training the subject is shifted to a problem with A relevant and B irrelevant, then the theory predicts all-or-none transfer. The expectation was that subjects who initially solved on cue A would transfer with no errors; those who initially solved on cue B (now irrelevant) would show no specific transfer and would learn the second problem at the same rate as appropriate control subjects. These expectations were supported. Positive transfer from RRC training was confined exclusively to the incidence of "zero errors." Those RRC trained subjects who made one or more errors in transfer learned no faster than did appropriate control subjects. As expected, the unconditional average errors in transfer were less when the more salient of the RRC's was retained as relevant in transfer. This lower mean resulted primarily from the high frequency of subjects who made zero errors, indicating the relative dominance of the more salient cue in the solutions of the initial RRC problem. The transfer results were quantitatively predicted by the sampling model. The model was also modified to handle some aspects of nonreversal shift learning.

In Chapter 5 our argument was extended to paired-associate learning. Colors and nonsense syllables acted as RRC's for the paired-associate response. Evidence for additivity of learning rates was found in PAL, and the tripartite division of subject-item protocols into solution types (color, syllable, or both) also resulted. The frequencies of solution types following RRC paired-associate training was predicted using the learning-rate estimates obtained from control groups who learned with the color or the syllable as the only relevant component. Although the initial literature review in Chapter 1 established the generality of selec-

205

tive learning in RRC (or compound-CS) situations, the paired-associate experiment demonstrated that our specific interpretation of "what is learned" is not restricted solely to experiments on discrimination learning.

The experiments in Chapter 6 examined the influence of cue salience and number of irrelevant cues upon the frequencies of solution types in RRC problems. In theory, increasing the number of irrelevant cues should lower the sampling probabilities of each relevant cue, thus producing slower learning and fewer two-cue solutions. This was found in both experiments. Similarly, if the salience of one of the relevant cues is increased by emphasis or enhancement of its discriminability, then the theory expects an increase in the proportion of subjects who learn that cue. This also was found in both experiments. In the first experiment in Chapter 6, variations in the discriminability of the size cue produced large variations in the types of solution. In the second experiment in Chapter 6, emphasizing the letter J, or the letter N, or both 50 percent of the time produced a high frequency of solvers on J alone, N alone, or on both cues, respectively.

In Chapter 7 the question whether overtraining on a RRC problem enhances the probability of a two-cue solution was considered. The effect of cue novelty was shown to depend on the number of preceding trials on the initial discrimination. Subjects learned a novel RRC if a large number of overtraining trials were given prior to its introduction. Two other experiments were run, using letters or geometric figures as stimuli with the same RRC cues throughout. Overtraining increased the proportion of two-cue solvers with geometric but not with letter stimuli. In the former case, the overtraining effect was large and statistically significant; in the latter case, there was no suggestion of an effect. A revised sampling rule is needed to fit both these results and those on blocking, since the three outcomes are incompatible with the current assumption. These particular results leave several issues unresolved, and further research is needed on this question.

Having briefly reviewed the results of our experiments, a few general questions raised by this line of research and consideration of other variables than those investigated are now discussed.

DO SINGLE-CUE AND DOUBLE-CUE SOLVERS DIFFER?

The title of this section reflects a question often raised about our findings. This question has not been specifically investigated but post-facto analyses relevant to the question are possible and will be reported here.

206

If one supposes that individual differences in this task are negligible, then the baseline theory says that in particular conditions it is a chance affair whether a particular subject learns one or two cues. Of course, comparing *across conditions,* the theory implies that the learning rate of a problem and the probability of two-cue solutions are positively correlated. But suppose that we entertain the opposite view, that the one-cue and two-cue learners differ in multiple ways. For example, two-cue solvers might be generally brighter, faster learners, less rigid in their stimulus scanning, might retain or remember several cues simultaneously in their sample focus, and so forth. If one supposes that subjects differ in their probabilities of sampling the two relevant cues, then the theory would imply that those with high sampling probabilities would most likely learn fast and learn both cues. This possibility was investigated by performing post-facto analyses on error (learning) scores for subjects who solved in the three exclusive ways. The question is whether the two-cue solvers had a higher average learning rate than did the one-cue solvers.

The post-facto analyses of error scores are summarized in Table 8.1 for the experimental conditions reported in Chapters 3 and 6. For each condition is shown the number of subjects who solved in the three different ways, their average errors during learning, and, where appropriate, an F test for the significance of the differences among the mean error scores of the three subgroups. The F was not computed in one case where the number of subjects was too small (group 0).

The results in Table 8.1 do not indicate a general relationship between error scores and the number of cues in the solution focus. The differences in error scores between groups are neither consistently large nor consistently in one direction, and in all but one case they show nonsignificant effects. Among those ten conditions having two or more subjects solving on one and on both cues, there are four cases where the two-cue solvers make the fewest errors, two cases where they make the most errors, and four cases where their mean errors fall between those of the other subgroups of one-cue solvers.

On the basis of these data, one cannot conclude that there were any systematic differences between the learning rates of one-cue and two-cue solvers. This is what should occur according to the baseline theory, especially if individual differences in parameters are small.

However, almost any outcome of the post-facto analysis could be consistent with the baseline theory supplemented by assumptions about individual differences either in sampling probabilities or in sample size. For example, individual differences in sampling probabilities would induce a positive correlation between learning rate and number of cues in the solution focus. Individual differences in the sample size, s, by itself

207

TABLE 8.1. Post-Facto Analyses of Errors during Learning for Subjects Who Solve the Redundant Cue Problem in the Three Exclusive Ways

Experimental Group	Solution Type	N	Mean Errors	F
S D	Shape	31	5.39	
	Dot	45	3.31	1.79 [a]
	Both	13	2.31	
L3	Size	3	4.33	
	Color	36	5.31	1 [a]
	Both	1	0	
M3	Size	9	3.89	
	Color	19	4.42	1 [a]
	Both	12	4.10	
H3	Size	9	4.44	
	Color	12	6.33	2.34 [a]
	Both	19	4.23	
M1	Size	9	2.67	
	Color	14	1.93	1 [a]
	Both	17	2.03	
M5	Size	8	11.50	
	Color	22	4.87	2.87 [a]
	Both	10	8.40	
0	J	0	—	
	N	1	3.00	—
	Both	27	3.70	
1	J	10	5.80	
	N	9	4.56	1 [a]
	Both	9	8.77	
2	J	12	14.83	
	N	14	8.14	1.89 [a]
	Both	2	15.00	
N	J	0	—	
	N	23	3.48	1 [a]
	Both	5	2.80	
J	J	22	4.91	
	N	3	16.33	5.06 [b]
	Both	3	5.33	
J, N	J	4	9.75	
	N	5	9.00	1 [a]
	Both	19	8.86	

[a] $p > .05$.   [b] $p < .01$.

would not cause any correlation if the theory is correct in supposing that s affects what is learned but not the learning rate. An outcome that would be embarrassing to the theory would be a consistent negative correlation between learning rate and number of cues in the solution focus—that is, if one-cue solvers made fewer errors. This particular outcome can be seen to occur infrequently in Table 8.1.

CONFIGURAL LEARNING

In our RRC experiments, although the values of the two relevant dimensions always appeared together, the two-cue solvers had little difficulty responding on test trials to either component presented in isolation. That is, in these experiments there was little evidence of configural learning—the compound pattern was not the only functional stimulus.

Animals and men of course can learn configural problems when the differential reinforcement contingencies demand it. For example, a dog that is reinforced to bell plus light but not to bell alone or light alone will learn this configural discrimination. Similarly, a subject reinforced for saying "1" to red circles or blue triangles, and "2" to red triangles or blue circles will learn (with some difficulty) this configural discrimination. In these cases, the functional stimulus is the conjunction of the two components taken together, and, after learning, either component alone is unable to cue the response (e.g., in the second illustration, to "red" the subject would give an equal distribution of responses 1 and 2).

One may ask: if such configural learning can occur when the reinforcement contingencies require it, why does it not occur at least to some extent in our simple case, where the contingencies do not demand it, that is where single-cue solutions will suffice? The answer is that the very behavior that distinguishes configural from nonconfigural learning (i.e., transfer from patterns to components) is explicitly extinguished during training of a configural discrimination. In fact, it is the presence of such pattern-to-component transfer early in training that makes configural discriminations relatively difficult to train, since these transfer tendencies must first be inhibited via extinction. Thus an accurate description of the relations appears to be this: transfer always occurs from compounds to at least one of the components, unless such transfer responding has been specifically extinguished during training.

There are certain kinds of evidence that would appear embarrassing to this conclusion. These could arise if following differential conditioning to a pattern and extinction (to zero) to one of its components, one were to find transfer to the nonextinguished component to be substantially less than the response to the pattern. A hypothetical example in the Pavlovian situation would be the following: reinforced trials to light plus tone randomly alternate with nonreinforced trials to light alone; upon testing after training, the response amplitude (say, in drops of saliva) is ten to light plus tone, zero to light alone, and only five to tone alone.

After writing the foregoing, we came upon a recent report by Guth (1967) with just such a finding using rats as subjects in a "go-no go" discrimination. Guth trained rats to press a lever for food reward with a tone and a light $(T + L)$ acting as discriminative stimuli. Following training on the $T + L$ compound, the animals underwent experimental extinction to one of the component stimuli. Subgroups then were tested on either $T + L$, T alone, or L alone. Control groups were trained initially on T alone and L alone and were then extinguished on one component. Testing on the compound or component stimuli was also carried out for these controls.

Guth reasoned in the same manner as above: if learning of the $T + L$ stimulus was by components and not by the pattern, then responding to the $T + L$ compound in testing should be the same as that to the unextinguished component. If, however, there was pattern learning, then responding to the $T + L$ compound should be greater than that to the unextinguished component, indicating that the pattern was not affected by extinction on one of the components. The latter results were obtained in the experimental conditions while the former occurred for the controls.

A variety of ad hoc reasons can be supplied for why this generalization decrement might occur. First, there is the "surprise" effect of the novel test stimulus (tone alone), eliciting an OR that interferes with the conditioned response. Second, there could be generalization of extinction from the extinguished component to the nonextinguished component. This could be either direct (primary generalization) or mediated. For example, a mediator causing decrement for a human subject could be the developing hypothesis "respond to two components, but don't respond to one component." There also could be a failure of extinction on components to generalize to compounds in a similar fashion.

Although our two-cue solvers responded correctly for the most part on the single-cue tests, we did not record response latencies or obtain confidence ratings to see whether the subjects would show a slowing of reaction and loss of confidence on the single-cue tests. More than likely such latency effects would be obtained, even if the single-cue test patterns were interpolated during a prolonged criterion run. Although latency may increase when one learned component is removed or altered,

210

classification accuracy should remain if the alternate learned component is intact. This suggests a possible correlation between whether or not a component is learned and whether its alteration produces a slowing of reaction time. That is, subjects who learn cue A alone might be unaffected by alteration of cue B on test trials, whereas those who learn both cues would have slower reaction times when either one of the cues is altered. Such slower reaction times, if obtained, would be explained in the terms of interfering OR's.

VARIATIONS IN SAMPLE SIZE

Throughout prior discussions, the sample size, s, has been treated as a fixed parameter which we had hoped would remain constant over the conditions within an experiment. It is fruitful to turn the issue around, however, to consider the sample size as a dependent variable, and to inquire about experimental variables that could reasonably be expected to influence the sample size or the average size of the sample focus. The variables that may be expected to influence s may be classified generally as those relating to the task itself, the prior training of the subjects, and individual differences among the subjects. Each of these is now discussed in turn.

TASK VARIABLES

These variables may be subdivided according to whether they refer to the experimental procedure or to the arrangement of stimuli. An example of a procedural variable that should affect the sample size is the exposure time of the stimuli. It takes time to scan and identify or encode several attributes of a complex stimulus. This process would be limited if the exposure time is limited. This analysis suggests conducting discrimination experiments wherein the stimuli are presented very briefly by a tachistoscope. Independent of the effect of exposure time upon learning rate in such a situation, the proportion of two-cue solvers is expected to decrease with shorter exposure times.

A covariate that should affect sample size in *brief* exposure situations is the physical proximity or contiguity of the several attributes in the display. For example, a subject would be more likely to sample the color and shape cues if the stimulus were a solid red circle rather than a patch of red on the right and an outlined circle on the left of the visual field. Although physical contiguity of independent dimensions of stimulus variation appears on obvious variable in brief-exposure situations, our results in Chapter 7 indicate that it may not remain a significant

determinant of s with long stimulus exposures. Although physical contiguity (i.e., "closeness" in the visual field) might be expected to affect the
degree of correlation in the sampling of stimulus attributes, we did not
find more two-cue solutions when the RRC's were in close physical
contiguity.

Other proximity considerations come to mind if we take the view
that human subjects are probably encoding these stimuli into verbal
descriptions of dimensions. Thus the pattern consisting of two large blue
circles is probably encoded verbally in just that form, "two large blue
circles." Following this encoding, dimensions then are selected for use in
hypothesis testing. This analysis suggests trying to manipulate the style
or manner of encoding by instructions to the subjects, and investigating
whether the encoding method affects learning rate and sample size as
inferred from two-cue solutions. In this regard, Harris and Haber
(1963) and Haber (1964) showed the relevance of encoding order and
method in studies of selective attention and short-term memory. It is also
possible that coding order reflects directly the attention values of cues so
that operations such as emphasis may, in turn, affect the coding order as
well as rate of learning of a given attribute.

One possibility is to require (via instructions) that the attributes be
described overtly in a particular order. One then could examine learning
rate as a function of the ordinal position of the relevant attribute in the
encoding order. The probability of learning both cues in a redundant
problem would probably decrease with an increasing separation between
these two attributes in the forced encoding order. If these effects were
obtained, the interpretation would be similar to that of physical proximity, that is, the covariation of sampling probabilities of cues used in the
solution focus.

Another way to increase the average sample size is to use a shifting
emphasizer, as was done in the second experiment of Chapter 6. In the
experiment that involved alternately emphasizing the two relevant cues,
the frequency of two-cue solutions was larger than could be predicted
from prior estimates of s. This discrepancy is difficult to understand if
one supposes, as does the model, that cues are admitted into the sample
focus only on error trials, because only one of the relevant letters was
emphasized on any particular error trial. In turn, the discrepancy suggests that an emphasized cue may be incorporated into a sample focus
on correct response trials as well and learned if it is a relevant cue. To
the extent that this happens, the effective sample size is increased above
the baseline assumed by the model.

Another task variable likely to affect s is the information load
involved in any subsidiary task in which the person engages while

212

working on the central, discrimination task. The sample focus is a temporary listing of several hypotheses the person is trying out at the moment, consisting of $k(1 \leq k \leq s)$ pairs of associates of the form: (red-A, blue-B), (square-A, circle-B), (small-A, large-B), and so on. Presumably this listing is held in a short-term memory storage from trial to trial, and is altered and revised according to how incoming information is evaluated. It is known that short-term memory has a limited capacity for holding or handling information (e.g., Murdock, 1961; Posner, 1963), and that the memory for a given item can be severely degraded by a complex subsidiary task in which the person must engage during the retention interval. If the short-term store has a fixed capacity and if much of that capacity must be expended for performance on the subsidiary task, then little capacity remains for working on the central, concept-identification task. Consequently, the greater the information load of the subsidiary task, the smaller should be the sample focus and the less frequent should be two-cue solutions. A variety of subsidiary, distracting tasks can be designed varying in their information load (cf. Posner & Rossman, 1965). For example, suppose that coincident with performing a discrimination learning task to stimuli shown in the left display window, the subject also is required to continuously (or intermittently, between trials) monitor the right display window and to (a) stamp his foot if a simple signal appears there, (b) read off random digits, (c) read off interfering descriptions of the figures, (d) add successive random numbers, or (e) memorize a list of nonsense syllables for a later recall test. Presumably the more "mental effort" required by the subsidiary task, the less the subject would learn in the RRC problem.

Effects similar to those conjectured above apparently can be produced by requiring the subject to work concurrently on several distinct concept-identification problems, with trials on each problem intermixed with trials on other problems in a random series. For example, three distinct problems involving geometric figures, flower designs, and letter clusters could be used, each classification separately depending upon one or two attributes. Such problems have been studied by Erickson, Zajkowski, and Ehmann (1966) and by Restle and Emmerick (1966). When several problems are thus interleaved, the total memory load on the subject is increased in several ways. First, the subject should have some interference and forgetting of which hypotheses were tried and rejected previously on a given problem, so his sampling of new hypotheses to test would tend more toward the randomness implied by ignorance of past information. Second, the multiproblem load would cause a restriction in the size of the sample focus effective on a given problem, since the sample foci for the other problems are also limiting

213

the available storage capacity in short-term memory. For these reasons, the percentage of two-cue solvers is expected to be less when a RRC problem is embedded in a concurrent, multiple-problem task.

Another task variable that might affect s is "time stress," wherein subjects are forced to respond to the stimulus series very rapidly. Since it probably takes longer to make a decision when more cues are in the sample focus, the pressure for rapid decisions should reduce the average size of the sample focus. Under time stress, the reinforcing event would be brief and be followed quickly by the next stimulus. The subject therefore will have less time to accurately process the information received on error trials (e.g., in haste he might choose an hypothesis that is inconsistent with the present trial's information). This reduction in study time should lower both the learning rate and the sample size. On the other hand, enforcing quick responses but holding constant the study time should mainly decrease the sample size and leave learning rate unaffected. In either case, a reduction in sample size should be accompanied by a reduction in two-cue solutions in a RRC problem.

PRIOR TRAINING AND SAMPLE SIZE

The parameter s is likely to be a variable that could be systematically manipulated by different training histories. A reasonable conjecture is that at the beginning of a concept task the subject "sets" s at the value that appears warranted by his past experience with a particular class of problems. For example, if a subject has learned a number of similar problems in which there was only one relevant cue, it seems likely that a bias toward single-cue solutions would persist into a RRC problem. Conversely, if he has previously learned a number of conjunctive problems, where the correct answer depended upon the joint value of two (or three or four, etc.) attributes, then this should bias him toward larger sample foci and more two-cue solutions.

AN ATTEMPT TO MANIPULATE SAMPLE SIZE

The foregoing conjectures were tested in a small study by Kathryn Nash at UCLA. Since the experiment is of a pilot nature, it serves mainly as an illustration of the method of investigating experiential effects on the focus sample size in RRC problems rather than providing a conclusive test of the foregoing ideas.

In Nash's study, the same stimuli used in the main experiment of Chapter 3 were employed; the attributes were the dot location, the shape, color, number of interior lines, and open-side positions of the figures, and the responses were A and B. Four groups of ten subjects each were run and the groups differed in terms of their pretraining experiences. All groups underwent the same final RRC transfer training with the shape and the dot attributes relevant and redundant (i.e., the problem of group $S + D$ in Chapter 3). After reaching a criterion of fifteen successive correct responses on the transfer problem, the subjects were tested for what they learned and then answered a questionnaire on their solution hypotheses.

In pretraining the stimuli were the same as in transfer. Group S was trained on a single-cue problem where only the color alone was relevant. Group R was trained on a different RRC problem with the color and interior lines as the relevant and redundant attributes (e.g., red figures always had two interior lines and blue figures always had one line). Group C learned a conjunctive problem in which the color and interior line attributes were relevant but only one of their four combinations determined the A classification. For example, only red *and* two interior lines determined category A; all other combinations determined category B. Thus a subject could solve this problem by paying attention only to a conjunction of two attributes. A fourth group of subjects served as a control (group N) and had no pretraining.

In the pretraining acquisition, additivity of cues was observed: group R, which had been trained on the color and number of lines as RRC's, learned faster than group S, which had only the color relevant. Conjunctive learning was considerably more difficult: group C required more trials and made more errors than either group R or group S. The mean number of errors to criterion (fifteen successive correct responses) for groups R, S, and C in pretraining was 1.6, 2.8, and 38.8, respectively.

In transfer, groups S, R, and N learned at about the same rate, although groups S and R showed slight warm-up effects; group C took longer to learn than these groups, presumably because subjects in this condition persisted in trying to find conjunctive-type solutions which entail a greater memory load. This was supported by the subjects' verbal reports and by the fact that four of the ten subjects reported their solution hypotheses in conjunctive form on the RRC problem even though one attribute was sufficient (e.g., "all circles with either one or two lines are in category A and all the rest were B's"). Thus the conjunctive pretraining apparently had some transfer effect regarding the form of the solution hypothesis. The mean number of errors to criterion in transfer for groups S, R, N, and C was 1.2, 1.4, 3.0, and 5.2, respectively.

Two questions of interest pertain to the effect of pretraining on the

215

size of the focus sample. First, subjects in group S were trained on a single-cue problem. If this pretraining is effective and persists in transfer, then s should equal one for each subject and no subject is expected to learn both of the RRC's; if, however, the training is less than fully effective, one would still expect a reduction in the number of subjects who solve on both the shape and dot cues, compared with controls who have no pretraining. Second, in group C, the subjects learned to base their solution hypotheses on two cues. If this pretraining is fully effective and transfers, then all subjects would have s equal to two or greater, and a larger number of two-cue solvers is expected in this group, relative to controls. In group C, all subjects are not expected to learn both of the RRC's since it is a random event as to whether or not a subject samples both RRC's on the same error trial. A third datum of interest is afforded by group R. In pretraining, these subjects learned a RRC problem with different relevant cues and then were asked to state their solution hypotheses before transfer. If individual differences in the sample focus size exist, then one might anticipate that those subjects who initially learn two cues will also learn both RRC's in transfer.

The subjects in the four groups were classified as having learned the shape, the dot, or both attributes. For all groups, subjects who stated a solution only on the shape sorted 99.5 percent correctly on shape tests and only 50 percent correctly on the dot tests; those who stated a solution only on the dots sorted 97.5 percent correctly on the dot tests but only 49.7 percent correctly on the shape tests; those who stated both dimensions in their solution hypothesis sorted 83.3 percent correctly on the shapes and 91.6 percent correctly on the dots. Once more, the verbalized solution and sorting test data are in close agreement. Overall, fourteen subjects learned only the shape attribute, twenty-three learned only the dots, and three learned both attributes. These data are in close agreement with the findings in Chapter 3. The respective percentages of shape, dot, and both solvers in the present study were .35, .57, and .08, compared to .35, .51, and .14 from group $S + D$ of Chapter 3.

The solution types within the experimental conditions were distributed as follows. As expected, no subject learned both cues in group S; nine others learned only the dots and one learned only the shape. This effect, however, was not clearly a result of pretraining $s = 1$ since the baseline number of two-cue solvers was low. In groups N and R, only one subject per condition learned both cues. The number of subjects learning only the dots and only the shapes in groups N and R were six and three, seven and two, respectively. Since the number of two-cue solutions was so small, the likelihood of increasing s should be larger. Despite this, group C showed only one subject who learned both cues, indicating that although subjects were effectively set toward conjunctive-type problem solving, their focus sample was not influenced in the way we had anticipated. It is possible that our pretraining of group C had another effect that militated against learning both the shape and the dot cues. This group was pretrained on the color and interior lines which are associated with the shapes and not the dots. In transfer, the nine subjects of group C learned *only* the shape cues. This result, if reliable, represents a kind of transfer of observing responses to an area or specific characteristic of the patterns. Finally, in group R, the single subject who learned both cues in transfer also reported learning two cues in pretraining, so that some weak evidence for individual differences in s is afforded by this study.

Although this experiment is of a pilot nature, and is not an ideal test in some respects of the several ideas previously outlined on how one might influence the sample size, it serves as a heuristic for research on experience and attention in concept identification and illustrates how the sampling theory can be useful in evaluating these effects.

In principle, a "learning set" effect on s should be demonstrable in a series of RRC problems. Presumably the probability of a two-cue solution on problem n would differ depending on whether a one- or two-cue solution occurred on problem $n - 1$. Starting on problem 1 with a homogeneous group of subjects with mean $s > 1$, the positive feedback of solution type upon s is such that over successive problems some of these subjects (selected at random) would "absorb" predominantly on two-cue solutions.

Another obvious way to influence s with human subjects is by instructions before the learning task. Instructions probably serve much the same role as does prior training; that is, they can be worded so as to bias the subject toward either type of solution. For example, if in a RRC problem with cues A and B the subject is told to "look out for" variations in relevant dimension A, this should lower the likelihood of a two-cue solution involving A and B. Similarly, informing the subject that there are two relevant cues, that he will be tested later on both, and that he should keep searching for other relevant cues even after he's learned one, and so on, will probably produce an increase in frequency of two-cue solutions (cf. Houston, 1967). Such instructions are half-way measures to giving a complete characterization of the problem to the subject, that is, telling him that cues A and B are relevant, which of course produces 100 percent two-cue solutions.

INDIVIDUAL DIFFERENCES IN SAMPLE SIZE

It is undoubtedly a truism to say that there are individual differences in sample size in particular learning tasks. The issue is not the existence of such differences, but rather whether and how such differences in s might be correlated with other abilities or characterological traits. For example, it has been often proposed that people with high chronic anxiety (e.g., as measured by the Taylor Manifest Anxiety Scale) are poor in perceptual scanning, in dealing with simultaneous information, and for such reasons may be expected to have lower average s values. Similarly, tests are available to measure traits like "perceptual rigidity," the scores of which presumably would correlate with s via a person's ability to scan and deal simultaneously with several alternative attributes in his sample focus. We prefer to interpret such test scores not as immutable, characterological traits, but rather as convenient summary indices of the perceptual processes shaped into a person by his training history. But this interpretive point is not at issue here.

Of the many individual covariates of s that one might examine, there are two likely candidates for contributing a large portion of the total variance. One of these is the magnitude of the orienting reflex (OR) which idexes the "impact" of a stimulus. It is known that individuals differ reliably in their average magnitude of the OR (Maltzman & Raskin, 1965). Moreover, Maltzman and Raskin found that magnitude of the OR to the stimuli of a paired-associate task correlated highly and positively with the rate of learning these paired associates. Conceivably a high OR is indexing a high level of alertness of the learner, and the latter enhances the learning and/or performance. However, an appealing hypothesis to pursue in later research is that OR magnitude indexes s in the concept-identification studies, so that, for example, two-cue solutions would be more frequent among those subjects having higher OR's.

A second trait variable is the mental age of the subject, particularly in regard to his immediate memory and linguistic facility. For example, young children or mental retardates would doubtless learn less in solving a RRC problem than would average adults, that is, they would have fewer two-cue solutions. But why? Possibly for the two reasons mentioned—immediate memory and linguistic facility—the average s-value is lower for the children and retardates than for the normal adult. Recall our earlier discussion that the focus sample was a list of attribute-value-response pairs held in a temporary or short-term memory from trial to trial. It seems plausible that limitations of short-term memory restrict the size of this listing that can be successfully carried from trial to trial. Therefore the poorer the immediate memory, the smaller will be the sample focus, and the less likely will be multiple-cue solutions in RRC problems. The factor of linguistic facility enters if we suppose, as aforementioned, that subjects are probably encoding the stimulus patterns in terms of verbal labels of the dimensions present. Although such discrimination problems do not require verbal encoding for their solution (e.g., animals or nonverbal retardates can solve them), the availability of the verbal description of the stimuli undoubtedly helps. There is sufficient evidence that verbalization (implicit or explicit) of stimuli aids in remembering them; indeed, Brown and Lenneberg (1954), Conrad (1964), Sperling (1963), and others have proposed and tried to show that auditory traces from implicit verbalization of input stimuli are an important aspect of their later recallability or recognition. So, by use of verbal encoding, one can increase the average size of the sample focus that can be remembered from one trial to the next. And by this means, labeling facility would be expected to influence s.

THEORETICAL ALTERNATIVES

Looking back over the general qualitative results, we seem to have reached something of a theoretical impasse. Not only do we want a theory that easily handles the effects of cue salience and problem structure, but also a model that will sometimes learn two RRC's and sometimes only one; that sometimes learns a second cue during overtraining and sometimes does not; that sometimes learns a partially valid cue and sometimes does not; that sometimes shows complete blocking and sometimes only partial blocking. Some of these phenomena are consistent with a one-look, all-or-none learning model; more are consistent with a multiple-look, all-or-none learning model; and some phenomena are consistent with a "total-look," incremental theory of the type Spence espoused (cf. Chapter 1). Obviously one would like to have a somewhat more general theory that by specialization will handle all the salient results without having to invoke ad hoc assumptions. We confess to a lack of any striking success along these lines, despite many hours of theoretical searching. However, the reader may find it informative for us to go through two theoretical alternatives if for no other reason than to indicate the nature of the explanatory difficulties.

First of all, the data rule out all simple one-look or one-hypothesis models wherein a reinforced hypothesis is always held for another trial (if it were not, then perfect solution is impossible with this scheme). Such a model will never handle two-cue solutions, overtraining effects, or partial blocking results. A multiple-look model such as ours, with cue elimination from the sample, will never handle overtraining effects or partial blocking results.

A MODIFIED MULTIPLE-LOOK MODEL

Let us consider a modification of our multiple-look model wherein the response rule is altered. Formerly, it was supposed that the subject may hold a sample focus of up to s locally consistent hypotheses, that hypotheses dictating an error were weeded out of the focus after correct response trials, and that the response to the focus was decided by an average probability taken over the hypotheses in the focus. This averaging response rule means that irrelevant hypotheses (or unlearned cues) could not have been in the sample focus during a long criterion run of successes—otherwise, errors would have resulted. Suppose that the response rule is altered as follows: the hypotheses (or cues) in the sample focus are ordered according to some measure of strength (e.g., the number of successive confirmations) and the response is determined solely by the strongest hypothesis in the focus. This assumption alone does not materially change the learning characteristics of the model in comparison to those of the averaging model. That is, maintaining the other assumptions (about focus reduction, resampling on error), the two different response rules yield the same quantitative predictions, that is, a geometric distribution of errors and of successes between errors.

A new system arises, however, if we combine the dominant-element response rule with a new assumption regarding operations on the focus sample following correct response trials. The new proposal is that a focus hypothesis that is disconfirmed on a correct response trial may be *replaced* with probability b by another "nonfocus" hypothesis (i.e., a cue with locally consistent response assignments), whereas the disconfirmed hypothesis is merely removed from the focus and not replaced with probability $1 - b$. Now, if $b = 0$, we have our earlier model where the sample focus is narrowed down with each disconfirming event. But consider the system when $b = 1$, when disconfirmed cues (on correct response trials) are replaced by other cues not currently in the focus.

First of all, with $b = 1$, the probability of solution (no errors) eventuating from a sample consisting of x relevant cues and $s - x$ irrelevant cues is x/s, exactly the same as before, and the distribution of successes before the next error (if any) is geometric with parameter p. This arises as follows: imagine a "consecutive confirmation" counter, attached to each hypothesis in the focus, which increments by one for each consecutive pattern for which that hypothesis is confirmed; when a hypothesis is disconfirmed on a correct-response trial, it is replaced by another locally consistent hypothesis whose success counter is set at 1. The rule is to respond according to that hypothesis in the focus having the largest success count, choosing randomly among those that may be tied for the maximum. After k successes in a row, any relevant cue that started in the focus will have a confirmation count of $k + 1$, a proportion p^k of the irrelevant hypotheses will also have a success count of $k + 1$, whereas the remaining proportion of focus hypotheses will have success counts less than $k + 1$ (so will not be used for responding). Since, in case of ties, the dominant hypothesis is chosen at random, the conditional probability of a $(k + 1)st$ success given an initial focus of x relevant and $s - x$ irrelevant cues (after the preceding error) will be

$$Pr\,(S_{k+1} \mid S_k \ldots S_1 E_0) = \frac{x + p^{k+1}(s - x)}{x + p^k(s - x)}$$

This is identical to the equations used in Chapter 2, and so the same statistical properties hold for this model. By further assuming that the latency of response is inversely related to the success count of the dominant hypothesis, the theory will fit results showing a decrease in latency during a run of successes.

The novel, important feature of this model is that it allows for continued testing of new hypotheses after the subject has already learned and is responding on the basis of the dominant, correct hypothesis. Phrasing it differently, it allows for the learning of a previously unlearned, redundant relevant cue while the subject's performance is being controlled by his first-learned relevant cue. Given that correct performance is being taken care of by the dominant (correct) hypothesis, the other available slots in the focus sample can be used for evaluating other hypotheses, essentially by cycling members of the population of nondominant hypotheses through these slots that are not affecting performance. Figure 8.1 illustrates a system with a two-hypothesis focus sample or short-term memory register. The correct hypothesis, H_1, is in the dominant position in the focus, whereas an irrelevant hypothesis, H_7, is currently occupying the second slot of the register. H_7 happens to have a lower success count or less seniority here since it has had fewer consecutive confirmations than H_1. The arrows from the H pool into and out of the second slot in the focus illustrate the continuing trial-and-error

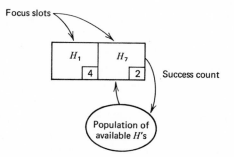

FIGURE 8.1. *Illustration of two-slot focus sample.*

search for another relevant cue. If H_7 were irrelevant, then there is probability p that it is confirmed and will stay another trial, probability qb that it is disconfirmed and replaced by another hypothesis drawn from the pool, and probability $q(1 - b)$ that H_7 is disconfirmed, is eliminated and not replaced, thus stopping all information gathering by the second slot of the system until the next error (if any) occurs with H_1 in the dominant slot. This last remark reflects the assumption that the system "resets" on an overt error trial, and that a new sample focus of size s (2 here) is drawn afresh.

Since the error-resetting features of this model are the same as our earlier model given in Chapter 2 (i.e., resample all slots, reset success counters to 1), the only new implications of this system regard what happens during the criterion and/or post-criterion run of correct responses in a RRC problem. It is clear that if $b = 1$, so that disconfirmed hypotheses are always replaced by other locally consistent hypotheses, then the model will eventually learn a second RRC if training is sufficiently extended. In fact, if the register has s slots, then with $b = 1$ and sufficient training, it can learn up to s redundant relevant cues, with some of these being learned after the criterion run. This learning of a cue in a nondominant position of the sample focus would be assessed, of course, by single-cue tests wherein the dominant cue is removed. The response rule is the same as before, that is, performance is controlled by that hypothesis in the focus which is dominant (has the largest confirmation count) provided it is applicable. By applicable we simply mean that the cue to which the hypothesis refers is present in the test stimulus pattern.

We have seen that if $b = 0$, the model will show no new learning after a criterion run, whereas if $b = 1$ it will eventually learn one or more RRC's after a criterion run. The former result obtains because when $b = 0$ the process during the criterion run progressively restricts or narrows attention to only the dominant hypothesis, and no further cue information can be gathered. The latter result obtains because when $b = 1$ the process keeps open all the $s - 1$ nondominant slots in the attention register, and uses them for collecting confirmation counts on alternative hypotheses. But what does the process do if b is neither 0 nor 1, but has some intermediate value like .5?

First of all, if there is only one relevant cue, then the effect of $b < 1$ following the last error is to progressively narrow the sample focus down to just that one relevant cue. Supposing that after the last error trial the sample focus consisted of one relevant and $s - 1$ irrelevant cues, the expected size of the sample focus at the beginning of the kth trial of the criterion run is

$$s_k = 1 + (s - 1)(p + qb)^{k-1} \qquad\qquad (8.1)$$

If $b = 1$, this remains constant at s, whereas for $b < 1$ it decreases to 1 at a rate which is faster the smaller is b. If there are $x < s$ different redundant relevant dimensions and all x appear in the last error sample, then Equation 8.1 describes the focus size when 1 is replaced by x.

The more interesting question when $b < 1$ is whether a relevant cue not in the focus at the beginning of the criterion run will ever get into the focus before attention becomes restricted to only those relevant cues with which it began on the last error trial. Metaphorically speaking, a "race" is involved: the focus of attention is being progressively narrowed, and the question is whether the other relevant cue will be sampled before the attention register becomes totally restricted. Let us consider calculations for a very simple case to see what is involved: suppose that $s = 2$, $b < 1$, at the start of the criterion run the sample focus consists of the dominant relevant cue and an irrelevant cue, and suppose that h denotes the probability that the second relevant cue is selected from the pool when a disconfirmed hypothesis in the second slot of the focus is replaced on a trial. We may characterize the "state" of this second slot by saying that on any one trial it holds either an irrelevant cue (state I) the other relevant cue (state R), or no cue (state N). States R and N are "absorbing" in the sense that if either of these occurs on any trial, then the process continues in that state for all subsequent trials. State I is transient or temporary, and Figure 8.2 enumerates in a tree diagram the possible transitions that can occur on a trial that begins in state I. The irrelevant hypothesis is confirmed and maintained for another trial with probability p, is disconfirmed and not replaced with probability $q(1 - b)$, is replaced by the relevant cue with probability qbh and with another irrelevant cue with probability $qb(1 - h)$. Starting in state I on the first trial of the errorless criterion

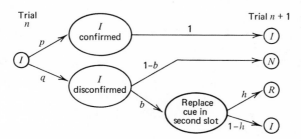

FIGURE 8.2. *Tree diagram of state transitions on a trial starting in state I.*

run, the probability that the process has absorbed in state R by the beginning of the nth trial of the criterion run can be shown to be

$$p_n(R) = \frac{bh}{bh + (1 - b)} \{1 - [p + qb(1 - h)]^{n-1}\} \qquad (8.2)$$

This increases with the length of the criterion run to a limit (the first term outside the brackets) which itself is an increasing function of b and h. If there are only two relevant cues and we let $p(2)$ and $p(1)$, respectively, denote the probabilities that the criterion run begins with either two or one relevant cue in the focus, then the proportion of eventual two-cue solvers given n criterion trials will be

$$Pr \text{ (2-cue solver)} = p(2) + p(1)p_n(R) = 1 - p(1)[1 - p_n(R)] \quad (8.3)$$

By proper choice of b and h, this proportion will increase significantly with the length of the criterion run; it therefore provides a way to account for an increase in two-cue solvers with overtraining while at the same time not implying that all subjects will become two-cue solvers. By the same token, the model allows for some learning in a "blocking" experiment, where a formerly irrelevant cue becomes relevant following an initial criterion run. This cue may be learned if the focus has not yet been severely restricted by the criterion trials before the redundant-cue training begins. For fixed b and h, the primary variable influencing the restriction of the attention focus is the number of criterion trials before the redundant phase begins. Thus the system is capable of explaining the result reported by Bruner, Matter, and Papanek (1955) that extended overtraining on cue A reduces the probability that the subject will learn anything about cue B in a later $A + B$ series of RRC trials.

Consider next the effect of partial validity of the B cue, established either during initial training (e.g., Babb, 1956; Bitterman & Coate, 1950) or during overtraining (e.g., Hughes & North, 1959). The average confirmation rate for a partially valid cue will be higher than a totally irrelevant cue; therefore, partially valid cues generally will have a longer staying time in the sample focus and a higher average confirmation count than will irrelevant cues. Hence, for suitable values of b, in transfer tests the system will show a "preference" for partially valid cues as opposed to strictly irrelevant cues, with the average extent of preference depending on the validity of the cue concerned.

From the foregoing, it appears that this dominant-element response model has the requisite flexibility to account for the major qualitative discrepancies from our earlier model. Still, considerable theoretical work is needed to fill in several lacunae of ignorance about the operation of the theoretical machine: this would include possibly a different cue-sampling rule, as it applies on error trials and for replacement of disconfirmed cues in nondominant positions of the sample focus (these would express h, $p(1)$, and $p(2)$ in Equations 8.2 and 8.3 as a function of the cue weights); it also includes working out the consequences of assuming a sample focus, s, larger than 2. A few preliminary remarks can be made about the effect of s, particularly as it influences the probability of the subject learning further relevant cues. Clearly, $p(R_n)$ will increase with s; the theory stated so far even implies a Markov process (similar to that graphed in Figure 8.2) for calculating $p(R_n)$, but the expressions are complicated. If the process starts with one relevant cue and $s - 1$ irrelevant cues in the focus, and one relevant cue plus many irrelevant cues outside the focus, then the "states" of the Markov chain are as follows: state R—the other relevant cue is now in the focus and thus will be learned; state N—the nondominant slots in the focus have all been eliminated and hence R will not be learned; state $I(j)$—there are j remaining slots in the attention register, all filled with irrelevant cues (where $j = 1, 2, \ldots, s - 1$). The process diagrammed in Figure 8.2 describes the transition possibilities for each single slot in the attention register, and the overall Markov process keeps track of the $s - 1$ nondominant slots in a manner relevant to calculating $p(R_n)$. Assuming the irrelevant cues have independent probability q of being disconfirmed on each trial, the transition probabilities for the general Markov chain are as follows: states R and N are absorbing, while state $I(j)$ has transition probabilities

$$p[I(j) \to R] = 1 - (1 - qbh)^j$$
$$p[I(j) \to N] = [q(1 - b)]^j \tag{8.4}$$

$$p[I(j) \to I(j - d)] = \sum_{i=d}^{j} \binom{j}{i} q^i p^{j-i} \binom{i}{d} (1 - b)^d [b(1 - h)]^{i-d}$$

The latter equation introduces sufficient complexities that the probability of reaching state R (learning the other relevant cue) within n criterion trials has not yet been derived. The more general case, for more than two redundant relevant cues with $s \geq 2$, is still to be derived. However, these details are not of material consequence in the present discussion.

The point here was to introduce some slight alterations to our earlier sampling model to obtain a model that for particular values of one parameter, b, will produce either our results or those somewhat discrepant from ours obtained under other circumstances. For these

225

purposes, the present level of specificity of the derivations has been sufficient.

AN INCREMENTAL-STRENGTH MODEL

To illustrate the range of theoretical alternatives we have considered, we will present an incremental-strength model which appears to have some promise of accounting at least qualitatively for many of the results. It is similar in spirit to Spence's (1936) theory of discrimination learning, except that the learning rate on a given cue is assumed to depend on the "degree of attention" to it, expressed as its ranking in a hierarchy of alternatives.

First, we represent the subject as holding and operating on a set of elementary hypotheses (really, cue-response assignments). With N binary dimensions there are $2N$ stimulus values and hence $2N$ elementary hypotheses. For example, in a simultaneous discrimination the two hypotheses with respect to a binary color dimension would be "choose red" and its complement, "choose blue." This representation is essentially the same as Spence's, except he called his units "approach response to stimulus component x."

Second, these $2N$ hypotheses have associated strengths or excitatory potentials, and we let $E_i(n)$ denote the strength of hypothesis i at the beginning of trial n of the experiment. The initial values, $E_i(1)$, correspond roughly to the cue weights we used in Chapter 2 and would be expected to vary with similar factors—cue salience, past training, and so forth. Ideally, at the beginning of a new problem with new cues, each hypothesis and its complement should start out at nearly equal strengths, since no specific response assignments have yet been reinforced.

We will consider two different performance rules for this system. The first rule is that the response is determined solely by the dominant (strongest) hypothesis in the hierarchy of applicable hypotheses. Response latency varies inversely with the strength of this dominant hypothesis. The alternate rule is that the response is determined by summing the strengths of all those hypotheses dictating response 1 to the stimulus pattern, and comparing this sum to the sum of the strengths of all those hypotheses dictating response 2 to the stimulus pattern. Whichever sum is larger, that response is made, and with a latency inversely related to the difference between the two sums. In most cases, these two rules dictate the same response, especially in conjunction with the learning assumptions given below. The implications of the "dominant hypothesis" rule are easier to envisage and so it is used in our discussion of this model. The summation or majority rule helps explain certain latency

226

results (e.g., those of Mahut, 1954, reviewed earlier) but appears to have no further advantages over the "dominant-hypothesis" rule.

Of principal importance are the learning assumptions for this model. We suppose that following each trial outcome each hypothesis is evaluated as having been confirmed or disconfirmed (there will be N in each class on each trial), and its strength will be increased or decreased accordingly. However, the amount of change in strength will reflect the relative strength of the hypothesis in the overall hierarchy of cues. As a first approximation to this kind of assumption, the learning operator for hypothesis i which holds rank r in the hierarchy will be written as

$$E_i(n + 1) = \begin{cases} (1 + \theta r^{-t})E_i(n) & \text{if } H_i \text{ confirmed as trial } n \\ (1 - \theta r^{-t})E_i(n) & \text{if } H_i \text{ disconfirmed on trial } n \end{cases} \quad (8.5)$$

In Equation 8.5, θ is some fraction between 0 and 1, r is the rank of H_i, varying from 1 (highest) to $2N$ (lowest), and t is a nonnegative number. The exponent $-t$ determines how much is learned about a hypothesis that occupies various positions in the strength hierarchy. For example, if $t = 0$, then all E's are altered with equal parameter θ; if $t = 1$, then the change in strength of the rth ranked hypothesis depends on θ/r, so that strong hypotheses are changed a lot but weak hypotheses are changed very little. If the parameter t is very large, then θ/r^t is negligible for all $r \geq 2$, so this value of t effectively confines the learning changes on a trial to only the first-ranked hypothesis.

It may be noted that the dominant-hypothesis response rule implies that the individual performance curve will show an abrupt jump from "chance" responding to perfect responding. That is, if the stimulus series is random, mean percentage correct responses will be at .50 over trials before the last error—a feature we have consistently found. Performance is at .50 whenever an irrelevant hypothesis occupies position 1, and changes to 1.00 as soon as a correct hypothesis moves into position 1. The nature of the learning operators in Equation 8.5 implies that once a correct hypothesis enters position 1, it will remain there so long as it continues to be reinforced.

Although the individual performance curve is expected to show only one step, from .50 to 1.00, the distribution of trials or of errors before this step is not geometrically distributed as in the Markov models. In fact, for almost all values of t, the probability that the step occurs increases continuously with trials. This is simply because the strength of the correct hypothesis is increasing steadily, whereas irrelevant hypotheses that fortuitously enter position 1 eventually have their strengths decreased by disconfirmations (error trials). If the hypothesis occupying position 1 is partially valid, being correct with some probability $p > .50$,

227

then it is expected to remain in position 1 for a larger number of trials, thus delaying the trial of solution. The critical event promoting a new H into position 1, of course, is an error (disconfirmation) on the current H in position 1. In a probabilistic situation in which no cue is perfectly valid (i.e., $p_i < 1$ for all H_i), the asymptotic state is that the H's will be ordered according to their validity or p values. If in addition t is large, the system can eventually arrive at always using the most valid H despite the occasional disconfirmations of it. This indeed is what Bourne (1963) observed with human subjects in a concept-identification task in which the most valid hypothesis still had $p < 1$. His subjects eventually came to respond always according to the most valid H, arriving at this at a faster rate the larger was $p - .5$.

Considering the implications of this system for RRC learning, it is apparent that its predictions for this case will depend on (a) the initial rank or strengths of the correct hypotheses, and (b) the parameter t, which determines how much learning is distributed throughout the hierarchy of alternative hypotheses. If H_a and H_b denote two different correct hypotheses and if $E_a(1) > E_b(1)$, then H_a will always enter position 1 sooner than will H_b, and so H_a will dominate responding eventually. Whether H_b will be learned depends on $t;$ if t is indefinitely large, then H_b will not be learned at all; if t is zero, then H_b will surely be learned, given sufficient trials on the RRC problem. By "learning of H_b" we mean that in a test situation in which cue a is removed, rendering H_a inapplicable, H_b would be the strongest applicable hypothesis in the hierarchy; hence, test responses would be determined by H_b. For our test situation, where all irrelevant cues are present on the test, the "learning of H_b" is equivalent to saying that it becomes the second strongest hypothesis in the hierarchy. If it were not, then on tests with the a cue removed the subject would respond (at chance) according to some irrelevant hypothesis that currently occupied the second position in the entire hierarchy.

Since $t = \infty$ produces only single-cue solutions, while $t = 0$ produces only two-cue solutions in a RRC problem, we may conjecture that intermediate values of t can produce both one- and two-cue solvers depending upon t, the initial strengths, and the number of training trials provided on a RRC problem. The larger is t and the poorer the initial rank of H_b, the less likely it is that it will be learned (attain rank 2) within a fixed number of trials. By extending the number of post-criterion trials, we increase the likelihood that H_b will be learned, so the system can account for cases in which overtraining increases the proportion of two-cue solvers. Under rather similar conditions on t, it can sometimes produce learning of a redundant relevant cue which was initially irrelevant (i.e., the blocking paradigm). However, because H_b will start the original criterion run in a more favorable position in the RRC paradigm than in the blocking paradigm (where H_b has been irrelevant), overtraining on a RRC problem should produce more two-cue solvers than will the redundant phase in the blocking paradigm. Comparing overtraining on a RRC problem to the beginning of the redundant phase of a blocking experiment brings out an interesting "self-embedding" feature of this model. Consider that the preliminary training has resulted in H_a being in the top position of the hierarchy, which implies that its complement (opposite), H'_a, is in the bottom position. The new correct hypothesis of interest, H_b, will begin this phase located in some position in the hierarchy, and we are concerned with calculating its path in percolating up into the second position, at which point we will say that H_b also will have been learned. We can now delete H_a and H'_a from the original hierarchy since they will maintain their relative positions, obtaining a subhierarchy of $2(N-1)$ hypotheses, and consider how H_b works its way to the top of this subhierarchy. But the process by which H_b moves to the top of this subhierarchy is precisely the same as the process by which H_a moved to the top of the original hierarchy, except the r in Equation 8.5 is replaced by $r + 1$. The same recursion would obtain for learning of a third, fourth, and so on, RRC except that r would be replaced by $r + i$ for the learning of the ith ranked correct hypothesis. Thus the effect of having performance controlled by a consistently correct H (the blocking paradigm) as opposed to changing irrelevant H's (original acquisition) is that the learning rate for the correct hypothesis of interest (H_b) is slower in the former case, and more so the more correct hypotheses (RRC's) that have been learned before the "blocked" RRC is introduced. These remarks follow directly from the nature of Equation 8.5 with $t > 0$.

A further confirmation of the model is provided by the Goodwin and Lawrence (1955) experiment which has been cited as opposed to Spence's incremental theory. Goodwin and Lawrence first taught rats a discrimination based on one cue (e.g., approach black, avoid white), and followed this by a nonreversal shift to a new relevant cue (presence or absence of chains in the maze arm) with brightness irrelevant. In the third phase, brightness again became relevant, with half the rats having the same black-positive, white-negative problem and half having the reversed or black-negative, white-positive problem. Goodwin and Lawrence found that the former subjects learned faster in phase 3 than did the reversal subjects. They argued that Spence's theory could not predict this result since the habit strengths to black and white should have been equalized by the phase 2 training during which black and white were

229

equally reinforced half the time. But for $t > 0$, the learning operators in Equation 8.5 do not imply equalization during phase 2 of the initial correct hypothesis and its complement. This is because the complementary (wrong) hypothesis begins phase 2 in the lowest rank of the H hierarchy where its learning rate is very slow, and it will take a very large number of trials for it to move up to the middle level of the hierarchy where the initial correct H will soon reside.

The basic disadvantage of this theory is that its predictions depend upon many unknown parameters, the $2N$ values of $E_i(1)$, θ, and t; and estimation procedures for these parameters are not presently known and would seem difficult to devise. The result is that quantitatively exact predictions are infeasible, and even qualitative predictions of interest can be grossly altered according to the values of some of the unknown parameters. In lieu of this, the theory can be employed as a convenient device for providing post hoc "explanations" for particular results. Monte Carlo simulations of various special cases (parameter values) of the theory have been run on simulated concept-identification experiments, and these have provided useful information about the properties of the general model and of the special cases investigated.

Our earlier remark, that the number of unknown parameters exceeds the usual degrees of freedom in the results of interest, may be viewed either as a note of despair about quantitative models in this special area, or as a challenge to devise experimental techniques that yield more relevant information regarding the quantities of concern to the theory. That is, the "classical" experimental paradigms, such as those reviewed and used here, may simply be of insufficient power or yield insufficient information to really test this theory. More efficient techniques for information extraction from human subjects learning concept tasks have been devised by Falmagne (1967) and by Levine (1966). Falmagne had her subjects assign "confidence ratings" to the $2N$ hypotheses after every trial in a concept-learning task, and showed that these ratings predicted quite well the response given by another group of subjects encountering the same sequence of concept cards. One could view these confidence ratings (about the probable correctness of each H) as monotone indices of the theoretical $E_i(n)$ values, although the monotone function relating the two variables is unknown. Investigations along this line seem likely to yield very useful information for models such as proposed here.

Comparing this strength model to the earlier one-look and multiple-look attention models, we see that they differ primarily in the manner in which learning is distributed each trial over the available cues. The one-look model provides for "learning" or hypothesis evaluation

230

only with respect to the hypothesis selected by the one-look on each trial. The multiple-look models extend this to allow for up to s hypotheses to be simultaneously and equally evaluated on a trial, with the remaining hypotheses being neither evaluated nor changed in strength on a trial. In other words, the learning rate is high for the s hypotheses in the focus sample but is zero for those outside the focus. The particular multiple-look model we developed in Chapter 2 had several advantages, but one of its disturbing flaws to our mind is that it has no learning rules for altering the cue weights in any permanent way. There, the w's defined at the outset of a problem (and tied to perceptual factors) were assumed to remain fixed throughout training; the concept of a sample focus provided a means for temporarily "increasing the weight" of those cues selected to be in it, but this was not a permanent change since, upon the next error, resampling of cues was presumed to occur according to the initial hierarchy of weights. Each error reset the effective weight hierarchy to what it was on trial 1. These assumptions lead to simple mathematics, and to simple geometric error distributions, but they obviously provide no mechanism for permanently altering cue weights or hypothesis strengths according to their reinforcement history.

The incremental-strength theory handles this matter directly by supposing that the hypotheses have their strengths altered on every trial, so that learning is coordinate with a reshuffling of the order of the H hierarchy in a manner sensitive to the sequence of stimulus-response confirmations embedded in a given problem. In place of the focus-nonfocus or one-zero learning-rate distinction, the incremental model provides for a continuous gradation in learning rate of an H, depending upon its position in the hierarchy of alternatives. The two panels of Figure 8.3 summarize the way in which attention, hypothesis evaluation, and learning gets distributed over the ranked hierarchy of cues or hypotheses. The left panel is for the one-look and multiple-look models, showing step functions at the point s, the size of the sample focus. In the right panel of Figure 8.3, the θ/r^t function of the incremental-strength theory is plotted for various values of t. As t increases, the strength theory approximates the one-look model, except for the assumed persistence in the altered strength of the H's.

Although this incremental-strength model handles the blocking and overtraining results we have been concerned with here, it encounters difficulties with other evidence which historically has been offered as support either for a two-process theory or for a noncontinuity theory as opposed to Spence's theory. First, unless t is large, it cannot handle our earlier presolution reversal studies (Bower & Trabasso, 1964b) with human subjects, wherein subjects reversed after every alternate error

231

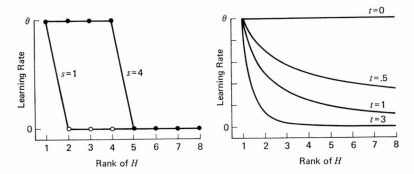

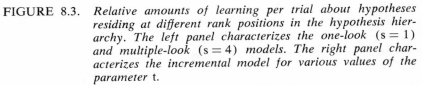

FIGURE 8.3. *Relative amounts of learning per trial about hypotheses residing at different rank positions in the hypothesis hierarchy. The left panel characterizes the one-look* (s = 1) *and multiple-look* (s = 4) *models. The right panel characterizes the incremental model for various values of the parameter* t.

(and told correct on that trial) made the same number of informed errors before solution as did control subjects who were never reversed. This is handled if t is large, effectively permitting no learning for non-dominant H's; but for large t, the model will not explain the overtraining effect we observed in the same situation.

Second, the incremental model encounters a range of difficulties because its elementary units of learning are stimulus component-response assignments rather than entire dimensional units. And the evidence tends to show that differential reinforcement to, say, two-color values raises the salience of the color dimension generally, not just the particular values used in training. This evidence arises particularly from studies of "intradimensional" versus "extradimensional" shift problems, wherein the same dimensions appear all at new values in the second problem with either the same or a different dimension being consistently reinforced. The fact that intradimensional shifts are learned faster than extradimensional shifts is most easily interpreted as showing that the preliminary training has raised the sampling probability of any values of the relevant dimension in this experimental context. A similar problem arises for this incremental theory in trying to explain the results of Lawrence's original experiments (1949, 1950) wherein high positive transfer occurred going from a successive to a simultaneous discrimination if the same cue dimension was relevant in both phases. Because the H's are defined in terms of procedure-specific responses (e.g., "choose black," or "if black, choose left" for simultaneous and successive problems, respectively), there is little basis for predicting transfer when the responses and H's are redefined.

A further difficulty is that the theory does not explain the fact that a reversal shift is learned faster than a nonreversal shift by adult human subjects. Moreover, overtraining on an initial problem should in theory only retard reversal learning, whereas in fact it has often been reported to facilitate such reversal. It was such facts as these that initially led investigators to formulate two-process or mediating-response theories, which separate the cue-sampling process from the instrumental response-conditioning process. And the present incremental-strength theory cannot deal with these facts any better than does Spence's original theory.

By this informal comparison then, the dimension-sampling model of the preceding section, with a dominant-response rule, would seem to come off slightly better and warrants further investigation. It associates the cue weights, the w's, with entire dimensions, and separates the cue-sampling process from the conditioning process by which responses are attached to the cues sampled (cf. Bower & Trabasso, 1964a). As with most theories in psychology, this one has its own set of failings and incompletenesses. For example, without further assumptions it produces no lasting changes in the cue weights due to learning; it lacks any substantive account of cue novelty effects; it provides no help in integrating the conflicting literature on overtraining reversal; it will not do pattern learning without further special assumptions, and so on. The informed and/or thoughtful reader can doubtless supply his own list of failings of the model. However, we feel that this theory is a small step in the right direction—at least, it is a step beyond our original model in Chapter 2—and that the gaps and incomplete parts of the theory can be filled in by future hypotheses and experimentation.

A more critical question is whether one should even attempt to construct a theory that is proposed to be valid for animals and men except for variations in the parameters. Though an attractive strategy, it may simply be unrealistic to expect even moderate success along these lines given the apparently vast differences between men and even primates in their categorization (or abstracting) capabilities and their competence in transforming information (cf. Lenneberg, 1967). Possibly more rapid advances will come from the development of learning theories having specific phylogenetic reference. Although the simple concept-identification task given to an adult human subject appears upon one characterization to be quite similar to, say, a brightness discrimination task given to a rat, there probably is little similarity in the information-processing mechanisms and their organization which these two subjects bring to bear upon their respective problems. Hence, by this argument, the theoretical description of the subject and his information processing should differ accordingly.

Although this question is easily posed, there is no hope for a definite answer, since it is one concerning strategy and guesses as to which direction of effort will prove more fruitful. In lieu of answering this general question, we believe that progress is made most easily by taking a specific task and a specific organism, and investigating that combination in detail with specific testable hypotheses. The results of one such enterprise have been reported in this book.

REFERENCES

Archer, E. J. (1962). Concept identification as a function of obviousness of relevant and irrelevant information. *Journal of Experimental Psychology,* **63,** 616–620.

———————, Bourne, L. E., Jr., & Brown, F. G. (1955). Concept identification as a function of irrelevant information and instructions. *Journal of Experimental Psychology,* **49,** 153–164.

Atkinson, R. C. (1961). The observing response in discrimination learning. *Journal of Experimental Psychology,* **62,** 253–262.

———————, Bower, G. H., & Crothers, E. J. (1965). *Introduction to mathematical learning theory.* New York: Wiley.

———————, & Estes, W. K. (1963). Stimulus sampling theory. In R. D. Luce, R. R. Bush, & E. Galanter (Eds.), *Handbook of mathematical psychology,* Vol. II, New York: Wiley, 121–268.

Babb, H. (1956). Proportional reinforcement of irrelevant stimuli and transfer value. *Journal of Comparative and Physiological Psychology,* **49,** 586–587.

Baron, M. R. (1965). The stimulus, stimulus control and stimulus generalization. In D. I. Mostofsky (Ed.), *Stimulus generalization,* Stanford: Stanford Univ. Press, 67–71.

Batchelder, W. H. (1967). A mathematical analysis of multi-level verbal learning. Tech. Rep. No. 104, Institute for Mathematical Studies in the Social Sciences, Stanford University.

Berlyne, D. E. (1960). *Conflict, arousal, and curiosity.* New York: McGraw-Hill.

Binder, A., & Estes, W. K. (1966). Transfer of response in visual recognition situations as a function of frequency variables. *Psychological Monographs,* **80,** No. 23 (Whole No. 631).

———————, & Feldman, S. E. (1960). The effects of experimentally controlled experience upon recognition responses. *Psychological Monographs,* **74,** No. 9 (Whole No. 496).

Bitterman, M. E., & Coate, W. B. (1950). Some new experiments on the nature of discrimination learning in the rat. *Journal of Comparative and Physiological Psychology,* **43,** 198–210.

235

Blazek, N. C., & Harlow, H. F. (1955). Persistence of performance differences on discriminations of varying difficulty. *Journal of Comparative and Physiological Psychology,* **48,** 86–89.

Bourne, L. E. Jr. (1963). Long-term effects of misinformation feedback upon concept identification. *Journal of Experimental Psychology,* **65,** 139–147.

―――――, & Haygood, R. C. (1959). The role of stimulus redundancy in concept identification. *Journal of Experimental Psychology,* **58,** 232–238.

―――――, & Haygood, R. C. (1960). Effects of intermittent reinforcement of an irrelevant dimension and task complexity upon concept identification. *Journal of Experimental Psychology,* **60,** 371–375.

―――――, & Pendleton, R. B. (1958). Concept identification as a function of completeness and probability of information feedback. *Journal of Experimental Psychology,* **56,** 413–420.

―――――, & Restle, F. (1959). A mathematical theory of concept identification. *Psychological Review,* **66,** 278–296.

Bower, G. H. (1961). Application of a model to paired-associate learning. *Psychometrika,* **26,** 255–280.

―――――. (1964). Notes on a descriptive theory of memory. Paper read at the Second Conference on Learning, Remembering and Forgetting, Princeton. To appear in D. P. Kimble (Ed.), *The anatomy of memory: Proceedings of the Second Conference on Learning, Remembering and Forgetting.* New York: New York Academy of Science, in press.

―――――, & Trabasso, T. (1964a). Concept identification. In R. C. Atkinson (Ed.), *Studies in mathematical psychology.* Stanford: Stanford Univ. Press, 32–94.

―――――, & Trabasso, T. (1964b). Reversals prior to solution in concept identification. *Journal of Experimental Psychology,* **66,** 409–418.

―――――, & Trabasso, T. (1964c). Working paper on concept identification. Unpublished manuscript.

Broadbent, D. E. (1958). *Perception and communication.* London: Pergamon Press.

Brown, R. W., & Lenneberg, E. H. (1954). A study in language and cognition. *Journal of Abnormal and Social Psychology,* **59,** 454–462.

Bruner, J. S., Matter, J., & Papanek, M. L. (1955). Breadth of learning as a function of drive level and mechanization. *Psychological Review,* **62,** 1–10.

Conrad, R. (1964). Acoustic confusion in immediate memory. *British Journal of Psychology,* **55,** 78–84.

D'Amato, M. R., & Fazzaro, J. (1966). Attention and cue-producing behavior in the monkey, *Journal of the Experimental Analysis of Behavior,* **9,** 469–473.

Deutsch, J. A., & Deutsch, D. (1963). Attention: Some theoretical considerations. *Psychological Review,* **70,** 80–90.

236

REFERENCES

Dodd, D. H., & Bourne, L. E., Jr. (1967). A direct test of some assumptions of a hypothesis-testing model of concept identification. Program on Cognitive Processes Rep. No. 101. Institute of Behavioral Science, University of Colorado.

Dulsky, S. G. (1935). The effects of a change in background on recall and relearning. *Journal of Experimental Psychology,* **18,** 725–740.

Eckerman, D. A. (1967). Stimulus control by part of a complex S. *Psychonomic Science,* **7,** 299–300.

Egeth, H. (1966). Selective attention. *Psychological Review,* **67,** 41–56.

Erickson, J. R. (1967). Hypothesis sampling in concept identification. *Journal of Experimental Psychology,* in press.

——————, Zajkowski, M. M., & Ehmann, E. D. (1966). All-or-none assumptions in concept identification. *Journal of Experimental Psychology,* **72,** 690–697.

Estes, W. K. (1956). The problem of inference from curves based on group data. *Psychological Bulletin,* **53,** 134–140.

—————— (1959). Component and pattern models with Markovian interpretations. In R. R. Bush & W. K. Estes (Eds.), *Studies in mathematical learning theory.* Stanford: Stanford Univ. Press, 9–52.

——————, & Burke, C. J. (1953). A theory of stimulus variability in learning. *Psychological Review,* **60,** 276–286.

——————, Hopkins, B. H., & Crothers, E. J. (1960). All-or-none and conservation effects in the learning and retention of paired-associates. *Journal of Experimental Psychology,* **60,** 329–339.

——————, & Suppes, P. (1959). Foundations of statistical learning theory: II. The stimulus sampling model for simple learning. Tech. Rep. No. 26. Institute for Mathematical Studies in the Social Sciences, Stanford University.

Falmagne, R. (1967). Analyse expérimentale et théoretique de l'apprentissage des concepts. Unpublished doctoral dissertation. Université Libre de Bruxelles.

—————— (1965). Un modèle mixte pour la situation identification de concepts. *Bulletin du Centre d'Études et de Recherches Scientifiques Psychologiques* (Paris), **3,** 219–241.

Friedman, M. P. (1966). Transfer effects and response strategies in pattern-vs.-component discrimination learning. *Journal of Experimental Psychology,* **71,** 420–428.

——————, Trabasso, T., & Mosberg, L. (1967). Tests of a mixed model for paired-associates learning with overlapping stimuli. *Journal of Mathematical Psychology,* **4,** 316–334.

Gardner, R. A. (1966). On box score methodology as illustrated by three reviews of overtraining reversal effects. *Psychological Bulletin,* **66,** 416–418.

Gibson, J. J. (1963). The useful dimensions of sensitivity. *American Psychologist,* **18,** 1–15.

—————— (1967). *The senses considered as perceptual systems.* Boston: Houghton Mifflin.

237

Goodwin, W. R., & Lawrence, D. H. (1955). The functional independence of two discrimination habits associated with a constant stimulus situation. *Journal of Comparative and Physiological Psychology,* **48,** 437–443.

Greeno, J. G., & Steiner, T. E. (1964). Markovian processes with identifiable states: General considerations and applications to all-or-none learning. *Psychometrika,* **29,** 309–333.

——————————, & Scandura, J. M. (1966). All-or-none transfer based on verbally mediated concepts. *Journal of Mathematical Psychology,* **3,** 388–411.

Gregg, L. W., & Simon, H. A. (1967). Process models and stochastic theories of simple concept formation. *Journal of Mathematical Psychology,* **4,** 246–276.

Guth, S. L. (1967). Patterning effects with compound stimuli. *Journal of Comparative and Physiological Psychology,* **63,** 480–485.

Guy, D. E., VanFleet, F. M., & Bourne, L. E., Jr. (1966). Effects of adding a stimulus dimension prior to a nonreversal shift. *Journal of Experimental Psychology,* **72,** 161–168.

Haber, R. N. (1964). Effects of coding strategy on perceptual memory. *Journal of Experimental Psychology,* **68,** 357–362.

Hammer, M. (1955). The role of irrelevant stimuli in human discrimination learning. *Journal of Experimental Psychology,* **50,** 47–50.

Hara, K., & Warren, J. M. (1961). Stimulus additivity and dominance in discrimination performance by cats. *Journal of Comparative and Physiological Psychology,* **54,** 86–90.

Harlow, H. F. (1945). Studies in discrimination learning in monkeys: V. Initial performance by experimentally naive monkeys on stimulus-object and pattern discrimination. *Journal of General Psychology,* **33,** 3–10.

Harris, C. S., & Haber, N. R. (1963). Selective attention and coding in visual perception. *Journal of Experimental Psychology,* **65,** 328–333.

Hebb, D. O. (1963). The semiautonomous process: Its nature and nurture. *American Psychologist,* **18,** 16–27.

Heidbredder, E. (1946). The attainment of concepts: II. The problem. *Journal of General Psychology,* **35,** 191–223.

Hergenhahn, B. R., Myers, C., & Capehart, J. (1966). Post-criterion insertion of a second relevant dimension in a simple discrimination problem. *Psychological Reports,* **18** (2), 547–551.

Hilgard, E. R. (1951). Methods and procedures in the study of learning. In S. S. Stevens (Ed.), *Handbook of experimental psychology.* New York: Wiley, 517–568.

Hill, F. A., & Wickens, D. D. (1962). The effect of stimulus compounding in paired-associate learning. *Journal of Verbal Learning and Verbal Behavior,* **1,** 144–151.

Holstein, S. B., & Premack, D. (1965). On the different effects of random reinforcement and presolution reversal on human concept identification. *Journal of Experimental Psychology,* **70,** 335–337.

238

REFERENCES

House, B. J., & Zeaman, D. (1960). Transfer of discrimination from objects to patterns. *Journal of Experimental Psychology, 59*, 298–302.

Houston, J. P. (1967). Stimulus selection as influenced by degrees of learning, attention, prior associations and experience with the stimulus components. *Journal of Experimental Psychology, 73*, 509–516.

Hughes, C. L., & North, A. J. (1959). Effects of introducing a partial correlation between a critical cue and a previously irrelevant cue. *Journal of Comparative and Physiological Psychology, 59*, 126–128.

Hull, C. L. (1920). Quantitative aspects of the evaluation of concepts: An experimental study. *Psychological Monographs, 28*, No. 123.

——————————— (1930). Simple trial-and-error learning: A study in psychological theory. *Psychological Review, 37*, 241–256.

——————————— (1943). *Principles of behavior.* New York: Appleton-Century-Crofts.

Imai, S., & Garner, W. R. (1965). Discriminability and preference for attributes in free and constrained classification. *Journal of Experimental Psychology, 69*, 596–608.

James, C. T., & Greeno, J. G. (1967). Stimulus selection of different stages of paired-associate learning. *Journal of Experimental Psychology, 74*, 75–83.

James, W. (1890). *The principles of psychology.* Vol. II. New York: Holt.

Jeffrey, W. E., & Cohen, L. B. (1964). Effect of spatial separation of stimulus, response and reinforcement on selective learning in children. *Journal of Experimental Psychology, 67*, 577–580.

Jenkins, H. M. (1966). The trouble with conditioning theories of discrimination learning. Paper read at the Eastern Psychological Association, New York.

Jones, L. (1954). Distinctiveness of color, form, and position cues for the pigeon. *Journal of Comparative and Physiological Psychology, 47*, 253–257.

Kamin, L. (1966). Conditioning to the elements of a compound stimulus. *18th International Congress of Psychology, Symposium 4*, 80–84.

Kelleher, R. T., & Gollub, L. R. (1962). A review of positive conditioned reinforcement. *Journal of the Experimental Analysis of Behavior, 5*, Supplement, 543–597.

Kendler, H. H., & Kendler, T. S. (1962). Vertical and horizontal processes in problem solving. *Psychological Review, 69*, 1–16.

Kintsch, W. (1964). Habituation of the GSR component of the orienting reflex during paired-associate learning before and after learning has taken place. *Journal of Mathematical Psychology, 2*, 330–341.

Köhler, W. (1941). On the nature of associations. *Proceedings of the American Philosophical Society, 84*, 489–502.

Krechevsky, I. (1932). "Hypotheses" in rats. *Psychological Review, 39*, 516–532.

Lashley, K. S. (1938). The mechanism of vision: XV. Preliminary studies of the rat's capacity for detail vision. *Journal of General Psychology, 18*, 123–193.

239

Lashley, K. S. (1942). An examination of the continuity theory as applied to discrimination learning. *Journal of General Psychology*, **26**, 241–265.

——————, & Wade, M. (1946). The Pavlovian theory of generalization. *Psychological Review*, **53**, 72–87.

Lawrence, D. H. (1949). Acquired distinctiveness of cues: I. Transfer between discriminations on the basis of familiarity with the stimulus. *Journal of Experimental Psychology*, **39**, 770–784.

—————— (1950). Acquired distinctiveness of cues: II. Selective associations in a constant stimulus situation. *Journal of Experimental Psychology*, **40**, 175–185.

—————— (1952). The transfer of a discrimination along a continuum. *Journal of Comparative and Physiological Psychology*, **45**, 511–516.

—————— (1963). The nature of a stimulus: Some relationships between learning and perception. In S. Koch (Ed.), *Psychology, a study of a science*. Study 11, Vol. 5. *Process Areas*. New York: McGraw-Hill.

Lenneberg, E. H. (1967). *Biological foundations of language*. New York: Wiley.

Levine, M. (1962). Cue neutralization: The effects of random reinforcement upon discrimination learning. *Journal of Experimental Psychology*, **63**, 438–443.

—————— (1963). Mediating processes in humans at the outset of discrimination learning. *Psychological Review*, **70**, 254–276.

—————— (1966). Hypothesis behavior by humans during discrimination learning. *Journal of Experimental Psychology*, **71**, 331–338.

—————— (1967). The size of the hypothesis set during discrimination learning. *Psychological Review*, **74**, 428–430.

Lindsley, D. B. (1957). Psychophysiology and motivation. In M. R. Jones (Ed.), *Nebraska Symposium*. Lincoln: Univ. of Nebraska Press, 44–105.

Lovejoy, E. P. (1965). An attention theory of discrimination learning. *Journal of Mathematical Psychology*, **2**, 342–362.

—————— (1966). Analysis of the overlearning reversal effect. *Psychological Review*, **73**, 87–103.

Luce, R. D. (1959). *Individual choice behavior : A theoretical analysis*. New York: Wiley.

Luria, A. R. (1960). *The role of speech in the regulation of normal and abnormal behavior*. New York: Lippincott.

Mackintosh, N. J. (1965a). Incidental cue learning in rats. *Quarterly Journal of Experimental Psychology*, **17**, 292–300.

—————— (1965b). Selective attention in animal discrimination learning. *Psychological Bulletin*, **64**, 124–150.

Mahut, H. (1954). The effect of stimulus position on visual discrimination by the rat. *Canadian Journal of Psychology*, **8**, 130–138.

Maltzman, I., & Raskin, D. C. (1965). Effects of individual differences in the orienting reflex. *Journal of Experimental Research in Personality,* **1,** 1–16.

Mandler, G. (1962). From association to structure. *Psychological Review,* **69,** 415–417.

Miles, C. G., & Jenkins, H. M. (1965). Overshadowing and blocking in discrimination operant conditioning. Paper read at Psychonomic Society, Chicago.

Murdock, B. B., Jr. (1961). The retention of individual items. *Journal of Experimental Psychology,* **54,** 86–90.

Murphy, J. V., & Miller, R. E. (1955). The effect of spatial contiguity of cue and reward in the object-quality learning of rhesus monkeys. *Journal of Comparative and Physiological Psychology,* **48,** 221–229.

Noble, C. (1952). An analysis of meaning. *Psychological Review,* **59,** 421–430.

Paul, C. (1965). Effects of overlearning upon single habit reversal in rats. *Psychological Bulletin,* **63,** 65–72.

Pavlov, I. P. (1927). Lectures. *Conditioned reflexes.* Oxford: Univ. Press.

Polson, P. G. (1967). A quantitative study of the concept-identification and paired-associates learning processes in the Hull paradigm. Unpublished doctoral thesis, University of Indiana.

Posner, M. I. (1963). Immediate memory in sequential tasks. *Psychological Bulletin,* **60,** 333–349.

———————, & Rossman, E. (1965). Effects of size and location of information transforms upon short-term retention. *Journal of Experimental Psychology,* **70,** 496–505.

Postman, L., & Riley, D. A. (1957). A critique of Köhler's theory of association. *Psychological Review,* **64,** 61–72.

Prokasy, W. F., Jr. (1956). The acquisition of observing responses in the absence of differential external reinforcement. *Journal of Comparative and Physiological Psychology,* **49,** 131–134.

Razran, G. (1965). Empirical codifications and specific theoretical implications of compound-stimulus conditioning: perception. In W. F. Prokasy (Ed.), *Classical conditioning: A symposium.* New York: Appleton-Century-Crofts, 226–248.

Reed, J. B. (1951). The speed and accuracy of discriminating differences in hue, brilliance, area, and shape. Tech. Rep. No. SDC-131-1-2. Mt. Holyoke College.

Restle, F. (1955). A theory of discrimination learning. *Psychological Review,* **62,** 11–19.

——————— (1957). Discrimination of cues in mazes: a resolution of the "place-vs.-response" question. *Psychological Review,* **64,** 217–228.

——————— (1959). Additivity of cues and transfer in discrimination of consonant clusters. *Journal of Experimental Psychology,* **57,** 9–14.

Restle, F. (1961). Statistical methods for theory of cue learning. *Psychometrika,* **26,** 291–306.

————————— (1962). The selection of strategies in cue learning. *Psychological Review,* **69,** 11–19.

—————————, & Emmerick, D. (1966). Memory in concept identification: Effects of giving several problems concurrently. *Journal of Experimental Psychology,* **71,** 794–799.

Reynolds, G. S. (1961). Attention in the pigeon. *Journal of the Experimental Analysis of Behavior,* **4,** 203–208.

Selfridge, O. G. (1959). Pandemonium: a paradigm for learning. In D. V. Blake and A. M. Uttley (Eds.), *Proceedings of the Symposium on Mechanization of Thought Processes.* National Physical Laboratory, Teddington, England. London: H. M. Stationary Office, 511–529.

—————————, & Neisser, U. (1960). Pattern recognition by machine. *Scientific American,* **203,** 60–80.

Shepp, B., & Zeaman, D. (1966). Discrimination learning of size and brightness by retardates. *Journal of Comparative and Physiological Psychology,* **62,** 55–59.

Sokolov, Y. N. (1963). *Perception and the conditioned reflex.* Trans. by S. W. Waydenfeld. London: Pergamon Press.

Spence, K. W. (1936). The nature of discrimination learning in animals. *Psychological Review,* **43,** 427–449.

————————— (1937a). Analysis of formation of visual discrimination habits in chimpanzee. *Journal of Comparative Psychology,* **23,** 77–100.

————————— (1937b). The differential response in animals to stimuli varying within a single dimension. *Psychological Review,* **44,** 430–444.

————————— (1938). Gradual vs. sudden solution of discrimination problems by chimpanzees. *Journal of Comparative Psychology,* **25,** 213–224.

————————— (1940). Continuous versus non-continuous interpretations of discrimination learning. *Psychological Review,* **47,** 271–288.

————————— (1942). The basis of solution by chimpanzees of the intermediate size problem. *Journal of Experimental Psychology,* **31,** 257–271.

Sperling, G. (1963). A model for visual memory tasks. *Human Factors,* **5,** 19–31.

Sperling, S. E. (1965a). Reversal learning and resistance to extinction: A review of the rat literature. *Psychological Bulletin,* **63,** 281–297.

————————— (1965b). Reversal learning and resistance to extinction: A supplementary report. *Psychological Bulletin,* **64,** 310–312.

Stein, L. (1966). Habituation and stimulus novelty: A model based on classical conditioning. *Psychological Review,* **73,** 353–356.

Stollnitz, F. (1965). Spatial variables, observing responses, and discrimination learning sets. *Psychological Review,* **72,** 247–261.

Suchman, R. G., & Trabasso, T. (1966a). Color and form preference in young children. *Journal of Experimental Child Psychology,* **3,** 177–187.

242

REFERENCES

Suchman, R. G., & Trabasso, T. (1966b). Stimulus preference and cue function in young children's concept attainment. *Journal of Experimental Child Psychology,* **3,** 188–198.

Sundland, D. M., & Wickens, D. D. (1962). Context factors in paired-associate learning and recall. *Journal of Experimental Psychology,* **63,** 302–306.

Suppes, P., & Schlag-Rey, M. (1965). Observable changes of hypotheses under positive reinforcement. *Science,* **148,** 661.

Sutherland, N. S. (1959). Stimulus analyzing mechanisms. In *Proceedings of the Symposium of the Mechanization of Thought Processes.* Vol. II. London: Her Majesty's Stationery Office, 575–609.

——————————— (1964). The learning of discriminations by animals. *Endeavor,* **23,** 140–152.

———————————, & Holgate, V. (1966). Two-cue discrimination learning in rats. *Journal of Comparative and Physiological Psychology,* **2,** 198–207.

———————————, & Mackintosh, N. J. (1964). Discrimination learning: Non-additivity of cues. *Nature,* **201,** 528–530.

Terrace, H. S. (1963). Discrimination learning with and without errors. *Journal of the Experimental Analysis of Behavior,* **6,** 1–27.

Theios, J., & Blosser, D. (1965). The overlearning reversal effect and magnitude of reward. *Journal of Comparative and Physiological Psychology,* **59,** 252–257.

Thompson, R. F., & Spencer, W. A. (1966). Habituation: A model phenomenon for the study of neuronal substrates of behavior. *Psychological Review,* **73,** 16–43.

Thorndike, E. L. (1928). *Adult learning.* New York: Macmillan.

Thurstone, L. L. (1927). A law of comparative judgment. *Psychological Review,* **34,** 273–286.

Torgerson, W. S. (1958). *Theory and methods of scaling.* New York: Wiley.

Trabasso, T. (1960). Additivity of cues in discrimination learning of letter patterns. *Journal of Experimental Psychology,* **60,** 83–88.

——————————— (1963). Stimulus emphasis and all-or-none learning of concept identification. *Journal of Experimental Psychology,* **65,** 395–406.

———————————, & Bower, G. H. (1964a). Component learning in the four-category concept problem. *Journal of Mathematical Psychology,* **1,** 143–169.

———————————, & Bower, G. H. (1964b). Memory in concept identification. *Psychonomic Science,* **1,** 133–134.

———————————, & Bower, G. H. (1964c). Presolution reversal and dimensional shifts in concept identification. *Journal of Experimental Psychology,* **67,** 398–399.

———————————, & Bower, G. H. (1966). Presolution dimensional shifts in concept identification: A test of the sampling with replacement axiom in all-or-none models. *Journal of Mathematical Psychology,* **3,** 163–173.

———————————, & Staudenmayer, H. (1967). Random reinforcement in concept identification. *Journal of Experimental Psychology,* in press.

243

Treisman, A. M. (1964). Selective attention in man. *British Medical Bulletin,* **20,** No. 1 (Exptl. Psychol.), 12–16.

Uhr, L., & Vossler, C. (1963). A pattern recognition program that generates, evaluates, and adjusts its own operators. In E. A. Feigenbaum & J. Feldman (Eds.), *Computers and thought.* New York: McGraw-Hill, 237–250.

Underwood, B. J. (1963). Stimulus selection in verbal learning. In C. N. Cofer & B. S. Musgrave (Eds.), *Verbal behavior and learning: Problems and processes.* New York: McGraw-Hill, 33–48.

—————————, Ham, M., & Ekstrand, B. (1962). Cue selection in paired-associate learning. *Journal of Experimental Psychology,* **64,** 405–409.

—————————, & Richardson, J. (1956a). Some verbal materials for the study of concept formation. *Psychological Bulletin,* **53,** 84–95.

—————————, & Richardson, J. (1956b). Verbal concept learning as a function of instructions and dominance level. *Journal of Experimental Psychology,* **51,** 229–238.

Warren, J. M. (1953). Additivity of cues in visual pattern discrimination by monkeys. *Journal of Comparative and Physiological Psychology,* **46,** 484–488.

————————— (1954). Perceptual dominance in discrimination learning in monkeys. *Journal of Comparative and Physiological Psychology,* **47,** 290–292.

Weiss, W., & Margolius, G. (1954). The effect of context stimuli on learning and retention. *Journal of Experimental Psychology,* **48,** 318–322.

Woodbury, C. B. (1943). The learning of stimulus patterns by dogs. *Journal of Comparative Psychology,* **35,** 29–40.

Woodworth, R. S., & Schlosberg, H. (1954). *Experimental psychology.* (Rev. ed.) New York: Holt, Rinehart, and Winston.

Wundt, W. (1894). *Logik: Eine Untersuchung der Prinzipien der Erkenntnis.* Vol. II. Stuttgart: Ferdinand Enke.

Wyckoff, L. B., Jr. (1952). The role of observing response in discrimination learning. Part I. *Psychological Review,* **59,** 431–442.

————————— (1951). The role of observing responses in discrimination learning. Unpublished doctoral thesis, Indiana University.

Yum, K. S. (1931). An experimental test of the law of assimilation. *Journal of Experimental Psychology,* **14,** 68–82.

Zeaman, D., & House, B. J. (1963). The role of attention in retardate discrimination learning. In N. R. Ellis (Ed.), *Handbook of mental deficiency.* New York: McGraw-Hill, 159–223.

AUTHOR INDEX

245

SUBJECT INDEX

Abstraction, 1–2, 11
Acquired distinctiveness of cues, 51, 147, 232–233
Afferent neural interaction, and compound-component learning, 7–9, 21
All-or-none transfer, 102
  in concept identification, 96, 150
  in verbal concept learning, 103–105
Attending, response hierarchy, 170–176, 226
  vs. using cues, 85–86
Attention, conservation of, 39
  goals for a learning theory of, 18–19
  in learning, history of, 2–11
  peripheral vs. central issue, 11
Attention span, *see* Focus sample
Attention value of cues, *see* Stimulus salience
Attribute, *see* Stimulus analyzer

Belonging, and stimulus selection, 86
Blocking, 82–85, 181–186, 224
  vs. attenuation of signal input, 15
  and incremental hypothesis-strength model, 228–229

Channel bias, 171
Choice axiom, of Luce, 22, 52, 81–82, 171–173
Coding, and stimulus selection, 212, 218–219
Color preference, and concept learning, 41–42, 173–174
Concept identification, and paired-associate learning, 111–113

Conditioned emotional response, as an index of stimulus control and blocking, 182
Confidence ratings, and configural learning, 210–211
  and correct responding, 56–57, 210, 230
  see also Response latency
Configural learning, 16–17, 139, 209–211
  hypothesis of, 19–20, 24, 35, 42
  see also Stimulus compound-component problem, and pattern discrimination
Conjunctive learning, 139–142
Constant ratio rule, of Luce, 81–82, 151
Continuity-noncontinuity issue, 5–6
Cue, *see* Stimulus *listings*
Cue weight, *see* Stimulus salience, representation of

Dichotic listening, review of, 4
Dimension, 232
  see also Stimulus analyzer
Discriminability, and compound-component transfer, 28–31, 35, 119–120, 149–151, 158–159
  see also Stimulus salience
Discrimination, 1
  conditional, 37
  see also Stimulus compound-component problem, and pattern discrimination
Discriminative control, *see* Stimulus dominance, Stimulus selection

249

253